Connie Cartwright Kwasha's

Cartwrights

of the
Southern United States

HERITAGE BOOKS
2009

HERITAGE BOOKS
AN IMPRINT OF HERITAGE BOOKS, INC.

Books, CDs, and more—Worldwide

For our listing of thousands of titles see our website
at
www.HeritageBooks.com

Published 2009 by
HERITAGE BOOKS, INC.
Publishing Division
100 Railroad Ave. #104
Westminster, Maryland 21157

International Standard Book Numbers
Paperbound: 978-0-7884-0491-7
Clothbound: 978-0-7884-8264-9

Dedication and Acknowledgements

This work is dedicated to Christie Lee Grooms, Rikki Michelle Cartwright, Terrence Zachariah Kwasha, Rachel Nicole Peterson, Jennifer Marie Peterson, and Howard Charles Kwasha---some of our rising generation of Cartwright descendants. And to their many 'cousins' who are spread far and wide. We are indebted to all those persons and organizations responsible for the preserving of records and information, who are too numerous to name here but without whom we might never have had access to much of the data which is presented in this volume. Many thanks are due to my husband Bruce Charles Kwasha for technical support in the use of computers for the work, and to my daughter Christie and my close friend Julie Powell for doing 'legwork' on my behalf when I could not make certain trips for obtaining bits of needed data. I would also like to dedicate the work to my parents, who were the salt of the Earth and seemed to believe that we were just 'plain people', about whom there was little to know. Their error was simply one of modesty.

Ronald Earl Cartwright
born
19 February 1923
died
25 January 1994

Carrie Harmon Cartwright
born
20 September 1920
died
12 February 1984

Table of Contents

Table of Contents

Introduction

As a result of my attempts to sort out my own Cartwrights from among a multitude of others, I have acquired enough data to provide a wide overview of most of the Cartwrights who were present in the areas of Maryland, Virginia, North Carolina and Tennessee during the early years of our country's settlement. It was obvious that a correlation of the data could be a very useful guide to others who might be trying to investigate the surname, and thus I undertook the project of organizing the information in order to present it to the public. I have included here a vast amount of data from sources already extant, the reason being to provide a single comprehensive volume for ease of survey. Also included, however, are a number of wills and other records which have not to my knowledge been previously published, or have only been abstracted in other sources.

There were mainly two sets of Cartwrights who spread through the pertinent regions---those who originated in Maryland, and those who came from the area of Princess Anne County, Virginia and Pasquotank County, North Carolina. Concerning the early generations of the latter group, a considerable amount of information has long since been published in the form of charts by the noted authority, Alice Granberry Walter. My purpose here is not to infringe upon her work, but in order to provide as complete a set of data as possible I will touch upon the Cartwright descent she has shown and then expand upon the family.

I have begun each of the two sections of this work with specific genealogical outlines which I have worked out through my own study, but the main purpose of doing so is to give a broad perspective of the Cartwrights in question and to provide an easy reference point for identifying a specific person who may be under discussion in later examinations. While the information as taken from verifiable sources is clearly stated, the outlines provided from my own study contain a few placements as to parentage which are theoretical,

1

and therefore the outlines should not be taken as concrete fact in themselves. Connections that are tentative are shown plainly within the context of the presentation, with qualifying remarks in parentheses and subsequent discussion of the reasoning behind the deductions. Being a person who loathes to enter even a tentative date or a sketchy middle initial unless there is a very clear basis for it, I have scrupulously avoided giving any information that is not shown well enough by the proper types of records to be valid. I myself have been confused by various bits of erroneous information in this search, and thus I have undertaken to examine the available sources with a critical eye and to present the clearest assessment possible. I do not believe that I have made any glaring errors of reasoning where I have offered my own opinion, but it has been my experience that most all genealogical work can be subject to corrections, and mine is certainly no exception.

Connie Cartwright Kwasha

Part I

The
Maryland Cartwrights

and
Their
Descendants

Matthew Cartwright

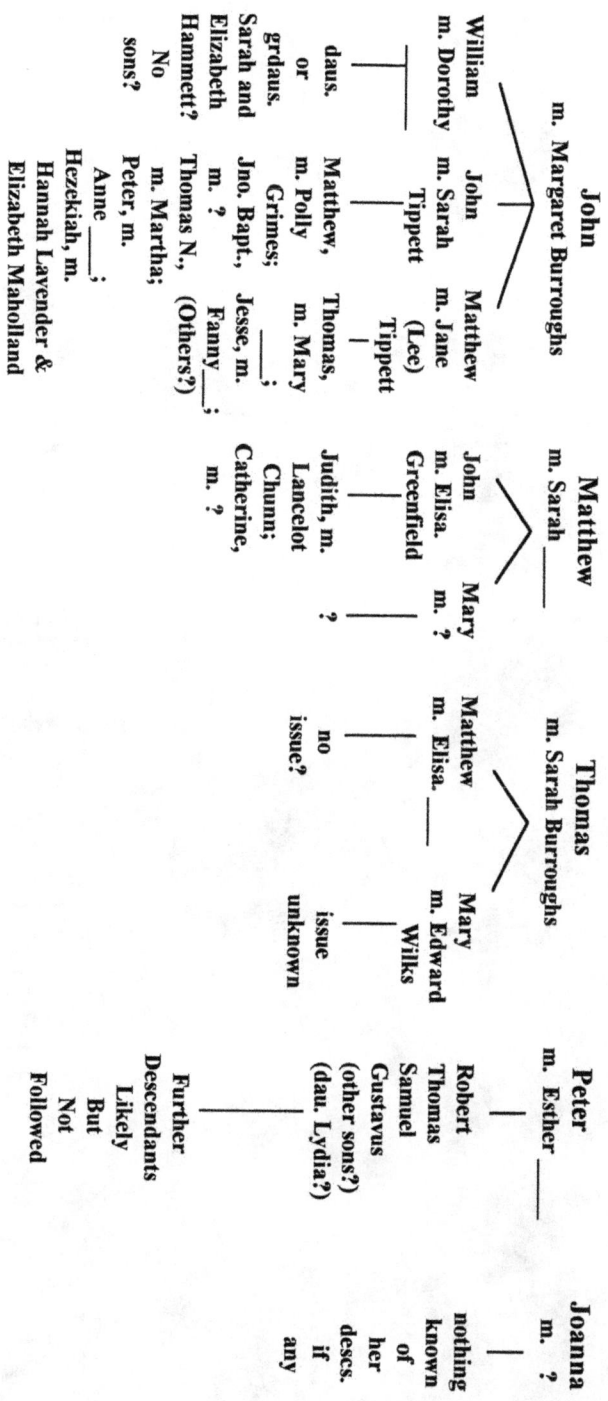

Children of Matthew Cartwright:

John m. Margaret Burroughs   Matthew m. Sarah ___   Thomas m. Sarah Burroughs   Peter m. Esther ___   Joanna m. ?

Under John m. Margaret Burroughs:

William m. Dorothy ___   John m. Sarah Tippett   Matthew m. Jane (Lee) Tippett   John m. Elisa. Greenfield   Mary m. ?

- **William m. Dorothy ___:** daus. or grdaus, Sarah and Elizabeth Hammett? No sons?

- **John m. Sarah Tippett:** Matthew, m. Polly Grimes; Thomas, m. Mary ___; Jesse, m. Fanny ___; Thomas N., m. Martha; Peter, m. ___; Anne ___; Hezekiah, m. Hannah Lavender & Elizabeth Maholland

- **Matthew m. Jane (Lee) Tippett:** Judith, m. ?; Jno. Bapt., m. Mary Lancelot Chunn; Jesse, m. ___; Catherine, m. ? (Others?)

- **John m. Elisa. Greenfield:** ? — no issue?

- **Mary m. ?:** ? — no issue?

Under Thomas m. Sarah Burroughs:

Matthew m. Elisa. ___   Mary m. Edward Wilks

- **Matthew m. Elisa. ___:** issue unknown

- **Mary m. Edward Wilks:** issue unknown

Under Peter m. Esther ___:

Robert, Thomas, Samuel, Gustavus (other sons?) (dau. Lydia?) — Further Descendants Likely But Not Followed

Under Joanna m. ?:

nothing known of her descs. if any

Known and Postulated Descent from Matthew Cartwright the Immigrant to Maryland

Chapter One

Cartwright Origins in Maryland

There were a number of Cartwright immigrants who came to the shores of Maryland during the earliest days of settlement in the colonies, as can be seen from the immigration lists and headright records. Unfortunately, the trail on most of them runs cold, either due to a lack of records which can connect them with later descendants or because of a clear demonstration that they left no male issue to carry on the name. There are several Cartwrights found in the seventeenth-and-eighteenth century records of Maryland for whom I have been unable to demonstrate either a specific progenitor or a further family line, and they are shown later in this chapter as 'unplaced' Cartwrights.

Most of those Cartwrights who are found to have spread south and west from Maryland seem to have originated with one man, a **Matthew Cartwright** who came to Maryland in 1671 and left a will to delineate his children. He was obviously a partriarch who generated a large number of descendants, and yet there is little directly-stated evidence which allows the lines to be traced to him from those later generations. My reasons for presenting the data herein with such a vast amount of commentary is that I hope to show, through the detailed examination in this work, which of those Cartwrights of North Carolina, Tennessee, and beyond were those who descended from this original Maryland immigrant, and how. Not everyone may agree with my reasoning, but the data is presented in such a way that it is easily separated from my commentary should anyone wish to examine the facts separately. It is my belief that we do not have to give up on trying to trace certain family lines merely because we do not have a trail of direct, documented proof. In this case it certainly seems possible to work out at least the probable lines on the basis of the clues that we do have. Thus I begin with a tentative genealogical outline that must be considered hypothetical in some respects, though that fact should not reflect upon the validity of the different pieces of data in themselves, which are taken from verifiable sources.

The information given for the first generation is clearly demonstrated by the will and other records concerning **Matthew Cartwright** the immigrant. I have found his birthdate stated variously as 1634 and 1638 in different published sources, for which I lack a knowledge of the original source of such information. Since both dates seem to frame a reasonable range for the approximate age of the man in question, I have chosen to note them both and have left the birthdate open, with a question mark.

The data shown in the outline for the subsequent generations is taken from a variety of sources which are given as clearly as possible hereafter and are detailed in the bibliography at the end of the chapter, with the proper footnotes inserted in the text.

I. Matthew Cartwright
b. ca 1634-1638?, Holland.
m. **Sarah** _____ , date unknown.
d. March 1688/9 St. Mary's County, Maryland.
Children: II-A.   **John Cartwright**, see further.
            II-B.   **Matthew Cartwright**, m. **Susannah** _____ .
                    Children: **John Cartwright** and **Mary Cartwright**. (abstract of will, given later.)
            II-C.   **Thomas Cartwright**, m. **(Sarah Burroughs?**
                    See references in my later commentary)
            II-D.   **Peter Cartwright**, m. **Esther** _____ .
                    Children: **Robert Cartwright, Thomas Cartwright, Samuel Cartwright,**

8

Gustavus Cartwright, and apparently
others. (will abstract given later)

II-E. Joanna Cartwright (no data on her)

The naturalization papers of Matthew Cartwright the
immigrant, as recorded in St. Mary's County, Maryland, are found in
the Maryland Archives, vol. 2, page 282; dated 19 April 1671.[1,2] He
stated on the record that he was born 'att Middlebourgh in the
Province of Zealand under the Dominion of the States Generall of the
United Provinces'. The 'Province of Zealand' is not to be confused
with either New Zealand or with Sjaelland, sometimes called Zealand,
which is the largest of Denmark's islands. The Province of Zealand
here in question is a small maritime island in the southwestern
Netherlands, a part of the Dutch Republic (Holland). The town of
'Middlebourgh' is the capital of the province and was a flourishing
trade center during Medieval times, now found with the spelling
'Middelburg'. The Province of Zealand is more currently called
'Zeeland', and has an area of only 691 square miles. It is one of
numerous small islands connected with each other and to the mainland
by bridges.[3]

II-A. **John Cartwright**
b. unknown, but probably ca 1670-75
m. (apparently) **Margaret Burroughs**, daughter of **John Burroughs**
     and wife **Mary**; date unknown
d. unknown
Children (apparently): III-A. **John Cartwright**, see further
                        III-B. **William Cartwright**, m.
                                Dorothy_____; d. Jan. 1755
                                St. Mary's County, Maryland.
                                Children: possibly daughters or
                                granddaughters named
                                Elizabeth and **Sarah**, but
                                apparently no sons.
                        III-C. **Matthew Cartwright**, see further. (I
                                am offering him as a son in this
                                family on an even more tentative
                                basis, but see discussion of the

9

reasoning for this throughout the
following chapters.)

III-A. **John Cartwright**
b. ca 1700?
m. **Sarah (Tippett?**, daughter of **Dennis Tippett; date of marriage**
   unknown. See abstract of Dennis Tippett's will, given
   hereafter, for the conclusion as to this marriage)
d. November 1780, Edgecombe County, North Carolina (that this
   John Cartwright and wife Sarah are not only the brother and
   sister-in-law of William and Dorothy, above, but are the same
   ones who are later found in Edgecombe County, North
   Carolina, seems evident from a variety of records, discussed
   hereafter.)
Children (birth order uncertain):
> IV-Aa. **Matthew Cartwright**, see further.
> IV-Ab. **John Baptist Cartwright** (little data on him,
>> though see references to him in Chapter
>> Two. If he had children, there were
>> evidently no males.)
> IV-Ac. **Peter Cartwright**, m. **Anne** _____.
>> Children: (birth order not known)
>> **Susannah Cartwright, John
>> Cartwright, Joshua Cartwright,
>> Jonas Cartwright, William
>> Cartwright, Sarah Cartwright,
>> Eleanor Cartwright, Peter
>> Cartwright, Ann Cartwright,
>> Elizabeth Cartwright**. (This son of
>> John moved on to Wilson County,
>> Tennessee, as did Hezekiah and Thomas
>> Notley, below. See the wills and other
>> records, given in Chapter Five.)
> IV-Ad. **Mary Cartwright**, m. _____ **Caulwell**. (No
>> data on her. She is named as Mary
>> Caulwell in her father's will, q.v.
>> Chapter Two.)
> IV-Ae. **Hezekiah Cartwright**, m. 1st. **Hannah**

10

Lavender[14]; m. 2nd. **Elizabeth Maholland**. Children: **Richard Cartwright, Peter A. Cartwright, Benjamin Cartwright, Matthew T. Cartwright, John Cartwright, Elizabeth (Cartwright) Lambert, Penelope Cartwright, James N. Cartwright, Hezekiah Cartwright, Hannah Cartwright, William Cartwright, Edward W. Cartwright, Mary (Polly) Cartwright, Nancy (Cartwright) McIntosh, Sally (Cartwright) McIntosh, Lucinda Cartwright**. (The daughters Nancy and Sally are called McIntosh in a settlement of Hezekiah's estate, which is the only evidence that I have found for their marriages. The marriages for a number of the other children of Hezekiah are noted in Chapter Five.)

IV-Af. **Sarah Cartwright**, (No data on her.)

IV-Ag. **Susanna Cartwright**, (No data on her.)

IV-Ah. **Thomas Notley Cartwright**, m. **Martha** _____. Children: **Samuel Cartwright, Thomas Cartwright, Hezekiah Cartwright, Sally Cartwright, Patsy Cartwright, Susannah Cartwright**. (His will, and other records such as marriage dates are examined in Chapter Five, dealing with the Wilson County, Tennessee Cartwrights.)

III-C. **Matthew Cartwright**
b. ca 1730-40, St. Mary's County, Maryland
m. (probably 2nd.) **Jane (Lee) Tippett**, widow of **Philip Tippett**, in Halifax County, North Carolina, ca 1775.

d. unknown (probably ca 1790-1800)

Children (apparently): IV-Ca. **Jesse Cartwright**, m. **(Fanny**
_____?) Children:
Unconfirmed, but probably:
**Jesse Cartwright, Thomas
Cartwright, Jane Cartwright**,
(possibly others.)

IV-Cb. **Thomas Cartwright**, see further

IV-Cc. (possibly others from a first marriage--
James?)

IV-Aa. Matthew Cartwright (Apparently son of John, IIIA. His
birthdate and wife's maiden name are taken from published
accounts which have been shown to contain errors, with the
original sources not accessed by me; and thus I must view the
data cautiously. See Chapter Five. His will verifies the other
data concerning this family.)

b. ca 1754? St. Mary's County, Maryland

m. **Polly Grimes**.

d. February 1812, Wilson County, Tennessee.

Children: (birth order uncertain)

V-Aa. **John Cartwright**, m. **Polly (Crutchfield,**
according to other published sources,
and partially confirmed by records I
have noted in Chapter Five. This couple
evidently went to Texas.) Issue.

V-Ab. **Elizabeth Cartwright**, m. **James Edwards**, 19
June 1800, Sumner County, Tennessee.
(Sumner County marriage records.)

V-Ac. **Sally G. Cartwright**, m. **Richard Hankins**, 7
February 1800, Sumner County,
Tennesssee. (Sumner County marriage
records.)

V-Ad. **Bethany Cartwright**, m. _____ **Jarney (or
Joyner)**, per will.

V-Ae. **Susannah Cartwright**, m. **John Hallum**, per
will and other records.

V-Af. **Mary (Polly) Cartwright**, m. **Pettus Ragland**,
per will. (In a few early published
sources, some of these children have
been have been confused with the
children of Hezekiah, Matthew's
brother, as to spouses, etc. The data
given here is the correct information as
found quite clearly in Matthew's will
and other records. See Chapter Five.)

IV-Cb. Thomas Cartwright (Apparently son of Matthew, IIIC.)
b. ca 1775-80, Halifax County, N.C.
m. **Mary** _____ (b. 1779, North Carolina; d. ca 1852, Tippah
County, Mississippi); m. ca 1800-1804, probably in Blount
County, Tennessee
d. January 1814, Blount County, Tennessee; Veteran of War of 1812
(possibly died from injuries sustained in that conflict. His will
given hereafter.)
Children: V-Ca. **Matthew Cartwright**, b. ca 1805 Blount
County, Tennessee; m. **Sarah** _____.
Children: **Martha A. Cartwright,
Sarah C. Cartwright** and **Rachel E.
Cartwright** (twins), **Maria J.
Cartwright, Elvina F. Cartwright**.
(Possibly others, all females, per 1830
and 1840 censuses of Lawrence County,
Tennessee and Tippah County,
Mississippi. The 1840 census shows
his household with one male and
nineteen females.)
V-Cb. **Sarah Cartwright**, b. ca 1806? (no data on her
after mention in father's will, q.v.
Chapter Three.)
V-Cc. **John Nelson Cartwright**, b. ca 1807; m. **Mary**
_____. Children: **James H.
Cartwright, William F. Cartwright,
Thomas F. Cartwright, John J.
Cartwright, Benjamin M.**

13

Cartwright, Theresa J. Cartwright.

V-Cd. **Nancy Cartwright**, b. ca 1808; never married.

V-Ce. **Mary (Polly) Cartwright**, b. ca 1810, never married, but apparently had two children called by the name of Cartwright: **James T. Asbury Cartwright**, and **Nancy A. Cartwright**.

V-Cf. **James R. Cartwright**, b. ca 1812; m. **Elizabeth Long** (per data of other researchers. I do not have the source of the maiden name for this wife, and have seen only deeds which name her as Elizabeth.) Children: **Thomas O. Cartwright, Mary P. Cartwright, Sarah J. Cartwright, Samuel C. Cartwright, John H. Cartwright, James M. Cartwright, Williams S. Cartwright**.

V-Cg. **Thomas Cartwright**, see further
(See Chapters Three and Four for references and further data on this family and the next generation, below.)

V-Cg. Thomas Cartwright, Jr.
b. 1813-14, Blount County, Tennessee
m. **Lavinia Rogers** ca 1841, Tippah County, Mississippi
d. unknown---out west. (official Probate 1852 Tippah County, Mississippi; but see my commentary in Chapter Four, in reference to the fact that he was actually missing at the time. Various clues suggest the probate might have resulted from a faked report of his death.)

Children:
VI-Ca. **Mary E. Cartwright**, b. ca 1842, Tippah County, Mississippi; m. **John J. Box**, 20 December 1858 in Tippah County, Mississippi.

VI-Cb. **James H. Cartwright**, b. ca 1845, Tippah County, Mississippi.

VI-Cc. **General Taylor Cartwright**, b. ca 1847,
Tippah County, Mississippi
VI-Cd. **Thomas R. Cartwright**, b. September 1850;
apparently died young, for he is not
found again in any records after the
1850 census. See written accounts
concerning this family, in Chapter Four.
VI-Ce. **William Lavert Cartwright**, see further

References for the following generations are 15 through 19 in the
Bibliography at the end of the chapter:
VI-Ce. William Lavert Cartwright
b. 23 May 1852 (Tippah County, Mississippi or out west---see later
discussion)
m. 1st. **Amanda J. Wallace**, 10 April 1871 Tippah County,
Mississippi; (she d. 15 November 1879); m. 2nd. **Harriett A.
Dowty**, 17 July 1881, Hardeman County, Tennessee.
d. 1 April 1928, Hardeman County, Tennessee (his tombstone dates in
the State Line Cemetery, Hardeman County, Tennessee---
Tippah County, Mississippi, are off by one year.)
Children of first marriage:
VII-A. **William Henderson Cartwright**, b. 28
September 1874, Hardeman County,
Tennessee; m. 1st **Cora Young**; m. 2nd
Fannie F. Minton; issue.
VII-B. **Roxanna Cartwright**, b. 24 June 1877,
Hardeman County, Tennessee; d. 14
November 1917; m. **Sam Barclay**;
issue.
VII-C. **Christopher Columbus Cartwright**, b. 1
November 1879; d. 15 February 1880,
Hardeman County, Tennessee.
Children of second marriage:
VII-D. **James Albert Cartwright**, b. 6 August 1882,
Hardeman County, Tennessee; m.
_____; issue.
VII-E. **Joshua Benton Cartwright**, b. 23 February
1884, Hardeman County, Tennessee, m.

Lena _____; issue.

VII-F. **Edward Leon Cartwright**, b. 7 March 1886,
Hardeman County, Tennessee, m. **Ruth**
_____; issue.

VII-G. **John Allen Cartwright**, b. 21 November 1887,
Hardeman County, Tennessee; m.
Manie Noonie Mellon 26 February
1912, Hardeman County, Tennessee; d.
26 July 1960, Washington County,
Tennessee; issue.

* * * * * * *

Source Materials and Commentary

The body of the rest of this chapter consists of the abstracts of records taken from sources relating to Maryland, and the discussion and commentary upon them which explains my reasoning for the placements given in the foregoing outline. The abstracts reprinted here are not given in chronological order, but rather as they seem to be relevant to each other. I might caution that one must pay close attention to the dates and the counties involved, in order to follow the reasoning by which I have postulated various family placements. A broad grasp of all the data is necessary in order to see why certain individuals are ruled out for certain relationships, in some instances requiring a knowledge of the data revealed several generations later. (It is hoped that experienced researchers will not be impatient with my explanations and admonitions, which may be helpful to those just beginning with genealogy.)

Wills and Inventories of Maryland[4,5]

The will of **Matthew Cartwright** the immigrant, dated 21st Feb. 1688/9---18th March 1688/9, St. Mary's County, Md. Names 'eldest son **John**', to whom is left 100 acres, part of a 400 acre tract at

'Chaptico', St. Mary's County; 'second son **Matthew**', to whom is left 100 acres of the same 400 acre tract; 'third son **Thomas**', who likewise receives 100 acres of the tract; and 'fourth son **Peter**', the same. To 'son **John** and to each of 3 sons at 18 yrs. of age, and to dau. **Joanna** at 16 yrs. of age, personalty'. To wife **Sarah**, dower rights. Executors are wife **Sarah** and **Jno. Turlinge**. Witnesses are **Jno. Nichols, Philip Tippet**, and **Edward Farr**. (See further abstracts, and the data in Chapter Two, concerning the Tippet family and their connections to the Cartwrights.)

The will of **John Burroughs**, dated 13th Mar. 1715/6---5th Dec. 1717, St. Mary's Co. names wife **Mary**, who is to receive '1/3 of personal estate absolutely, and dwelling plantation during life'; at her decease to eldest son **John**; to eldest son **John**, personalty and tract where he now lives, excepting that part conveyed by deed of gift to daughter **Margaret Cartwright**. Lands conveyed to youngest son **Richard** and to dau. **Margaret** aforesaid, confirmed. To daughter **Sarah Carter** during life, north part of dwelling plantation. Residue of personal estate divided among six children. There is no mention of an executor. Witnesses: **John Cartwright, William Hulse**, and **Samuel Johnson**. (Two of the mentioned six children are not named, but see reference to will of Sarah Carter, given shortly, which names a sister Elizabeth. There is nothing here which specifically proves that the John Cartwright shown is the 'eldest son John' of the immigrant Matthew. The facts of the proximity in the same county, the date which seems appropriate, and the absence of evidence of any other Cartwright males to account for him is what has prompted me to identify him thus.)

The will of **Matthew Cartwright**, dated 6th May 1714---15th May 1714, St. Mary's County, Maryland, names son **John** who receives plantation, and daughter **Mary**, who is to receive it if **John** should die without issue. Wife **Susannah**, executrix, receives life interest in plantation, and personal estate jointly with son and daughter. Brother **Peter** is to have charge of daughter's share of estate until she attains 16 yrs. of age or marries. Witnesses are **Jno. Sanders, Thos. Orphin**, and **Michael Wikley**. (The reference to 'brother Peter' is

17

what identifies this Matthew as the 'second son' of the immigrant. The indication is that the son John named here is young, unmarried, or at least without children at the time.)

The will of **Peter Cartwright**, dated 25 November 1748---22 July 1751, Charles County, Maryland: names 'my two sons, **Robert** and **Thomas**', tract in St. Mary's County near the head of Chaptico Bay, known as 'Western Addition'. If either of them should die without heirs then the right shall devolve on son **Samuel**, and if he dies without heirs then to the next surviving sons, etc. To son **Gustavus**, Negro girl **Lucy**. To wife **Esther Cartwright**, Negro man **Roger**, in addition to her thirds. Son **Thomas Cartwright** and wife **Esther Cartwright**, exs. Witnesses: **Sam Chunn, Peter Dent, John Tuel**. (The reference to the land at Chaptico Bay in St. Mary's County is what identifies this Peter as the 'fourth son' of Matthew the immigrant. The implication here seems to be that there might be more sons of Peter who were not named. Obviously no daughters are named, but this does not exclude the possibility that there were some, and in fact it seems there was at least one daughter. See later references.)

An inventory of the estate of **Peter Cartwright**, 17 August 1751---12 October 1751, Charles County, Maryland. Appraisers are **Benjamin Chunn** and **John Waters**. Creditors are **Thomas Midgley** and **Francis Parnham**. 'Next of kin' are **Samuel Cartwright** and **Lydia Vawdry**. Executors are **Esther Cartwright** and **Thomas Cartwright**. (Peter's descendants seem to remain distinguishable from those in St. Mary's County, despite some common connections with other families. We cannot rule out the possibility that some of the Cartwrights discussed hereafter may have been sons of Peter, but my commentary will show various apparent placements by process of elimination.)

The will of **Sarah Carter**, 'widow', dated 21 November 1733---3 August 1757 St. Mary's County, Maryland: To daughter **Mary Cartwright**, parcel of land I now live on called 'Mere Chance'. To daughter **Mary**, Negro girl **Priscilla** and Negro woman **Jane**. If **Jane** should have children then said child or children shall be equally divided

18

between my three children **Mathew** (sic), **Mary** and **Elizabeth**. To son **Matthew Cartwright**, Negro boy **James**. To grandaughter **Elizabeth Herbut** (perhaps this should be Hubert), Negro child. Also to children **Matthew, Elizabeth**, and **Mary**, Negro girl **Jane**. To son in law **John Edwards**, Negro boy **Thomas** to his heirs begotten on the body of my daughter **Elizabeth**. To sister **Elizabeth Burroughs**, free power during her life to dwell on any part of the land whereon I now live called 'Mere Chance'. Daughter **Mary Cartwright**, executrix. Witnesses: **Jno. Burroughs, Laurence Lant, John Hubert**. (The implications here are numerous. Sarah Carter must have been married previously to a Cartwright, though such a husband must have died well before 1714, when she is already called Sarah Carter in the will of her father, John Burroughs. Sarah refers to two of her children as Cartwrights. Though the testators in such early wills often referred to their children's spouses simply as sons or daughters along with their own children, it certainly does not seem from the wording in this will that the Matthew Cartwright in question was a son-in-law married to the daughter Mary, but rather that they were both Sarah's own children, thus indicating the previous Cartwright marriage. There is no statement as to whether the daughter Elizabeth was a Cartwright or a Carter, but it seems that the latter is the case, simply from the fact that the testator distinguishes Mary and Matthew as Cartwrights and does not mention the same in reference to the daughter Elizabeth. Which Cartwright may have been the first husband of Sarah Burroughs Carter is not readily apparent; but by process of elimination it seems likely he was the 'third son, Thomas' of the immigrant, since that Thomas seems to be unaccounted for as far as a wife or children are concerned. We will see by other records that there don't seem to be any other Cartwrights in the area who can account for him. The further implications in this will of Sarah Carter are that the daughter Elizabeth also must have been married more than once, for there is reference to a grandaughter Elizabeth Herbut or Hubert, and also the reference to son-in-law John Edwards. While in many cases these early wills contain the designations 'in-laws' to refer to step-children, etc, in this case it is clearly a reference to the current meaning of the term, for the testator mentions 'John Edward's heirs begotten on the body of my daughter Elizabeth'. It is difficult to tell from these references which is the current husband of Elizabeth, and which is the deceased one. But see next the inventory of a Matthew Cartwright who was clearly the same as the one mentioned in this will, and in which inventory one of the next of kin, along with Sarah Carter, is named as Elizabeth Edwards. Sarah Carter's will was written in 1733 but she clearly did not die until 1757; while her son Matthew died in 1751. Although it is possible that the Elisabeth Edwards named in the latter's inventory is a daughter of Elizabeth Carter Edwards rather than the first Elizabeth herself, the indication seems to be that the daughter of Sarah Carter who was named Elizabeth married first a Hubert and then John Edwards. Finally, as mentioned earlier, Sarah Carter's will names her sister, Elizabeth Burroughs, thus identifying one of the two Burroughs siblings who were not named in the will of their father.)

An inventory of the estate of **Matthew Cartwright**, 28 March 1751---5 June 1751, St. Mary's County, Maryland, names the 'next of kin' as **Sarah Carter** and **Elisabeth Edwards**. Appraisers are **Thomas Mattingly, Jr.** and **William Bond**. Creditors are **Philip Key** and **Zachariah Bond**. Administratrix/Executrix is **Elisabeth Cartwright**. (Here is the bit of evidence that the Matthew Cartwright who was a son of Sarah Burroughts Carter had neither brothers nor, evidently, children. Both are merely presumptions on the basis of this meager record alone, but it is usually the children who are named as 'next of kin' in these inventories, if there are children in evidence. It has been my observation that brothers, sisters, and other relatives are named as the next of kin only when there are no children or when the children have predeceased the parent or are shown in other capacities in the same case, such as below with the inventory of Sarah Carter herself. Although it is possible there were minor children of this Matthew who were too young to be considered in a legal sense at the time of his death, the naming of mother and sister as 'next of kin' seems a strong indication that there were no offspring. The executrix Elisabeth Cartwright was of course most likely Matthew's wife, children or no.)

An inventory of the estate of **Sarah Carter**, 25 August 1757---3 August 1758, St. Mary's County, Maryland, names appraisers as **Zachariah Bond** and **Meverell Lock**. Creditors are **Merler Swann** and **Joseph Burroughes**. 'Next of kin' are **Margret** (sic) **Cartwright** and **Richard Burroughes**. Administrators/Executors are **Edward Wilks** and his wife **Mary Wilks**. (Margaret Cartwright, and Richard Burroughes are Sarah's siblings, as shown earlier in her father's will. Joseph Burroughs may have been the final missing sibling in the Burroughs family, or else he was probably a son of one of Sarah's brothers, Richard or John. Evidently the daughter Mary Cartwright had married Edward Wilks since the time her mother's will was written, for she is named in said will as executor and thus there is little doubt this is the same Mary who is shown as executor along with husband Edward Wilks.)

The will of **Philip Key**, dated 10 March 1764---1 September 1764, St. Mary's County, Maryland, refers to land '....that I bot. from **Edward Welsh** and to which **Matw. Cartwright** and **John Cartwright** released their right and that I bot. from the same **Matw. Cartwright**......' (This is a very long will, describing numerous tracts of land and from whom each was bought or acquired. The reference to the land in which Matthew and John Cartwright had a 'right' may be an indication that one of the wives of an early Cartwright in St. Mary's County was of the maiden name Welsh, with said land descending to the Cartwright men in that manner. Matthew the immigrant's wife was Sarah, with maiden name unknown; and his son Matthew's wife was Susannah, also with her maiden name unknown. There is no indication of the relationship between the two Cartwright men mentioned here, so they could have been brothers or father and son, etc. And with the reference being merely to land bought of them, it does not necessarily indicate that either of them is still alive at the time of this will. The land is not described, except that the reference occurs in a paragraph which mentions other land lying in St. Mary's County, so it may be that it is distinguished thus from land mentioned that was in Charles County, etc. With the facts thus observed, it is my own tentative opinion that the two Cartwrights here mentioned, John and Matthew, may be those whom I have presumed to be sons of the 'eldest son John' of the immigrant, who married Margaret Burroughs. There are no other apparent families within this St. Mary's County group which seem to have both John and Matthew named as sons in the same family. Though there is no direct evidence that the 'eldest son John' had any children at all, the examination of all these

21

Cartwrights as a whole leads me to believe that his children are as I have given them. Later clues by association, discussed in Chapter Two, seem to indicate that the John Cartwright of generation III who died in North Carolina had a brother named Matthew, or at least a close relative by that name who was not the same as his own son Matthew. And the only family here which seems able to account for them in such a configuration is that of the elder John.)

A **William Cartwright** is found as one of the appraisers in the inventory of the estate of **Charles Leach**, dated 7 April 1750---5 June 1750, St. Mary's County, Maryland. The other appraiser is **Meverell Lock**. Creditors are **James Keech** and **George Bowles**. Next of kin are **William Leach** and **Joseph Fowler**. Executrix is **Sarah Leach**.

An inventory of the estate of **William Cartwright**, 13 January 1755---24 March 1755, St. Mary's County, Maryland, names appraisers **Thomas Brome** and **John Edwards**. Creditors are **Thomas Hutchinson** and **John Urquhart**. 'Next of kin' are **Elisabeth Hammett** and **Sarah Hammett**. Administratrix/Executrix: **Dorothy Cartwright**. Another inventory or account made in August of the same year gives no further information.

The will of **Dorothy Cartwright**, dated 10 February 1769---6 June 1770, St. Mary's County, Maryland: Names only 'brother **John Cartwright**' and 'sister **Sarah Cartwright**'. They are also made executors. Witnesses: **John, Joseph**, and **James Hammett**. (This would make it seem that Dorothy had no children, although the strong implications of William's inventory, above, are that the females Elisabeth Hammett and Sarah Hammett may have been daughters or grandaughters. Thus, the men John, Joseph, and James Hammett may also have been grandchildren. Otherwise, there is no way to tell who the Hammetts were in relation to these Cartwrights. Since Dorothy names no children, it seems just as possible that the Hammetts were other relatives such as neices and nephews, possibly children of an unknown sister of William; or else that they were Dorothy's own relatives. But it seems likely that Dorothy was a Rudd, per one of the inventories shown below.)

An inventory of the estate of **Basil Boothe**, 5 December 1750---6 February 1753, St. Mary's County, Maryland, shows **William Cartwright** as the Administrator/Executor. Appraisers are **Thomas Broome** and **Thomas Greenfield**. Creditors are **W. McWilliams** and **Stourton Edwards**. 'Next of kin' are **James Keech** and **Stephen Cawood**.

An inventory of the estate of **James Rudd**, 18 January 1756, St. Mary's County, Maryland, shows appraisers **N. T. Greenfield** and **Thomas Greenfield**; creditors **Thomas Reeder** and **Stephen Caywood**; and 'Next of kin' are **Elener Cowood** (perhaps this should be Eleanor Caywood?) and **Dorothy Cartwright**. Administrator/Executor is **John Burroughs**. (Jr., evidently.)

An inventory of the estate of **Samuel Keech**, 20 June 1751---7 August 1751, St. Mary's County, Maryland, shows **William Cartwright** as one of the 'Next of kin', along with **Mary Burroughes**. Appraisers are **Meverell Lock** and **John Edwards**. Creditors are **Cornelius McCaffeny** and **Francis Parnham**. Executrix is **Dorcus Keech**.

The will of **Henry Greenfield**, dated _____---6 December 1748, St. Mary's County, Maryland: To brother **Thomas Greenfield** 43 pounds st. (sterling) and all tobacco he now owes me. To brother **George Greenfield**, that the moiety (?) or half tract of land called 'Good Luck' now joining to said **George Greenfield's** land and a horse called Jolley and a small gunn (sic). To cousin **Catharine Cartwright**, negro girl called **Priss** and her increase. **Elizabeth Barber's** daughter called **Rebecca**, 25 pounds st. at age 16. Witnesses: **James Forbes, Nathl. Parran, Nathl. T. Greenfield**.

An inventory of the estate of **Henry Greenfield**, 30 March 1749---6 June 1750, St. Mary's County, Maryland, names **John Cartwright** and **N.T. Greenfield** as 'next of kin'. Appraisers are **Samuel Sothoron** and **Richard Sothoron**. Creditors are **George Maxwell** and **N. T. Greenfield**. Administrator/Executor is **Thomas Greenfield**.

An inventory of the estate of **George Greenfield**, _____---5 December 1750, St. Mary's County, Maryland, names **Elizabeth Cartwright** and **Rebecca Greenfield** as 'next of kin'. Appraisers are **Meverell Lock** and **Samuel Sothoron**. Creditors are **John Wheatly** and **George Maxwell**. Administrator/Executor is **Thomas Greenfield**.

An inventory of the estate of **John Cartwright**, 22 April 1755---3 June 1758, St. Mary's County, Maryland shows appraisers to be **John Edwards** and **Thomas Brome**. Creditors are **John Chesley** and **Thomas Greenfield**. 'Next of kin' are listed as **Judith Cartwright** and **Catherine Cartwright**. Administrator/Executrix is **Elisabeth Cartwright**. (This inventory and the others above, when taken together, seem to indicate that Elisabeth, the wife of the John Cartwright mentioned here, was a sister of the Greenfield brothers Henry, George, and Thomas; Nath'l. T. Greenfield may have been another brother, or he may have been the father of the family. The Catherine Cartwright mentioned in the will of Henry Greenfield as 'cousin' is clearly the daughter of John and Elizabeth Cartwright, along with Judith. I believe this John Cartwright to be the son of 'second son Matthew' of the immigrant, per the reasoning in the discussion below.)

Commentary---The preceding abstracts not only establish that William Cartwright and the John Cartwright who had a wife named Sarah were brothers, but that the latter was not the same as the John Cartwright who married into the Greenfield family. The references show at least some association between all of the Cartwrights with both the Burroughs and the Greenfields, but the stronger indication is that William Cartwright's closest connection was with the Burroughs. Though such brief references are hardly proof in themselves of the relationships, when taken along with the many other things which must be noted and applied, the most reasonable conclusion is that the brothers William and John Cartwright, with wives named Dorothy and Sarah respectively, were sons of John Cartwright and Margaret Burroughs. We have seen from the discussion of the will and inventory of Sarah (Burroughs) Carter that she had been previously

24

married to a Cartwright, and that apparently the only Cartwright he could have been was Thomas, the 'third son' of the immigrant. The only Cartwright children in that union were apparently Matthew and Mary, with no John or William. Her husband could not have been the 'second son Matthew', whose wife was named Susannah and who named children *John* and Mary, not Matthew and Mary. Neither could her husband have been Peter, whose wife was Esther. The 'eldest son John' of the immigrant Matthew seems to have married Sarah Carter's sister Margaret, with Sarah already called by the name Carter in her father's will and John Cartwright clearly not deceased at that point since he signed as a witness on said will. Therefore the previous Cartwright husband of Sarah Burroughs Carter who died before 1714 *must* have been Thomas, the 'third son' of Matthew the immigrant, and they were the parents of Matthew and Mary, not William and John.

Further, the above abstracts show that the John Cartwright in the Greenfield connection had a wife named Elisabeth, probably sister of the Greenfields mentioned, and that he died in 1755, and therefore could not have been the same as the John who was a brother of William. All of this makes it seem likely that the John Cartwright with wife Elisabeth Greenfield was the son John named in the will of Matthew the 'second son' of the immigrant. Since the 'fourth son Peter' of the immigrant did not mention sons John *or* William, none of the men in question seem to have come from his family. Even though there is an indication of sons who were not named in Peter's will, the ones who inherited the land in St. Mary's County and thus might have been found again in that area were Robert and Thomas. Finally, it seems that the only other early Cartwrights who are found mentioned in the proximity of St. Mary's County left no sons at all (see the unplaced Cartwrights, later), so there is little danger of confusing any of the Cartwrights of the above abstracts with descendants of anyone other than the original Matthew. Since the indication is that the immigrant's sons were all quite young at the time of his death in 1688/9, it is unlikely that they could have had sons of their own who were old enough to be the men named in most of these records. In light of all these facts and observations, it appears that the only son of Matthew Cartwright the immigrant who could have been the father of the brothers William and John Cartwright is the 'eldest son John' who

25

evidently married Margaret Burroughs; and that the only Cartwright who could have been the first husband of Sarah Burroughs Carter was the 'third son Thomas'.

There is more to explore here, for there are families of persons who become even more important for following the trail of the Cartwrights once we find them in North Carolina. Lest we have to 'come back' to Maryland in the next chapter, I think it more appropriate to give the references here:

The will of **John Lee**, dated 17 January 1757---9 June 1757, St. Mary's County, Maryland: He gives to eldest daughter, **Eliza. Gibson**, a breeding sow; to daughter **Susanna Bowling**, a breeding sow. Daughters **Henerita** (sic) **Hobson, Sarah Tippett, Jane Tippett**, and **Mary Fanning** each receive one ewe and lamb. To son **Thos. Lee**, bed and covering. To wife, **Mary Lee**, the rest of the estate. If wife marries, then she should have no more than her thirds and the rest to be divided between 'my two sons **Thomas Lee** and **John Lee**'. Wife **Mary**, executrix. Witnesses: **Thos. Cooce, Francis Yates**. (We will see that the evidence indicates that the Jane Lee Tippett mentioned is the wife and then the widow of a Philip Tippett in North Carolina, and the records there will show that she married second Matthew Cartwright, whom I have tentatively identified as a son of John Cartwright and Margaret Burroughs. Also, the daughter Susanna Bowling seems to have married twice more, eventually to a Cartwright. See below.)

The will of **Mary Lee**, dated 4 May 1761---29 September 1761, St. Mary's County, Maryland: Sons **Thomas** and **John Lee** are given slaves. Daughters **Henrietta Hobson** and **Susanna Maddox**, 'the tobacco notes that were burned in **Lieciellin's** (?) warehouse. May be meant for **Lieciellin's**, in the year 1759, to be divided between them'. (? This passage unclear in meaning.) To daughter **Jane Tippet**, some slaves. Daughter **Sarah Tippet**, 2,000 lbs. tobacco. Daughter **Elizabeth Gibson**, riding chair. To daughter **Mary Fanning**, 2,000 lbs. tobacco. Son **Thomas Lee** to pay all the above tobacco legacies, except the burned tobacco, out of his part; to have tract 'I now live on', and if no heirs, then same to son **John Lee**. Remainder to be

26

divided between sons **Thomas** and **John Lee**. Ex: **Thomas Lee**. Witnesses: **James Jordan, Thos. McWilliams, Joshua Gibson**. (The daughter Susanna clearly had married twice at this point---first to a Bowling, since she was called by that name in her father's will; and then to a Maddox, since she is named that here. Evidently her husband was Notley Maddox---see next.)

The will of **Notley Maddox**, dated 23 April 1761---3 November 1761, St. Mary's County, Maryland: names wife **Susanna**, 'use of plantation I now live on unless she remarries' then to descend to daughter **Judith Warren Maddox**. The will refers to an unborn child, and if it is a son then the land to go to him; 'also a strip of land lying on the south side of said plantation, part of tract willed me by my father. And in default of heirs of above-named children, to descend to my brother **Townley Maddox** and heirs'. Also to daughter **Judith Warren Maddox**, slaves. Wife is executrix. Witnesses: **John Edin, James Willson, Josias Fanning**. 23 April 1761---3 November 1761. (There were a number of men named Notley Maddox in Maryland, but most of them had wives of other given names, and the Fanning name certainly provides a clue for identifying this one in the connection to the Lee family, since one of the other daughters had married a Fanning. Further, see the abstract of the inventory of the estate of this Notley Maddox, given next. It would appear that Susanna soon married yet a third time, to John Cartwright. I do not know which John Cartwright he might have been, since all the other John Cartwrights in evidence seem to have been accounted for. He could have been a son of Peter; or by this time, possibly an adult grandson of one of the four original sons of Matthew the immigrant. Susanna herself would not necessarily have been very old at this point, since these three marriages all seem to have occured within a short span of five years. It is my guess that she and her sisters as named in her father's will in 1757, though all married, were quite young and that Susanna was still in her twenties at the time of the third marriage to John Cartwright. We will see from later evidence that her sister Jane Tippet may have been a mere teenager when named in her father's will in 1757 as Jane Tippett, for she married Matthew Cartwright ca 1775 and apparently bore more children.)

An inventory of the estate of **Notley Maddox**, 30 March 1762---27 May 1762, St. Mary's County, Maryland, names the executors as **John Cartwright** and his wife **Susannah Cartwright**. Appraisers are **Samuel Briscoe** and **Edward Turner**. Creditors are **William Divan** and **Leonard Bond**. 'Next of kin' are **John Maddox** and **William Maddox**. (For a fuller treatment of the Maddox family, see 'Maddox', by W. N. Hurley, Jr.; Heritage Books, Inc., Bowie, Md.)

The will of **Dennis Tippett**, dated 13 February 1773---15 October 1773, St. Mary's County, Maryland, names daughter **Elizabeth Taylor**; son **John Tippitt** (sic); daughter **Sarah Cartwright**; son **Notley Tippitt**, executor; son **Joseph Tippett**, executor and his wife **Eleanor Tippett**; daughter of the latter, **Mary Magdalene**; son **James Tippett**, son **Dennis Tippett**, executor; **Butler Tippett** (not called a son here, but identified as such in another abstract, below). Witnesses are **John Horrell**, **Thomas Nicholls**, and **Elisha Herbert**. (Although John Cartwright and his wife Sarah were apparently already in North Carolina by the time this will was written, as will be seen when the records of that state are examined, it seems probable from a number of clues that the Sarah Cartwright mentioned in this will of Dennis Tippett is said wife of John Cartwright who moved to North Carolina. The close connection there with the other Tippett family of Philip and his wife Jane Lee is a strong piece of evidence, even though we don't know what the relationship might have been between Philip Tippett and Dennis Tippett. On the other hand, that is basically all the evidence we have, along with the obvious name, the fact that the age would be about correct, and the simple fact that there is a lack of any other identity for either woman. That Sarah, the daughter of Dennis Tippett, would have been old enough to be the Sarah who was wife of John Cartwright of Edgecombe County, North Carolina is evidenced by the fact that Dennis Tippett's children were likely all born during the time period of the 1720's to early 1730's, as shown by the abstracts below where his son Butler is named in the will of William Halliewell. John and Sarah Cartwright of Edgecombe County, North Carolina had sons born at least by 1747 or so, and if Sarah was born around 1730 or before, that would be a reasonable correlation of ages. See Chapter Two.).

Since we have already seen well enough the Tippett family connections to the Cartwrights who are under examination, it would be well to touch upon the few other references to Tippetts that I have found in the same Maryland sources:

A **Nicholas Tippett-Typpett** signed as a witness on numerous early wills in Maryland. There is no indication in any of the references of relationships with those for whom he signed, and his name as a witness in those many instances are the only mentions of him which I have found.

A **Thomas Tippett** signed as a witness on the will of **Notley Maddox**, St. Mary's County, Maryland dated 24th February 1715--- 3rd April 1716. (This is an earlier Notley Maddox than the one discussed above, and thus at least some sort of brief Maddox connection is found before that of the marriage of Susannah-Lee-Bowling-Maddox-Cartwright as shown in the wills of her parents, John and Mary Lee. Needless to say, I have examined all the references to the Maddox family that I could find, and have come upon no explanations for the connections to the Tippett and Cartwright families, other than the mentions already given in this work. Nor do any of the published sources that I have examined concerning the Maddox family give any detail concerning Tippetts or Cartwrights, except for some Cartwright marriages in later generations. Said Cartwrights of later years seem to have originated among Peter's family.)

In the will of **William Haliewell** (Holliwell, Hollaway), St. Mary's County, Maryland dated 2nd February 1729---13th February 1729 there is mention made of 'Jane, dau. of **Phillip Tippet**'; and '**Butler**, son of **Dennis Tippet**.' (These were mentioned along with others who were apparently not children of the testator, who names no wife or children. None of the other names connected with this will are familiar or found elsewhere in connection with the Tippetts or Cartwrights. The Jane Tippett here should not be confused with Jane Lee, the wife of Philip Tippett of the later records which are to be studied. The Philip Tippett in the Haliewell will may be the same one who signed as a witness on the will of Matthew Cartwright the

29

immigrant, or he may be a son or nephew of same. In any case, clearly there were several Philip Tippetts in the lines of the family. The reference here which names both Philip Tippett and Dennis Tippett with children by 1729 is at least a slight clue that the two may have been brothers, but it isn't likely this Philip is the one found later in North Carolina. The latter did not name a daughter Jane in his will and his children would all have been much younger than those mentioned here, so it is possible he was a son of the Philip Tippett named here, or of another brother in the family. See later references which indicate a Philip Tippett in connection with a Henry Tippett.)

The will of **John Suttle**, St. Mary's County, Maryland dated 19 September _____ ---19 November 1751 names daughter **Elizabeth Tippet**, along with son **John Suttle**, son **William Suttle**, and 'the heir of deceased dau. **Mary Ann Wathing**'. The son **William** had sons of his own named **William** and **John Baptist Suttle**, and daus. named **Eleanor** and **Mary Ann**. Son **William** is executor. Witnesses: **Richd. Millard, William Wathin** (sic), **Charles Hollon**.

The will of **Thomas Greaves** (Graves?), dated 14 September 1759---6 November 1759, St. Mary's County, Maryland names **Ucill Tipit** as a legatee, and a **Philip Tippet** signed as a witness. It is a fairly long will, and no relationship was stated, but it is possible or probable that the wife of the Philip Tippett mentioned was a daughter of the testator, and thus that Ucill Tipit was a grandson.

The will of **Edward Davis**, dated 20 March 1759---13 June 1764, Charles County, Maryland, names daughters **Susannah Tippet** and **Ann Tipet** (sic) among numerous other children. Witnesses were **Sam Amery, Lydia Amery**, and **Eleanor Amery**. (There is a Cartwright-Amery marriage noted later in this Chapter; though what the exact connection here might be, I have not determined.)

A **James Tippet** is mentioned in the will of **George Medford** of Kent County, Maryland as one who mortgaged tracts of land to the testator. 4 September 1761---17 October 1761.

30

An inventory of estate for **Henry Tippett**, St. Mary's County, Maryland dated October 7 1767---November 10 1767 names appraisers **Joseph Edwards** and **Thomas Dent**, creditor **John Tippett**, and next of kin **Philip Tippett**. Administrator is **Jonathon Tippet**. (Whether the creditor, next of kin, and administrator were sons of Henry, or brothers, or a combination of both, is unknown. But judging from the date, this Philip Tippett certainly could be the one whom we will see later in Halifax County, North Carolina. Men by the names of John Tippett and Jonathon Tippett are seen later along the trail, as well.)

The will of **Andrew Mills**, dated 28 September 1771---20 January 1772, St. Mary's County, Maryland, names **Elizabeth Tippitt** among his children, with **John**, **James**, and **Charles** (Mills?). Also mentioned is **Mary Tippitt**, along with several others of varying surnames and concerning whom the relationship is not clarified.

It is fruitless to speculate as to which of the many women named as Tippetts in the foregoing abstracts may have been the wife of Dennis Tippett who named daughter Sarah Cartwright, but it seems likely that one of them was said wife of Dennis. Since Dennis Tippett's only daughters were named Sarah and Elizabeth, one might guess that the mother of the family must have been either Sarah or Elizabeth, but that would still leave a number of choices from the above families and is mere conjecture. There may be more information to be had upon questions such as this among other records of Maryland to which I have not had access for study.

Miscellaneous references:

A **John Cartwright** signed as a witness on the will of **John Sothoron** of Charles County, Maryland, dated 18th March 1711---1st May 1719. The testator names son **John Jonson** ('Southern' given in parentheses); to him goes 'land bought from **Edward Barber** by **John Johnson**, father of wife' (other land mentioned, but this tidbit given only for the reference to relationships. The implication is that the son 'John Jonson', alias Southorn or Sothoron, must have been born out of wedlock to the testator's wife before their marriage; but whether he was John Sothoron's own son or was merely adopted by the man is not clear.) Son **Samuel**; son **Richard**; son **Charles**; daughter **Ann**; daughter **Mary**; younest son **Benjamin**. Wife **Mary**, executrix. Other witnesses are **Thos. Hunt** and **Thos. Cooksey**. (There is no indication of any relationship to John Cartwright. He may have been one of those already discussed, or may have been one of the sons of Peter Cartwright who were not named in his will, since this is a Charles County record. It seems likely however, considering the date, that this was the same 'eldest son John' of Matthew the immigrant, who married Margaret Burroughs, even though the record occurs in Charles County, which neighbors St. Mary's.)

Peter Cartwright signed as a witness on the will of **Henry Norris** of Charles County, Maryland, dated 5th January 1713---25th January 1713. Entire estate goes to son-in-law **John Fairfax** who is executor, to pass to 'grandchild, son of same'. The other witnesses are **Robert Saintclar** and **Jon Slye**. (Undoubtedly the Peter Cartwright here is the same as the son of the immigrant Matthew.)

The 'State of His Lordship's Manors' Rent Rolls for 1766, 1767, and 1768[6] shows a tract of 376 and 3/4 acres posessed by **Maj. Zachariah Bond** in St. Mary's County, and leased to **Lydia Vadry** since January 16, 1752; the section of the report requirng an entry for 'terms or lives' on which the lease is based lists **Lydia Vadry**, **Thos. Cartwright**, and **Gustavus Cartwright**. Their ages are given as **Lydia** 36, **Thomas** 46, and **Gustavus** 28. (These are clearly children of Peter Cartwright, the 'fourth son' of Matthew Cartwright the immigrant, who left a will in Charles County and named the two men here in question among his sons. Since Lydia Vadry or Vawdry was mentioned as next of kin along with son Samuel Cartwright on Peter's inventory, she may have been a daughter who was not named in Peter's will, and who married a Vadry/Vawdry/Voidry. The surname is found with the latter spelling in respect to several other individuals, connected with the Maddox family.)

The only early marriage[7] which I have found for any of the Cartwrights mentioned in the foregoing records is that of **Lancelot Chunn** and

Judith Cartwright, 4 May 1753. (This Judith being probably the same one as the apparent daughter of John Cartwright and Elisabeth Greenfield, listed as one of the next of kin on the inventory of that John Cartwright's estate.) Again, I am sure there may be sources for early marriages in Maryland that I have not checked.

A **John Cartwright** is listed among the officers of the Troops of Horse in the St. Mary's County Militia, per a muster roll from the years 1732 through 1749.[21] He is shown as a clerk in the 4th Troop under the command of Coll. George Plater. There is no way to be certain which John Cartwright this might have been. Even the now-familiar names of others found in the same troop does not help to distinguish whether this John Cartwright was the 'eldest son John' of the immigrant, or perhaps the John Cartwright who married into the Greenfield family. John Burrows (sic) is listed as Cornet in the same troop, and the Captain of the troop was Thomas Greenfield. The lieutenant was Meverell Lock.

* * * * * * *

Unplaced Cartwrights of Maryland

Early Cartwright Immigrants[8,9]
(only those who arrived at or were destined for Maryland are listed)

Cartwright, Demetrius   Immigrated 1657
Cartwright, Elizabeth   Transported 1663, wife of
                              Demetrius
Cartwright, Henry   Transported 'many years
                              prior to 1650' (Since there
                              is a Henry Cartwright found
                              in Virginia records during
                              this time period, I presume
                              this Henry is the same, who
                              moved into Virginia rather
                              than staying in Maryland.)
Cartwright, James   Transported 1668
Cartwright, Mary   Transported 1676

33

Cartwright, Thomas	Transported 1676
Cartwright, Jno. age 19	to Maryland and/or Virginia, 1699
Cartwright, Matthew	to Maryland 1666-1750
Cartwright, Peter	to Anapolis, Maryland 1725 (just as a for instance, this could have been the son of Matthew the immigrant who had merely made a trip abroad and returned, or he could be an entirely different Peter Cartwright.)
Cartwright, Thomas	to Maryland, 1726 (same possibility as above)
Cartwrite (sic), **Hannah**	to Maryland and/or Virginia, 1728

Wills and Inventories of 'unplaced' Cartwrights and others[4,5]

The will of **Demetrius Cartwright** dated 27th December 1676---13th January 1676 in Calvert County, Maryland, names **Susanna Floyd**; her son **William Floyd**; **Alice**, wife of **Samuel Graves** and their sons **Samuel** and **John**. **Susanna Floyd** and **Alice Graves** aforesaid are the heirs, executors, and residuary legatees of the estate. Overseers are **Jno. Yoe** and **Jno. Taylor**. Witnesses: **Edward Armstrong**, **Henry Hollis**, and **Jno. Yoe**. (No wife is mentioned, indicating that the wife Elizabeth named in the immigration lists must have died before Demetrius. There is no direct statement in the will to the effect that the two female legatees named are daughters, but it seems evident that they are. Clearly, this Cartwright did not leave a male line; but there may have been some relation between him, the original Matthew, and the Charles Cartwright mentioned below. Possibly, for instance, they were all brothers or cousins of about the same age. There do not seem to be any extant naturalization papers for Demetrius and Charles.)

The will of **Charles Cartwright** dated 11th July 1692---15th November 1692, Talbot County, Maryland, names wife **Sarah**, executrix, and daughter **Sarah**, still in her minority. Residual legatees are brother-in-law **Robert Harrison**, his son **John**, and his other children. Witnesses: **Henry Adcocke, Wm. Ganan, Geo. Taylor**. (Here again, it seems evident that this Cartwright did not leave any male issue.)

A **William Cartwright** signed as a witness on the will of **Thomas Peck**, dated 25th September 1734---16th November 1734, Dorchester County, Maryland. The only legacy is to **Robert Spedding** and heirs, land called 'Willoughby's Neglect' and 100 acres of 'Fox Hill' on Muddy Creek. No executor is mentioned. Other witnesses were **John leCompte** and **Peter Noell**. (There is no indication of a relationship to William Cartwright, and the testator does not mention a wife and children. This William Cartwright, whose own inventory is given below, is clearly not the same William who is discussed earlier and who resided in St. Mary's County.)

An inventory of the estate of **William Cartwright**, _____---18 February 1752, Dorchester County, Maryland. Appraisers are **Thomas Foster** and **John Smith**. Creditors are **Thomas Allcock** and **Alexander Frazar**. 'Next of kin' are **Ann Cartwright** and **William Cartwright**. Administrators are **Joseph Allford** and **Mary Ann Cartwright**. (Mary Ann Cartwright evidently being the wife, with Ann and William apparently being children of the deceased.)

A **John Cartwright** signed as a witness on the will of **Rachel Harris**, dated 24 November 1756---27 May 1757, Frederick County, Maryland. The testator names children **Thomas**, **Ruth Belt**, **Benjamin**, **Sarah Tayneyhil**, **Samuel**, and **Rebeckah Perry**. Grandaughter **Elizabeth Belt**. Son-in-law **Wm. Taneyhill** (sic). The other witness is **Joshua Busey**. Executors are **Thomas Harris** and **Wm. Taneyhil**. (There is no indication of any relationship to John Cartwright, nor whether this John might be connected to those in St. Mary's County.)

An inventory of the estate of **Matthew Cartwright**, 26 May 1772---10 August 1772, St. Mary's County, Maryland. Appraisers are

Edward Turner and **Samuel Maddox**. Creditors are **John Briscoe** for **James Buchanan & Co**. 'Next of kin': **John Cartwright**. Administratrix: **Teresia Cartwright**. (I have not been able to place this Cartwright family, but at the date mentioned the deceased Matthew could have been a son of one of Peter's family, namely perhaps a son of Robert or Thomas who inherited the land in St. Mary's County.)

A **Hannah Cartwright** signed as a witness on the will of **Sarah Bordley**, widow, dated 4 September 1769---25 October 1769, Cecil County, Maryland. The testator names children **Stephen** and **Mary**. Brothers **Andrew** and **Daniel Pearce**. Sister **Rachel Pearce**, guardian of daughter. Brother **Andrew Pearce** guardian of son. Executor is brother **Andrew Pearce**. The other witness is **Robt. Lusby**. (There is no indication of any relationship to Hannah Cartwright. This Hannah may be of the Kent County families shown in the records of St. Paul's Parish, shortly hereafter.)

The will of **Francis Posey**, dated 23 February 1772---23 April 1774, Charles County, Maryland, names daughter **Ann Cartwright**, with son **John Posey**, daughter **Mary Ann Kensman**, daughter **Elizabeth Gill**, son **Thomas Posey**, son **Francis Posey**, son **Belain Posey**, son **Richard Posey**, son **Jacob Posey**, and son **Benjamin Vernal Posey**. Wife **Ann Posey** is executrix. Witnesses are **George Elgin**, **George Keech**, and **Peter Harront Roby**. The will also names 'negro wench **Pat**', to son Francis; 'Negro wench **Grace**', to son Belain; 'Negro wench **Sue**', to son Jacob; and 'Negro girl **Rachel**', to son Benjamin. (None of the other names in the rather long will give any indication of which Cartwright may have been the husband of this Ann, though merely from the fact that it occurs in Charles County, a good guess would be that Ann was probably the wife of one of Peter's sons.)

Miscellaneous Records:

The 1750 Assessor's Field Book of Baltimore County, Maryland[10] shows a **'Maray' Cartwright** who 'lives on **Calep Goodings** land'.

The records of St. Paul's Parish, Kent County, Maryland[11] reveal two families of Cartwrights whom I have not been able to place as to progenitors---**Thomas** and **Mary Cartwright**, with a number of children; and **Abram** and **Mary (Ayres) Cartwright**, with several children also. The **Thomas Cartwright** and **Abram Cartwright** mentioned here could have issued from one of the sons of **Matthew** the immigrant, or they could have been descendants of some other early Cartwright immigrant:

> **Samuel Cartwright**, son of **Thomas** and **Mary Cartwright**,
>   b. September 27 1746.
> **Margret Cartwright**, daughter of Ditto, b. January 2 1748/9.
> **Hugh Cartwright**, son of Ditto, b. April 8 1750.
> **Sarah Cartwright**, daughter of **Thomas** and **Mary**
>   **Cartwright**, b. June 11 1752.
> **Abram Cartwright** and **Mary Ayres**, m. Nov. 174_
> **Mary Cartwright**, daughter of Do, b. October 2 17__
> **Rachel Cartwright**, daughter of Do, b. December 12 175_
> **Elizabeth Cartwright**, daughter of Do, b. January 9 1754.
> **Isaac Cartwright**, son of Do, b. July 1756.
> **Abram. Cartrite** (sic), son of **Abram.** and **Mary Cartrite**, b.
>   January 6 1759.
> **Sarah Cartrite**, daughter of Ditto, b. February 26 1761.
> **Hannah Cartrite**, daughter of Do., b. July 4 1763.
> **Jacob Cartrite**, son of **Abrm.** and **Mary Cartrite**, b.
>   December 8 1765.

With apparent relevance to the **Thomas Cartwright** shown above, there is this notice found in a newspaper of the times, dated Thursday 28 February 1754[12]:

> '**Thomas Cartwright**, in Kent County, beat a servant to death a few days ago. **Cartwright** has absconded.'

The only further marriage of any seeming relevance, other than those already mentioned, is the marriage of **Jesse Cartwright** and **Margaret Amery** 13 December 1753, Charles County, Maryland[7]. (Since it pertains to Charles County, this Jesse may have been a descendant of Peter.)

The ancestor lists of the National Society of Colonial Dames[20] refer to a **John Cartwright** who was in Maryland as early as 1602; m. **Jannecke Lawrence**. (I have not looked into the records of said society to investigate the orginal source of the information. It seems from the Dutch flavor of the wife's name that there might possibly be a connection to the immigrant Matthew. Perhaps this John was an earlier member of his family.) Also found in the above cited volume is a **John Cartwright** of Md.-Va. 1720-1780, with wife named **Sarah Mills**. (Since, as stated, I have not investigated the sources for the information, I cannot comment in detail on the identity of the John Cartwright identified here. I must presume he is not intended to be the same as the one whom I have placed as brother of William Cartwright, and son of John of generation II, in the outline previously given; and whom I have also placed as the John Cartwright who died in Edgecombe County, North Carolina in 1780. There is no evidence that the John Cartwright of Edgecombe County, North Carolina was ever in Virginia, except perhaps if he traveled down to North Carolina by that route. However, the the identical death dates and the fact that some other sources have shown the John Cartwright and Sarah Mills, above, as the parents of the Matthew Cartwright who eventually settled in Wilson County, Tennessee makes me believe that various bits of data concerning both are somewhat mangled, if not entirely erroneous. The parentage of Matthew Cartwright of Wilson County, Tennessee will be discussed at later points in this volume. There is no proof as to that parentage one way or the other, but the 'preponderance of evidence' will be examined.)

On 25 November 1669, 1300 acres of land called 'Essenton' was surveyed for **Demetrius Cartwright** in Prince George's County, Maryland.[21]

This is the extent of the data that I have found concerning Cartwrights in Maryland during the early years. This is not to say that there cannot be other sources containing mentions of Cartwrights, undiscovered by me. Nor have I followed up on those Cartwrights

38

who remained in Maryland beyond the mid-eighteenth century, since I have been mainly concerned with tracing those who moved on to other areas after that time frame. Several of Peter Cartwright's children seem to have remained in Maryland, as shown by the later censuses there. But from here on, we will examine the Cartwrights found in North Carolina and Tennessee who seem to have descended from Matthew Cartwright, the immigrant to Maryland.

Bibliography of Sources for Chapter One

1. 'Colonial Maryland Naturalizations' by Jeffrey A. Wyand and Florence L. Wyand. Genealogical Publishing Co., Inc. Baltimore, Maryland 1975
2. 'To Maryland from Overseas' by Harry Wright Newman. Ibid, 1984.
3. Encyclopedia Brittanica, Fifteenth Edition
4. 'Maryland Calendar of Wills', compiled by Jane Baldwin and others. Family Line Publications, Rear 63 East Main Street, Westminster, Maryland 21157. 1991. (Multiple-Volume set.)
5. 'Abstracts of the Inventories of the Prerogative Court of Maryland' by V.F. Skinner. Ibid, 1989. (Multiple-volume set.)
6. 'Maryland Records, Colonial, Revolutionary, County, and Church, from Original Sources' by Gaius Marcus Brumbaugh, M.S., M.D., Litt. D.. Genealogical Publishing Co., Inc. Baltimore, Maryland 1975
7. 'Maryland Marriages 1634-1777' compiled by Robert Barnes; Ibid. 1978
8. 'The Early Settlers of Maryland' by Gust Skordas. Ibid. 1986.
9. 'Passenger and Immigration Lists Index' edited by P. William Filby with Mary K. Meyer. Gale Research Co., Book Tower, Detroit, Michigan. 1981.
10. 'Inhabitants of Baltimore County 1692-1763' compiled by F. Edward Wright. Family Line Publications, Westminster, MD. 1987.
11. 'Maryland Eastern Shore Vital Records 1726-1750', by F. Edward Wright. Ibid. 1983.
12. 'The Maryland Gazette, 1727-1761, Genealogical and Historical Abstracts', by Karen Mauer Green. The Frontier Press, Galveston, Texas 1990.
13. 'Genealogical Abstracts of Revolutionary War Pension Files' abstracted by Virgil D. White. The National Historical Publishing Company, Waynesboro, Tennessee. 1990.
14. 'North Carolina Revolutionary Soldiers, Sailors, Patriots & Descendants' compiled by Joseph T. Maddox and Mary Carter. Published by Georgia Pioneers Publications, Albany, Ga. (No date. Original sources of information not given in this work.)

15. Family Bible records of the William Lavert Cartwright family, photocopies and partial originals of which are in possession of the author.
16. Photocopies and/or certified copies of vital records: death and marriage certificates for William Lavert Cartwright; John Allen Cartwright.
17. Federal Census records of 1850, 1860, 1870 and 1900 for the counties of Hardeman, Tennessee and Tippah, Mississippi; available on microfilm rolls from the National Archives, Washington, D. C. for purchase or interlibrary loan; or for hourly research at any of the regional branches of same.
18. Cemetery inscriptions, State Line Cemetery of Hardeman County, Tennessee and Tippah County, Mississippi.
19. Interviews (numerous) 1955-1994 with Ronald Earl Cartwright, J W Cartwright, Edward Leon Cartwright, John Allen Cartwright, all deceased. Interviews 1955 to present with Laurene Cartwright Bridges of Memphis, Tennessee.
20. 'Seventeenth Century Colonial Ancestors of the Members of the National Society Colonial Dames XVII Century, 1915-1975' compiled by Mary Louise M. Hutton, with Supplements for 1975-1988. Genealogical Publishing Co., Inc. Baltimor Md. 1991.
21. 'Sidelights on Maryland History' by Hester Dorsey Richardson. Originally published 1913; reprinted by Genealogical Publishing Co., Inc., Baltimore, Md. 1967, 1995.

Chapter
Two

Maryland Cartwrights in North Carolina

There are of course a great many Cartwrights to be found in the early records of North Carolina. Most of them derive from the Princess Anne County, Virginia--Pasquotank County, North Carolina Cartwrights, who will be discussed in Part II of this work. There is, however, one Cartwright whom I have found in the early records of the state who was clearly of Maryland origins. **John Cartwright** of Edgecombe County, North Carolina was a patriarch who generated a large number of descendants, most of whom spread west on the fringes of the frontier movment and are found in Tennessee and even further by the turn of the nineteenth century. As I have shown in the first chapter, I believe that this John Cartwright was the son of the 'eldest son John' of Matthew Cartwright the immigrant. John Cartwright of Edgecombe County, North Carolina had eight children, and most of his sons were found later in the area of Wilson County, Tennessee with numerous descendants of their own. The few published accounts that I have seen which relate to members of this family seem confused and contain some errors. The data given here will help to clear up some of those errors; and hopefully my own commentary will provide a reasonably sound theory as to certain linkages that cannot be made otherwise. At the very least, a full discussion of this group of Cartwrights is in order.

The earliest indications of the family that I have found are a number of deed records in Halifax County, North Carolina[1]; and it will be seen later by the will of **John Cartwright**, in Edgecombe County, that they are all of the same family, sons of said **John**---with the apparent exception of a **Matthew Cartwright** who is found in the Halifax deeds. John Cartwright of Edgecombe County had a son named Matthew, but the Matthew Cartwright mentioned in the Halifax deeds seems to have been too old to be that son. Though closely connected with the sons of John, he is clearly not the same Matthew who is found with that set of brothers later in Wilson County, Tennessee. Thus, I have tentatively identified this older Matthew as a probable *brother* of John Cartwright, and therefore likely a son of the first John and his wife Margaret Burroughs.,

First, the deed abstracts from Halifax County, North Carolina are given below in chronological order, with the inclusion of records involving the Tippetts, who have obvious connections to the family. (Inconsistencies in spelling have merely been copied as found, and since these excerpts have been taken from a published transcription of the records, it may be presumed that the original compilers likewise copied the names as found.):

Granville Grant (of land in Halifax County) to **Matthew Cartwright** of Halifax Co., 3 July 1760. 200 acres, joining **Giles Hedgepeth, John Alston, Spann**. **Thos. Child** for **Granville**. (Agent making grant) Witnesses: **Thos. Jones, Jos. Montfort**. Jan. Ct. 1763 CC: **Jos. Montfort**.

Lewis Kirk of Halifax Co. to **John Cartwright** of Granville Co. (no day) Jan. 1768. 100 pounds proclamation money. 220 acres, joining Great Creek, **Hedgepeth, Robert Tucker**. **Lewis Kirk, Sarah Kirk** (signed) Witnesses: **Peter Cartwright, John Baptist Cartwright**. Jan. Ct. 1768. Examined by **Egbert Haywood, Sarah Kirk** relinquished her right of dower. CC: **Jos. Montfort**. (Although this deed describes John Cartwright as being of Granville County, I have found no other references to him or any Cartwrights at all in Granville County. It was formed from Edgecombe County in 1746, rather than

43

the other way around, and Halifax was also formed from Edgecombe, in 1758. Although the father, John, died in Edgecombe in 1780 and clearly owned lands there, I have likewise found no mention of any of the Cartwrights in the other records of that county, except to show that sons Thomas and Hezekiah resided there at the time of the 1790 census.)

Thomas Good, planter of Halifax Co. to **Philip Tippet** planter of same. 6 Mar. 1770. 33 pounds 5 shillings proclamation money. 400 acres, joining **John Bass, Evans, Brantley, Merritt,** Cowhall (Creek?). **Thos. Good** (signed). Witnesses: **Zachariah Greenwall, Peter Cartwright, Lucy Good.** May Ct. 1770. CC: **Jos. Montfort**.

John Evans of Dobbs. Co. to **Phillip Tippett** of Halifax Co. 29 Aug. 1771. 30 pounds proclamation money. 234 acres, joining **Reed. John Evans** (X). Witnesses: **Benj. Haynie, Samuel Simpson, Zupariah Bond.** Nov. Ct. 1771. CC: **Jos. Montfort**.

John Cartwright, Jr. signed as a witness on a deed of **Thomas Stewart** of Halifax Co. to **John Hamilton,** merchant of Virginia. 24 Oct. 1771. (Evidently this John Cartwright, Jr. is the same as John Baptist Cartwright.)

Matthew Cartwright of Halifax Co. to **George Morris** of same. 17 Jun 1774. 70 pounds proclamation money. 200 acres, joining **Giles Hedgepeth, Joseph John Alston, Span. Matthew Cartwright** (signed). Witnesses: **Robert Williams, William Morris, Bettey Morris.** Aug. Ct. 1774 CC: **Jos. Montfort**.

Jane Tippett of Halifax Co. to **Nathan Spears** of same. 4 Feb. 1774. 6 pounds 6 shillings 8 pence proclamation money. 25 acres which was part of land **John Evans** acquired 27 Apr 1753, joining her own corner, Flax Pond Branch, Cowhall Branch. **Jane Tippett** (signed). Witnesses: **Tobias Whitehead, Zachariah Reves** (X), **Jesse Haynie.** Nov. Ct. 1774. CC: **Jos. Montfort**.

Matthew Cartwright to his son-in-law Erasmus Tippet. 30 Jan. 1777. For "love, good will, and affection." 200 acres, joining John Bass, Evans, Brantley, Merritt, Cowhall Swamp. Matthew Cartwright (X). Jane Cartwright (X). Witnesses: Thomas Dew, Jacob O'Daniel (X), Parker Savage (X). May Ct. 1777. CC: Ben McCullouch.

John Cartwright of Edgecombe Co. to George Morris of Halifax Co. 27 Nov. 1777 200 pounds proclamation money. 220 acres, joining Great Creek, Jiles Hedgepeth, Robert Tucker. John Cartwright (X). Witnesses: William Morris, Matthew Cartwright, George Morris. May Ct. 1778. CC: Ben McCulloch.

Erasmus Tippet to his brother Erastus Tippett. 15 Jun. 1778. For "love, good will, and affection." (no acres)? which said Erasmus Tippett had received from his father-in-law Matthew Cartwright, the same tract which Thomas Good had sold to Phillip Tippett 1770. Erasmus Tippett (signed). Witnesses: Wm. Spear (X), Matthew Cartwright (X), Jane Cartwright (X). Nov. Ct. 1778. CC: Ben McCulloch.

William Edwards of Halifax Co. to Erasmus Tippett of same. 18 Nov. 1782. 200 pounds. 80 acres, joining James Perry, Ready Branch, Elm Bass, Champion, Jesse Haynie. William Edwards (signed). Witnesses: Joab Cotton, Henry Josey. Aug. Ct. 1782. CC: Wm. Wooten. P.R., Wm. T. Ballard.

Erasmus Tippett and Lucy his wife of Halifax Co. to Joab (Joal?) Cotten of same. 18 Nov. 1782. 400 pounds proclamation money. 240 acres which had been part of a patent to Benjamin Foreman May 1768, and which had been conveyed from William Foreman to Hester, Phareby, and Lucy Foreman, on south side of Mill Swamp, joining Ann Melton, Thos. Pope, Benjamin Foreman, Jr.. Erasmus Tippett, Lucy Tippett (X). Witnesses: Wm. Wooten. Aug. Ct. 1782. CC: Wm. Wooten. Public Register Wm. T. Ballard.

Erastus Tippett of Halifax Co. to **Erasmus Lee Tippett** of same. 12 Aug. 1783. 25 pounds specie. 200 acres which had been part of 400 acres acquired by **John Evans** 22 Sept. 1760, on Cowhall Swamp. **Erastus Tippet** (signed). Witnesses: **Epr. Dicken, Nathan Spear, Lewis Haynie.** Nov. Ct. 1783. CC: **Wm. Wooten.** P. Regr. **Jno Geddy.**

Erastus Tippitt, Elizabeth Tippitt, Matthew Cartwright, and **Jane Cartwright** to **Thomas Dew.** 11 Aug. 1786. 80 pounds. 160 acres, joining **John Barnes,** Poplar Branch, **Nathan Spears, John Evans'** old patent line, **Hood. Erastus Tippitt, Elizabeth Tippitt** (X), **Matthew Cartrite** (X), **Jane Cartrite.** (sic). Witnesses: **Jesse Haynie, Nathen Spear** (X) Aug. Ct. 1786. CC: **Wm. Wooten.** Note: (by compilers of abstracts) 'body of deed indicates that the women named are wives of said men.'

Erasmus Lee Tippett of Halifax Co. to **Jonas Shriver** of Edgecombe Co. 20 Feb. 1785. (no amount) 1 negro girl **Dinah,** "which negro was taken by Exe'or to satisfy a debt of cost of the just agent **Matthew Cartwright** brought by **James McMullen** and **Wm. McMullen.**" **Erasmus Tippett** (signed). Witnesses: **James Jones, J. Haynie, Benjamin Coffield.** Aug. Ct. 1786. CC: **Wm. Wooten.** (The meaning here is difficult to determine. It would seem that Jonas Shriver was the 'executor' who took Dinah, but for whose estate is unclear. Evidently, Matthew Cartwright had incurred some debt by acting as the administrator of Philip Tippett once he had married the widow Jane. Erasmus was apparently paying the debt with Dinah, since he had received the property of his father, Philip Tippett, from Matthew Cartwright and was liable for his father's debts.)

Erastus Tippett of Halifax Co. to **Nathan Speir** of same. 29 Jul. 1786. 100 pounds. 47 acres which was part of land acquired by **John Evins** 22 Feb. 1760, joining Poplar Branch, Cow Hall Branch. **Erastus Tippett, Jane Cartwright, Elizabeth Tippett** (X), **Matthew Cartwright** (X). Witnesses: **Benjamin Haynie, Thos. Dew, Jesse Haynie.** Nov. Ct. 1786. CC: **Wm. Wooten.**

Erasmus Lee Tippett and his wife **Lucy** of Halifax Co. to **Thomas Lowery** of Edgecombe Co. 27 May 1786. 200 pounds. 300 (350?) acres which had been patented by **John Evins** 10 Dec. 1760, joining **John Bass, Nathan Spear, Evans'** old line, **Brantley, Isam Hill,** Cow Hall (Branch?). **Erasmus Lee Tippett, Lucy Tippett**. Witnesses: **Epm. Dicken, Jesse Haynie, Benjamin Dicken, Phillip Rauls** (X). Nov. Ct. 1786. CC: **Wm. Wooten**.

Obviously there are many points of important information to be derived from the above abstracts:

---Some of the given names alone of the Cartwrights involved is an indication that they originated among the Maryland Cartwrights. The names Matthew, John, Peter, and Thomas, of course, are so common as to prove nothing (although the names Peter and Matthew are not found among the Pasquotank Cartwrights in the early generations). But the name John Baptist certainly is somewhat unique and is clearly a name of Maryland usage. Further, as we will see in the will of **John Cartwright** hereafter, there was a brother in this family named **Thomas Notley Cartwright**, which name is virtual proof of the family's Maryland beginnings. **Thomas Notley** was the governor of the colony of Maryland during the time frame of the immigrant **Matthew Cartwright** who settled there[2]. **Governor Notley** was evidently much revered in a personal way, for numerous families in the colony named children after him, although he had no issue of his own.

---It is evident that the **Matthew Cartwright** here in question was an adult by 1760, when he took his own Granville grant, and thus was born at least by 1739. That he was even considerably older is indicated later by the census records which will be examined. **Peter** and **John Baptist Cartwright** are shown to be adults by 1768 when they signed as witnesses on a deed of their father's, which means they must have been born at least by 1747 or so. We don't know that the latter two men weren't even older as well, but it is less likely considering that their dates of death are after the year 1800, as will be seen later. Just as important and apparently clinching the belief that the Matthew Cartwright mentioned in the Halifax deeds was much older than the sons of John, is the evidence of the other Matthew Cartwright who comes into prominence later as the probable son of

47

John. The indications concerning the second Matthew (later of Wilson County, Tennessee) is that he was considerably younger than the one in question here and had a different wife and children. It seems much more likely that he was the one who was the brother of the men Peter, Thomas Notley, and Hezekiah, since they were *all* found later in Wilson County, Tennessee and closely interacted with each other there. (See the genealogical outline given in Chapter One, and the discussion of the Wilson County Cartwrights in Chapter Five.)

---The connection to the Tippett family is another clear proof of the Maryland origins of this family of Cartwrights, and the fact that the two families remain closely intertwined during a total of two or three further migrations provides a means of tracing the descent of these Maryland Cartwright when there is otherwise no documentary proof as to their origins or the relationships. The **Phillip Tippet** who is found here in Halifax County cannot be the same as the one who signed as a witness on the will of the immigrant **Matthew Cartwright** in Maryland, nearly a hundred years earlier. But he may have been a grandson or a nephew, etc. of the previous **Philip Tippett**. **Jane** and the men **Erastus** and **Erasmus** are the widow and sons of this later **Philip Tippett**, as will be clarified when his will is explored shortly hereafter. The content of some of the Halifax deeds make it evident that the widow **Jane (Lee) Tippett** married **Matthew Cartwright**, before 1777. The references to the relationship between **Matthew Cartwright** and the men named **Erasmus** and **Erastus** as 'sons-in-law' was obviously the usage meaning 'step-sons', and certain references to the land also make the relationship clear. The marriage between Matthew Cartwright and Jane Tippett is another of the reasons why I have postulated the **Matthew Cartwright** in question as the brother of the elder **John**, rather than the son. **Jane** herself had to have been at least in her late thirties at the time of said marriage, and the implications of some type of family relationship between **Philip Tippett** and **Sarah (Tippett?) Cartwright** would have made the **Matthew** who was a son of **John** and **Sarah Cartwright** perhaps a nephew or at least a younger cousin of the **Philip Tippett** in question---and thus of **Jane** by marriage. While it wouldn't be unheard of for a man to marry such an aunt who was related only by blood, or to marry an older cousin, it just doesn't seem likely that the **Matthew** who married **Jane (Lee) Tippett** was the same as the son of

John and **Sarah Cartwright**. Again, the **Matthew** who was the son of **John** and **Sarah** must certainly be the one found with the other sons later in Wilson County, Tennessee, and who did *not* marry Jane Tippett.

---It is seen that the wife of **Erastus Tippett** was named **Elizabeth**, and that the wife of his brother **Erasmus Lee Tippett** was **Lucy Foreman**. It would appear that Lucy's father was **Benjamin Foreman** and that her probable siblings were **Benjamin Foreman, Jr, William Foreman, Hester**, and **Phareby**. (I have noted a Foreman family, which was likely the origin of this one, in the earlier Maryland records; but since we are more concerned with the Cartwrights and their closer connections here, I have not attempted further research concerning the Foreman surname.)

---There are at least some indications of connections to the other families such as Evans, Haynie (or Haynes), and Spear or Spears, whose names occur frequently in these transactions with the Cartwrights and Tippetts, and some of which are also found in close proximity in Tennessee, later. **Nathan Spear**, for instance, is found in connection with them here and not only later in Blount County, Tennessee, but further in Lawrence County, Tennessee after yet another migration. It seems likely that some of the females in either the Cartwright or the Tippett family may have married into one or more of these families, though I have found nothing to confirm such speculation. We also see in these Halifax deeds such surnames as Bond, Dew, Edwards, Wooten, and Merritt, which are all names that can be found in earlier Maryland records. Such repeated names along the trail may merely indicate that various neighbors followed each other in their pioneer movements, but it seems likely that there were familial relationships which extend rather far back in time, in some of the cases.

---Since several parcels of land were sold by the Tippetts and Matthew Cartwright in the year 1786, this may be when they were readying to leave the area. See later references to census records which show their positionings as of 1786 and 1790.

The will of **John Cartwright** in Edgecombe County, North Carolina[3], as mentioned, clarifies this family of Cartwrights. The will was written October 12, 1780 and proved in the November Court of that year. The abstract from which I have taken the data is itself long and detailed, and since I am not reproducing an original I will not try to repeat my source word for word. Named are wife **Sarah**; daughters **Mary Caulwell, Susannah**, and **Sarah**; sons **John Baptist Cartwright, Matthew Cartwright, Thomas Notley Cartwright, Peter Cartwright**, and **Hezekiah Cartwright**. Also named is 'my negro fellow **Primus**'. Aside from references to the testator's 'plantation' and tracts surrounding it, mention is made of 'land lying between the lines of **Peter Hines, Sr**. and **Peter Cartwright**, adjoining the testator's plantation; a tract of land bought of **Charles Evans**; 80 acres of land bought of **Jacob Johnson**; and 'my lands in Johnston County'. Aside from various individual bequests to the children and the mention of land already given to **Peter Cartwright** by deed of gift, the will distinguishes 'my four sons **Peter, Matthew, Thomas**, and **Hezekiah**' with a bequest of tools, not naming the son **John Baptist Cartwright** in this bequest. (Nor giving him any other bequest. But he had not gone elsewhere or died at the time of this will, for he was living in the next county, Halifax, as is seen by the census records given hereafter. It may be that he had previously been given the land that had been purchased by his father in Halifax in 1768.) Sons **Matthew Cartwright, Thomas Notley Cartwright**, and **Hezekiah Cartwright** are named as executors. Witnesses are **Peter Hines, Jr**. and **Henry Hines**. (One might speculate that the Hines connection could mean that there was a marriage of one of the Cartwrights to a Hines, since the surname of Hines is also found in all the same places as the Cartwrights, from Maryland to points west. The wills of both Peter Hines, Sr. and Peter Hines, Jr. are extant in Edgecombe County and give no indication of of a marriage connection to the Cartwrights, but since neither will names a wife and the men do not seem to have named all family members, the possibility of a marriage between the families is not ruled out. We have already seen that it is likely the wife of the elder John Cartwright was Sarah Tippett, daughter of Dennis Tippett in Maryland, and thus she was not likely the source of the connection. But as will be seen, we do not know the maiden names of the wives of Peter Cartwright and Thomas Notley Cartwright.)

Despite the references to Johnston County, North Carolina, I have not found any mention of Cartwrights there other than a state grant to a **John Cartwright** in 1782. This could not have been the elder John, since he died in 1780. And though it might have been John Baptist Cartwright who is mentioned in the grant, there seems no way of determining that. He clearly lived in Halifax County in 1786, as will be seen in the census records.

Obviously pertinent to the data under discussion is the will of **Philip Tippett**, found in Halifax County, North Carolina records.[4] It is dated 1770, with day and month not given. Proved May Ct. 1772. It names **Erasmus Lee Tippett** and **Erastus Tippett**; **Mary Lee Tippett** and **Cloey Lee Tippett**, (or Clara Lee?) referring to them as 'sons and daughters'; and wife **Jane Tippett**, who is made executrix. Witnesses are **Thomas Good** (a name found in some of the deeds given earlier) **Benjamin Haynes** (this name appears to be the same as 'Haynie' in the deeds, but which spelling is correct is difficult to tell), and **Elizabeth Bond**. (Bond is clearly a Maryland name.)

The use of the name 'Lee' for a middle name in this Tippet family is one of the important clues as regards the origins of Jane, who married first Philip Tippett and then Matthew Cartwright. As we have seen from the will abstracts given in Chapter One, she was apparently the daughter of John and Mary Lee of St. Mary's County, Maryland, named in their wills:

Reiterating the will of **John Lee** of St. Mary's County, Maryland, it names eldest daughter **Elizabeth Gibson**, daughter **Susanna Bowling**, daughter **Henerita** (sic) **Hobson**, daughter **Sarah Tippit**, daughter **Jane Tippit**, daughter **Mary Fanning**, son **Thomas Lee**, son **John Lee**, and wife **Mary Lee**. (It is possible that the Sarah Tippit mentioned here was the wife of Dennis Tippett, and thus that they were the parents of John Cartwright's wife Sarah. If Philip Tippett was a brother of Dennis, it would thus explain the two families' migrations together to North Carolina, for Philip and Jane Tippett would be the uncle and aunt of John Cartwright's wife, Sarah.)

The will of Mary Lee, as shown, merely clarified the same names, correcting 'Heneriter' as **Henrietta** and showing the second marriage of the daughter **Susanna Bowling** by naming her as a **Maddox**.

There is a further clue to the identity of Philip Tippett's wife Jane as the one who was daughter of John and Mary Lee in Maryland,

51

by the fact that it seems her sister **Henrietta** also came to Halifax County, North Carolina. The latter is found on the 1786 census for the county, as will be shown shortly---as head of her own household and, rather humorously, once again called 'Heneriter' rather than Henrietta.

The names **John Tippett** and **Jonathon Tippett** are also in evidence along the trail, and they might have been brothers of **Philip Tippett**, since these names are all found together in the inventory of a **Henry Tippett** in Maryland, shown earlier. A **John Tippet, Sr.** 'of Roane County North Carolina' is found in a record among Granville County, North Carolina wills[6], appointing 'my son **John Tippett, Jr.** of Roane County my attorney to transact all my business for me....' Witnesses: **Benjamin Bearden, Richard Hudspeth**. January 26, 1795. In Rowan County, North Carolina[7] is found the will of a **John Tipet** (sic), dated 26 May 1796, with no probate date. It names wife **Susannah**, sons **John, Luke, Thomas**, and **William**, daughers **Sarah, Nancy, Elizabeth**, and **Susannah**. Executors are **Susanna Tipet** and **William Tipet**. Witnesses **William Silvers** and **John Leathers**.

See also census records abstracted below, in reference to various Tippetts in North Carolina; and there is a **Jonathan Trippet** or **Tippett** found later in Blount County, Tennessee along with some of the Cartwrights and the sons of **Phillip Tippett**, which see in Chapter Three.

Further tidbits concerning the Cartwrights who were sons of John in North Carolina are the notation of **Peter Cartwright** and wife **Ann** as witnesses on the will of a **James Taylor** in Edgecombe County, August 10 1782---May Ct. 1782; and the signing of **Peter Cartwright, Thos. N. Cartwright**, and **Hezekiah Cartwright** as witnesses on the will of **John Stokes**, dated May 8, 1783---Feb. Ct. 1784, also in Edgecombe County.[3] (Recall that one of the sisters of Sarah Cartwright, if she was the daughter of Dennis Tippett, was named as Elizabeth Taylor. Though no wife was named in the will of the James Taylor mentioned here, and I have found no other identifying records, it is not far-fetched to assume that this may have been a connection to the family of the said Sarah's sister Elizabeth. It may be that nearly all of the children in the two families of the Lees

52

and Tippetts came to North Carolina, for there are Gibsons, Lees, and Fannings in evidence in Halifax County as well.)

I found no other reference to either Cartwrights or Tippetts among the will records of Halifax County, aside from Phillip Tippett's will. As far as I can determine, all other references to Cartwrights in other parts of North Carolina, except for those already mentioned in this study, involve those of Pasquotank descent. A close examination of the works of Grimes and Olds[8,9], and of the wills listed in Thornton Mitchell's Testator Index[10], reveals no other Cartwrights save those clearly of Pasquotank origin.

There are several pertinent references to military service which should be noted here. One source[11] (for which I was not able to find a reference to the *original* sources of the information given) lists the following:

Cartwright, Hezekiah (RS-Pvt-NC) 1761-1818, m.1st **Hannah Lavender**; m. 2nd **Elizabeth Mulholland** (Clearly, he is the same Hezekiah who is both a son of John Cartwright of Edgecombe County, North Carolina, and the one who moved to Wilson County, Tennessee, as will be seen in Chapter Three, although the second wife's maiden name seems more properly to be 'Maholland'. This is the only source that I have seen which gives the name of Hezekiah's first wife.)

Cartwright, Matthew (R-Pat-NC) 1754-1812 m. **Polly Ginnes**. (This is apparently meant to be the same as the Matthew who went to Wilson County, Tennessee and is found there along with the brothers Peter, Thomas Notley, and Hezekiah; but as mentioned, there are numerous errors in some published material concerning this Matthew. The name of the wife Polly is given in most other places as 'Grimes' rather than 'Ginnes'. I personally tend to believe that there is some mixing of information on two the different Matthews in this military record, as well. For instance, a man born in 1754 would have been of a ripe age to be a soldier during the Revolutionary conflict, so why would he have been merely a Patriot? It seems more likely that the older Matthew Cartwright, born as early as 1725, must have been the Patriot who was mentioned in whatever original record it was which provided this data.)

53

From another source[12] of military information, I have taken the following data, the first abstract making no mention of North Carolina but given here because of its brief relevance (I was not able to find a key for the abbreviations used in these abstracts):

Tippet, Notley, BLW #11770=100-1 Feb 1790 to **Ann Tootle** adm'x, **James Williams & Joseph Dawson** adm'rs of **James Tootle** "late assignee of sol", sol had srv as a Pvt in the Md line. (Likely this is the same Notley Tippett who is named as a son of Dennis Tippett in the latter's will.)

Tippet, Erastus, NC line, S39108, appl 4 Jan 1819 Lawrence Co Tn, sol enl in Halifax Co Va, (clearly this is in error---it should be Halifax Co. *North Carolina*, not Virginia); on 5 Oct 1820, sol stated he was age of 60 on 1 Aug 1819 & he then had a wife **Judith** & referred to children: **Ross, James, John, Jane & Nancy** & he stated his youngest son was age of 17 yrs. (Obviously, the wife Judith must have been a second wife, since we have the earlier records proving that Erastus's wife during the time just after the Rev. War was named Elizabeth. It seems likely that the children named are not all the children of Erastus Tippett, and that there were probably older children from his first marriage, for there are indications of others later in Blount County. That this is the same Erastus Tippett as the one we are studying elsewhere is obvious not only from the unusual name but because of the continuity of his connections with the Cartwrights through all their migrations, including the area of Lawrence County, Tennessee. Erastus is shown in another source[13] as being ten years older than the reference to his age here would suggest, but likely that is an error, especially since it seems from various clues that his mother Jane was quite young when named in her father's will as Jane Tippett in 1757. It is my belief that she herself was born around 1740, and that Erastus could not have been born in 1750.)

Census records provide the last references that I have found for the Cartwrights and Tippets before they leave North Carolina and are found in Tennessee. **Matthew Cartwright** and **John B. Cartwright**, along with the Tippetts and others of interest, are found on the State Census of North Carolina for 1784-1787.[14] As the last entry on page one of a list for District No. 3 of Halifax County, taken by Lemuel Hogun 1st February 1786, we find **Erastus L. Tippett** (this should undoubtedly be **Eras_m_us**, who is always the one distinguished with the middle initial L.; also because Erastus himself is listed nearby), whose household shows one white male 21 to 60 years old, one white male under 21 or above 60, 2 white females (all ages included) and one black person (sex not distinguished) 12 to 50 years old. At the top of page 2, (meaning next door, since the Halifax list was not alphabetized as some of those for the other counties were) we find **Matthew Cartwright** with 4 white males either under twenty-one or above sixty (Matthew himself evidently being above sixty at this point, since he certainly could not have been under twenty-one), 2 white females, and one black person either under 12 or above 50. (These numbers would account for the two sons Thomas and Jessee Cartwright whom I have ascribed to this Matthew in the genealogical outline and who will be discussed in the next chapter. They were evidently born after 1774 to the union of Matthew Cartwright and Jane Tippett, as will be seen by their apparent ages. There is no way of knowing who the other male and the second female in this household were, but they were probably other children of Matthew Cartwright, or the female could have been one of the daughters of Jane from her marriage to Philip Tippett. That this Matthew Cartwright on the 1786 census is not the other Matthew who was son of John and later died in Wilson County, Tennessee, is obvious from the data that is known on each of the men. If the latter Matthew was genuinely born in 1754 he certainly would not have been either under twenty-one *or* above sixty, and there is no male listed for the age group which would have been correct for him. Further, the said Matthew who was younger had only one son, as shown by his will which will be explored later in Chapter Five.)

Farther down on page 2 of the same census list, we find **Erastus Tippett**, with one white male 21 to 60 years old, 3 white males under 21 or above 60, one white female, 2 blacks 12 to 50 years old, and 5 blacks under 12 or above 50. Next door to him is **John B. Cartwright** (certainly this must be John Baptist Cartwright) with one white male between 21 and 60 years old; no other males; two white females; no blacks. (This reference is the basis for assuming that John Baptist Cartwright had no sons. He would have been at least in his mid-forties by this time, and if he had sons they probably would be evident here. Although it is possible that he had sons who had already left his own household, if so they don't seem to be in evidence anywhere.)

On page 3, the same district, we find **'Henerritter' Hopson**, and undoubtedly this should be **Henrietta Hobson**, the sister of **Sarah Tippett Cartwright** from Maryland, as mentioned. 'Henerritter's' household shows only one male, either under twenty-one or over 60, two females, and one black person. Not found on this 1786 census are Peter Cartwright, Thomas Notley Cartwright, and Hezekiah, but they appear to have lived at that time in Edgecombe County, for which no list seems to be extant. We see on this census of Halifax County, North Carolina all those who were seen to be connected with the Cartwrights and Tippetts in the deed abstracts given earlier, such as Nathan Spear, the Haynies, Thomas Good, etc. As well, there are others who were probably from Maryland---many Edwards families are listed, a number of Taylor families; several Lees, including a John Lee who might have been Jane Lee Tippett's brother; and other Maryland surnames such as Gibson, Fanning, Graves, Lock, Bond, Maddox, etc. There are a number of names on this census which will be found later as connections of the Cartwrights both in Blount County, Tennessee and in Wilson County, Tennessee---names such as Partin, James, Edwards, Joiner, Franks, Barnes, Rogers and so forth.

On the 1790 Federal census[15], **Thomas** and **Hezekiah Cartwright** are shown in Halifax District of Edgecombe County, North Carolina. **Erasmus Tippett** is still in Halifax County. **Erastus**, however, is in Richmond County, North Carolina---well on his way to the frontier country. His household numbers show one male over the age of sixteen, five males under sixteen, and four females, with no slaves. The only **Matthew Cartwright** listed on the 1790 census for North Carolina is in Pitt County, and the numbers in his household make it likely he was the younger Matthew who turns up later in Wilson County, Tennessee---one male over sixteen, one male under sixteen, five females, and three slaves. (Perhaps the elder Matthew was deceased by this time, or else he had already moved on to Tennessee, since we will shortly find the men who seem to have been his sons in Blount County, Tennessee.) Also on this 1790 census is a **John Tippett** in Granville County, apparently the same one mentioned earlier as being of 'Roane County, North Carolina', but with the

56

record found among Granville county data. There are Tippetts named **James**, **John**, **Joseph**, and **William** in Jones County, North Carolina.

Most of the other Cartwrights who are found on the 1790 census can be identified as those of Pasquotank (and Camden, which was taken from Pasquotank.) There is, however, an **Elizabeth Cartwright**, apparently a widow with several children, found in Rutherford County, North Carolina. I have found no indication of whether she had any connection to the Cartwrights under discussion here.

Neither **Peter Cartwright** nor **John Baptist Cartwright** are found on the 1790 census, but Peter seems to have been the first one to have moved on to Tennessee, and may have already gone there by 1790. And there is a John 'Cartist' listed in Halifax County who perhaps should be John (Baptist) Cartwright, with only himself shown in the household. It seems possible, judging from this, that the two females shown in the household of John B. Cartwright on the 1786 census could have been his mother and one of the sisters, or else both sisters, who were indicated in his father's will as being unmarried. A John Cartwright who is probably the same John Baptist Cartwright is found in Edgecombe County on the 1800 North Carolina census, and if so it rules him out as the apparent deceased husband of the Elizabeth Cartwright in Rutherford County, for she is still listed there in 1800 as well.

The preponderance of evidence seems to indicate that John Baptist Cartwright had no family, and I feel fairly confident in ruling him out as the father of the two Cartwrights who are found in Blount County, Tennessee, to be explored in the next Chapter. The fact that the latter originated among the Cartwrights of Halifax and Edgecombe counties in North Carolina is clear, as will be seen. But the data given in Chapter Five will show that neither could Peter, Thomas Notley, Hezekiah, nor the younger Matthew who appears to have been their brother have been the father of the Cartwrights of Blount County, Tennessee. It seems obvious then, from the weight of the evidence shown here and to be explored shortly, that the elder Matthew Cartwright who resided in Halifax County, North Carolina and who married the widow Jane Lee Tippett, must certainly have been the father of the Blount County, Tennessee Cartwrights.

Bibliography of Sources for Chapter Two

1. 'The Deeds of Halifax County, North Carolina' abstracted by Dr. Stephen E. Bradley, Jr.. South Boston, Va. 1989. (Multiple-Volume set.)
2. 'Sidelights on Maryland History' by Hester Dorsey Richardson; originally published Baltimore 1913; reprinted by Genealogical Publishing Co., Inc. 1967, 1995.
3. 'Abstracts of the Wills of Edgecombe County North Carolina 1733-1856' by Ruth Smith Williams and Margarette Glenn Griffin. Published by Joseph W. Watson, 406 Piedmont Ave., Rocky Mount, N.C. 27801; 1980.
4. 'Genealogical Abstracts of Wills 1758 through 1824, Halifax County, North Carolina' by Margaret M. Hoffman; published by the Roanoke News Company, Weldon, North Carolina.
5. 'Maryland Calendar of Wills' compiled by Jane Baldwin and others; Family Line Publications, Westminster, Maryland. 1991.
6. 'Abstracts of the Wills and Estate Records of Granville County, North Carolina 1746-1808' by Zae Hargett Gwynn; published by Joseph W. Watson, 406 Piedmont Ave., Rocky Mount, N.C. 1973.
7. 'Abstracts of Wills and Estate Records of Rowan County, North Carolina 1753-1805' by Mrs. Stahle Linn, Jr. C.G., Box 1948 Salisbury, N.C. 28144; 1980.
8. 'Abstracts of North Carolina Wills' by J. Bryan Grimes, Secretary of State; originally published Raleigh, North Carolina 1910; reprinted by Genealogical Publishing Co., Inc. 1967, 1975, 1980; and reprinted for Clearfield Company, Inc. by Genealogical Publishing Co. 1991.
9. 'Abstracts of North Carolina Wills' by Fred A. Olds, originally published Oxford 1925; reprinted Southern Book Company, Baltimore 1954; Reissued Genealogical Publishing Co., Inc. Baltimore, 1965, 1968, 1972, 1978, 1983; reprinted for Clearfield Company, Inc. by Genealogical Publishing Co., Baltimore 1990.
10. 'North Carolina Wills, A Testator Index' by Thornton W. Mitchell; Ibid, 1987-1993.
11. 'North Carolina Revolutionary Soldiers, Sailors, Patriots, and

Descendants' compiled by Joseph T. Maddox & Mary Carter; published by Georgia Pioneers Publications, Albany, Georgia (No date. No references to original sources of information.)

12. 'Genealogical Abstracts of Revolutionary War Pension Files' abstracted by Virgil D. White. The National Historical Publishing Company, Waynesboro, Tennessee. 1990.

13.. The Pension Roll of 1835, originally published in 1835 as Senate Document 514, Serial Nos. 249-51. Reprinted in four volumes 1968 by Genealogical Publishing Co., Inc., Baltimore, Md.

14. 'State Census of North Carolina 1784-1787' transcribed and indexed by Mrs. Alvaretta Kenan Register. Genealogical Publishing Company, Inc., Baltimore, Md. 1974.

15. 'Heads of Families at the First Census of the United States, Taken in the Year 1790'. First published Government Printing Office, Washington, D.C. 1908; reprinted Ibid. 1966-1992.

16. 'Index to the 1800 Census of North Carolina' compiled by Elizabeth Petty Bentley. Ibid. 1977.

Chapter
Three

The Cartwrights of Blount County, Tennessee

The first indication of Cartwrights in Blount County is the presence of the name **Thomas Cartwright** on the tax list of 1801[1]. He is found with no land and one white poll. On the same list are found surnames which become significant in connection with this Cartwright, such as Franks, James, and Barnes. A look back at the state census of 1786-87 for Halifax County, North Carolina shows that many of these people were there, as well. Here we continue to find names that go all the way back to Maryland, such as Bond, Edwards, Taylor, Hines, though still without any clue as to a relationship. Interestingly, there are a number of Caulwell/Cauldwell families on the early tax list for Blount County, Tennessee, and it should be remembered that one of the daughters of **John Cartwright** in Edgecombe County, North Carolina was named in his will as '**Mary Caulwell**', indicating that she had married a man of that name.

These bits are mere clues, but the fact that the **Thomas Cartwright** found on the tax list of Blount County must have come from among those in Halifax and Edgecombe counties in North Carolina becomes evident from the demonstration that the Tippetts are present in Blount County, and they remain closely connected with this Thomas Cartwright's family. Though no Tippetts are listed on the

1801 Blount County tax list, **Erastus Tippett** is found on an earlier list of 1800 for the county, and both he and **Erasmus** are found on the later 1805 tax roll[2]. Further, the court records which are to be explored shortly show that Erastus was in Blount County as early as 1796. He may have been the instigator of the move, since he would have been considerably older than the Cartwrights here, whom I believe to have been his half-brothers. The fact that he was in Richmond County, North Carolina at the time of the 1790 census indicates that he had headed west before others in the family, with the possible exception of **Peter Cartwright**, as mentioned earlier.

There is a marriage of a **Jenny Tippet** to **Daniel McKenzey** on record in Blount County dated 20 December 1798[3]. I believe Jenny may have been a daughter of Erastus's first marriage, for the children of Erasmus will be accounted for by records concerning his death, and there is a demonstrated connection between **Daniel Mckinzey** and **Erastus Tippett**, as will be seen when the deeds of the county are examined. There were several McKenzies (sic) in Richmond County, North Carolina at the time of the 1790 census when Erastus was there, including a **Daniel McKenzie** whose household showed three males over sixteen and three females, with one slave. This family may have been that of the **Daniel McKenzey** who married **Jenny Tippett** in Blount County, Tennessee.

The details of the 1805 roll for Blount County show **Thomas Cartwright** *and* a **Jesse Cartwright**, along with both **Erastus** and **Erasmus Tippet**. Listed also are **James Tippet** and a **Jonathon Trippet**, with the latter name possibly being a mistranslation of Tippet, since I have found it thus confused for Erastus in other records. The James Tippett who is listed could have been the son of Erastus who was named in the military record given in the previous chapter, but as we will see, his brother Erasmus also had a son named James. Found on the 1805 tax list as well is a man named **George Rogers**, who becomes a significant connection to the families in question, later. He should not be confused with a man of the same name who is found in the neighboring county of Sevier.

The same **Thomas Cartwright** mentioned above is found on the rosters for the War of 1812, in the company of **Col. Samuel Wear** of Blount County[1]. **George Rogers** is found on this roster as well, in the same company; but other sources have claimed the George Rogers on the roster is the one who resided in Sevier County. Since it is a Blount County list which contains the name, I have some question in my own mind as to the validity of the latter claim, but the two men are clearly different ones. Whatever the resolution as to the military record, the names of **Thomas Cartwright** and **George Rogers** are the only ones relevant to the present study that I have found on such lists for the area and time frame.

Thomas Cartwright left a will in Blount County, recorded 1814.[4] The will was written 15 January 1814, but when it was proved is unclear due to the lack of such dates on the court records as they stand today. No proving date is given on my copy, which came from a will book that was evidently transcribed by clerks at some point and contained the records from the year 1814. The will is given here in full, and I have reproduced it with the same punctuation, (or lack thereof), with no heading:

In the name of God, amen. I **Thomas Cartwright** of the state of Tennessee and county of Blount being very sick and weak in body but in perfect mind and memory thanks be given unto God calling unto mind the mortality of my body and knowing that it is appointed for all men once to die do make and ordain this my last will and testament; that is to say principally and first of all I give and recommend my soul into the hands of almighty God that gave it, and my body I recommend to the earth to be buried in a decent Christian burial at the discretion of my executors, nothing doubting but at the general Resurrection I shall receive the same again by the Mighty Powers of God and as touching such worldly estate wherewith it hath pleased God to bless me with (sic) in this lifetime I give, devise, and dispose of the same in the following manner and form. First I give and bequeath to my dear beloved wife **Mary Cartwright** all my lands and tenements as well as all my personal estate for the purpose of raising her (our?) children on, during her widowhood and if she should marry before the youngest child becomes of age, then and in that case, then the land to be given to my four sons to be equally divided between them. Namely, **Matthew** and **Nelson**, **James** and **Thomas**. And all the personal property I wish my wife **Mary** to draw one third thereof and the rest of the property I wish to be equally divided among all my children the four boys and three girls. Namely, **Sarah**, **Nancy**, **Polly**. N.B. I wish it be understood that if **Mary** never marry I wish my sons to have the land and the other property divided as above ---Likewise I constitute, make, and ordain **Mary Cartwright, William Barnes,** and **Henry Franks** the sole executors of this my last will and testament and I do hereby utterly disallow, revoke, and disannul all and every other former testaments, wills, legacies, bequests and executors by me in any wise before named, willed and bequeathed, ratifying and confirming this and no other to be my last will and testament in witness whereof I have hereunto set my hand and seal this fifteenth day of January eighteen hundred and fourteen.

Thomas (X) Cartwright
(Seal)

Signed sealed and delivered
in the presence of us.....................................**Leeroy Nobles**
Elisha James
Jesse (X)Cartwright

(A note written written with rather curious punctuation, apparently by the clerk, says 'interlined before signed. before assigned. with these words. Estate, wish, and the figure 3')

The names of the executors on a will, of course, are always interesting as possible clues to other family relations. A **William Barnes** is found in the earlier deed records of Halifax County, North Carolina[5], though there is no reference there to any connection with the Cartwrights:

William Barnes and **Mary** his wife of Halifax Co. to **John Bell** of same. 1 Sept. 1773. 100 pounds proclamation money. 323 acres on south side of Kehukey Swamp, joining **Killingsworth**, Blackburns Branch, **William Drew, Stinston. William Barnes, Mary Barnes** (signed). Witnesses: **Theophilus Cotton, Jesse Dickson, Wm. Grimmer**. (This last name could be Grimes, as that surname is found frequently in the records of Halifax County, with variant spellings; while 'Grimmer' seems to appear only in this one instance.) Aug. Ct.

1774. Examined by **David Sumner**, Esq., **Mary Barnes** relinquished her right of dower. CC: **Jos. Montfort**.

The fact that William Barnes was named executor of Thomas Cartwright's will leads me to wonder if Thomas's wife Mary was a Barnes. There seems no other evidence to confirm or refute the idea. As for the other names found on this will, they were also found in Halifax County, North Carolina at the time of the censuses mentioned earlier. There were members of a Franks family, possibly being the origin of the Henry Franks who was the third executor of Thomas Cartwright's will. One of the witnesses, **Elisha James**, was found in Halifax County himself, and there was a Francis Noble who may have been a relation of the Leroy Nobles who signed as a witness. **Leroy Noble**, however, was a justice in Blount County, Tennessee for a time, and may have been signing only in that capacity and as a neighbor, since it will also be seen that he owned land bordering that of Thomas Cartwright. As is seen from later records, men with the surnames of James and Franks married into the Rogers family, as did the son of the testator Thomas Cartwright. All these families are found together later in Lawrence County, Tennessee; but before getting into a greater discussion of that area, there are a number of other references concerning the Cartwrights and the families connected with them in Blount County.

First, a check of early Blount County deeds[6,7] reveals only a few transactions of interest, yet they are important for placing persons there at a specific time and for identifying the land owned and sold. (Many of the deeds were recorded years after the fact of the actual transactions, which explains why there are several mentions of land adjoining that of Thomas Cartwright well after the time that he was deceased.):

Erastus Tippet (clearly it *should* be Erastus, though transcribed as 'Wester' Tippet, with a question mark. The name was undoubtedly illegible to the transcriber.) signed as a witness on a deed of **Sollomen Arsbills** to **Henry Shields**, 8 Dec. 1802---3 Nov. 1803, 320 acres for $700.

There is a reference to **'Tippet's Spring'** in a deed of **George Buck** or **Beck** to **John Jackson**, 10 Jan. 1813---16 April 1816. $330 for '150 acres on south side of the Stoney Ridge, includes Tippet's Spring, adj **Moses Hughes'**. One of the witnesses was **William Barnes**.

A deed of **William Griffith** to **John Franks**, 7 Sept. 1814---1 May 1816, $200 for 94 acres in Hickory Valley, adj **Thomas Cartwright**, **George Cook, Bennett James, Jacob Franks**. Granted to **William Griffiths** 26 Jun. 1807. No witnesses. (Here we see that the James and Franks families were neighbors of Thomas Cartwright, which may have been the only connection at this time. Clearly the Thomas Cartwright mentioned here was the same one who died in 1814. It becomes evident from various later sources that there was another Thomas Cartwright in Blount County, but he was apparently one of Jesse's children and not an adult as yet in the time frame to which these deeds refer. The Thomas who was a son of Thomas, Sr. was a mere infant at this time.)

Nicholas Stevenson to **John Simpson**, 2 Aug. 1813---23 Jan. 1817, $500 for 126 acres in Hickory Valley, adj **Leroy Noble, David Partten, Thomas Cartwright, Jacob Franks, Henry Bond**. Witnesses: **Mahlen Stevenson, Holly Stevenson**. (Here we see again the surname Bond, which was found in the same areas as the Cartwrights both in North Carolina and in Maryland.)

Robert Hughes, executor of **Aleson/Allison Washum**, dec'd, to **Jesse Cartwright**, 30 Dec 1811, $320 for 160 acres adj **Samuel Montgomery, Thomas Cartwright, David Parkins** (I believe this should be Parton or Partten, as shown in the other deeds above) old line. Witnesses: **Henry Ron, Robert Wilson**. 7 May 1819.

Archable Johnston and **John B. Cusick**, guardian of the heirs of **James Williamson**, dec'd, to **John Adamson**, 26 Mar. 1821, $200 for 160 acres in Hickory Valley, being tract granted to **Williamson** as assignee of **David Parkins**, corner to **Allanson Washam** and **Thomas Cartwright**, adj **Nicholas Stephenson, Samuel Winters**.

Signed: **Archer Johnston. John B. Cusick.** Witnesses: **Samuel M. Gautt, Wm. W. Berry.** 20 Jan. 1824.

Henry Franks to **James Mitchel**, 30 Sep. 1823, $800 for 94 acres on Tennessee River. Witnesses: **George R. (X) Benett, Jim (X) Cartwright, Moses (X) Robinett.** 17 Feb. 1824. (This Jim Cartwright may have been one of Jesse's children, since the James who was son of Thomas Cartwright would not have been old enough to be signing on a deed at this date, as is shown by later census records which give his approximate year of birth. But there are other possibilities. We must keep in mind that there was a Cartwright male who is unaccounted for in the household of Matthew on the 1786 census of Halifax County, North Carolina; and there is some indication that James Cartwright and Jesse Cartwright may have had connections to a group of Cartwrights in Virginia, which complicates the matter somewhat. See Chapter Nine for discussions of this.)

Erastus Tippett of Rhea Co. to **Daniel McKinsey**, 23 Sept. 1811 $40 for 12 acres adj **William Barnes, Daniel McKinsey, Moses Hughs.** Witnesses: **Wm. Lowrey, Jr., J. Gardner.** 23 Sept. 1811. (Here we see that Erastus is already moving around again. But if he actually lived in Rhea County for any length of time, I find no other record of him there. As for the Daniel McKinsey shown here, he is undoubtedly the same Daniel McKenzey who married Jenny Tippett, as shown earlier.)

William Wallace, Sherriff, to **William Tuck**, 20 Mar. 1833, $9.24 for 117 acres in Hickory Valley adj **Thomas Cartwright, George Cook, Bennett James, Jacob** (name omitted, but probably Franks) Public sale 27 Aug. 1831 for taxes for 1828 and 1829, amounting to $1.10 for the two years, returned in the name of **Elizabeth Wooden.** Witnesses: **Sam Wallace, J.J. Walker.** 22 Apr. 1833. (This smacks of taking advantage of a poor widow, for sure. 117 acres for $9.24 was quite a bargan, even back then. Or at least it was judging by what was paid for other parcels of land in this same neck of the woods. One might think some charitable neighbor could have lent Elizabeth a dollar and ten cents for the taxes. In any case, I am presuming that this name *Wooden* is the same as 'Wooten' which is found earlier in Halifax

County, North Carolina and earlier still in Maryland, for there are other references to this family found later in the same places as the Cartwrights. It seems that William was probably a son of Elizabeth Wooden or Wooten, and that he apparently married a daughter of Jesse Cartwright, per the record cited below.)

One reference to **Jesse Cartwright** is a court record[8] showing that he had died by 1834. On 24 March 1834, the interest that **Jesse Cartwright** had in the deceased **Jesse Cartwright's** land was levied on by **Morgan G. Maupin.** (County Court Minutes of Blount County, Vol. 1, pg. 58.) A **William Woodin** had an interest in the above estate, which was levied on by **George Griffiths.** Obviously the second Jesse Cartwright must have been the son of the deceased; and it seems evident that the elder Jesse Cartwright had died quite some time before 1834, for he is not listed on the 1830 census for the county, while a **Fanny Cartwright** of about the right age to have been his widow is found on that census[9]. As stated in relation to **William Wooden**, it seems evident that he must have married one of the elder Jesse's daughters, for there is a marriage record found for **Jane Cartwright** to **William Wooden**, 12 December 1829, Blount County, Tennessee.[3] (The name Jane being obviously another clue that these Cartwrights were of the Matthew Cartwright and Jane Lee Tippett union.)

Other early marriages in the general area around Blount County, taken from various sources[3,10] which may be pertinent and have not already been noted:

Preston Cartwright to **Susan Jane Brotherton**, 25 September
 1837, Blount County, Tn.
William Cartwright to **Mary Drake**, 14 August 1828, Jefferson
 County, Tn.
David Cartwright to **Sarah White**, 12 April 1839, Monroe
 County, Tn.
Joseph C. Carterright (sic) to **Nancy Davis**, 20 October 1829,
 Rhea County, Tn.
James Tippett to **Catsey Ramsey**, 30 December 1809, Roane
 County, Tn.

Benjamin Tippitt to **Amy P. Morris**, 10 August 1818, Roane
County, Tn.

Janey Tippett to **Samuel Selby**, 25 February 1822, Roane
County, Tn.

Alesey Tippit to **Adam Gardenhire**, 24 December 1813, Roane
County, Tn.

Sarah Tippit to **Soloman Copeland**, 12 July 1819, Roane
County, Tn.

Also, **Erastus Tippett** was the surety on a marriage of **Jesse
Wallace** to **Margaret Isom**, 7 September 1801 in Blount County.[11]
What his relationship was to the two parties in the marriage is not
known, but it can be seen from some of the foregoing deeds that there
were Wallaces in the county who were likely friends and neighbors.
(And much later there is an intermarriage between a Wallace and a
Cartwright of this family line.)

Some of those noted in the above list of marriages are the
children of **Erasmus L. Tippett** and wife **Lucy**, as shown by the
records of his estate to be examined shortly. None of the Cartwrights
mentioned in the marriages were the children of Thomas, since we will
see shortly that they all moved to Lawrence County, Tennessee with
the possible exception of the daughter named Sarah. **Preston,
William**, and **David Cartwright** may possibly have been children of
Jesse Cartwright, or of Jim if the latter was of the older generation
instead of being one of Jesse's children himself. As for **Joseph C.
'Carterright'** of Rhea County, he may have been of the Cartwrights in
question here or he may have originated among those found in the
counties of Smith and then Franklin, who will be discussed at the end
of Chapter Five. There are a number of other Cartwright and Tippett
marriages in the areas surrounding Blount County, dated in years later
than those shown above, making it likely that they are later
descendants of Jesse Cartwright's family and of Erasmus Tippett's
family, since both of the latter seem to have remained in the area.

A **Thomas Cartwright** made a deposition in the case of
James R. Sexton, who was petitioning for divorce in Blount County
in 1831.[12] The abstract shows the Thomas Cartwright in question as
being age 23 when the deposition was taken, 24 August 1831.
Obviously this could not have been the Thomas who died in 1814, and

neither could he have been the son of same, Thomas, Jr., who is shown by later censuses to have been born that same year, probably just before his father died. This leads me to believe that the Thomas of the depostion in this divorce case was a son of Jesse Cartwright.

I have found in one regional library a booklet which gives a list of state militia officers from the area surrounding Blount County who served in the 'Cherokee disturbances and Removal' of 1838, and the list contains the names of **Thomas** and **Jesse Cartwright**. Unfortunately, the booklet seemed to have been a local contribution and the copy to which I had access did not give any information whatsoever on the author or compiler, nor concerning a publisher or the original source of the information. If the list was indeed accurate, then the Thomas and Jesse Cartwright named must surely have been the elder Jesse's sons, since both the elder Thomas and the elder Jesse had died before the time of the Cherokee Removal. Again, the children of Thomas had all moved west long before 1838. And since there are other references to indicate both a Thomas Cartwright and Jesse Cartwright of a second generation in Blount County, it would seem that we have at least some pretty certain evidence that Jesse Cartwright had at least three children---Thomas, Jesse, Jr., and Jane who married William Wooden or Wooten. That there were more seems likely.

It should be noted here that **Erasmus Tippett** and his wife **Lucy (Foreman)** moved over to Roane County and remained there, for Erasmus died in Roane County, apparently in January of 1822. There is an inventory of his estate on record for the January 1822 session of court, with a final estate account and settlement in January of 1823.[13] I will give the inventory and settlement here in full, as they both give considerable information of genealogical value:

January Term 1822
State of Tennessee
Roane County

An inventory of the estate of **Erasmus L. Tippett** Deceased taken this 29th day of January 1822. To wit one Black woman of the name of **Elizabeth**, one negro man of the name of **Richard**, one negro woman of the name of **Milley**, two negroe boys one of the name of

George & one of the name of **Jacob** & two negro girls one of the name of **Eliza** and one of the name of **Harriet**, one boy of the name of **James** (T. or L.); two head of horses & seventeen head of cattle, one wagon & thirty head of hogs & three beds and bedsteads & one pen of corn & two stacks of fodder & three trunks & one box & four spinning wheels & seven chears (?) and loom & one grinding stone and four pots and two ovens & one set of fire dogs & one shovel & two (stays?) & thirty books of different kinds & one looking glass & two pairs of (?) & two coffee mills & cupboard & cupboard ware & three piggins & one hackle & one set of knives and forks one shotgun & one table & one candle stick & eight (old?) barrels & one lot of cotton & one parsel of bacon & seven weeding hoes & two axes & one matock (sic) & four plough(shares?) & one pair of (?) and (?) & one iron wedge & four pairs of drawing chains & two leather collars & one log chain & one half of the improvements taken by me (? the latter passage unclear)

James Tippett
Administrator

January Sessions 1823   E. L. Tippet Settlement

      We the undersigned commissioners appointed by Court to settle with acts (sic) **Richard Richards** Administrator of the estate of **Erasmus L. Tippet** having (promised?) to perform that duty on the examination of the papers laid before us by said administrator that the following vouchers to wit:

A receipt from **Lucy Tippit** (sic) widow and relict of said Deceased for	$12.00
A receipt from **James Tippit** for	$12.00
A receipt from **Benjamin Tippit**	$12.00
A receipt from **A. Gardenhire** by his wife **Alsy**	$12.00
A receipt from **S. Copland** by his wife **Sarah**	$12.00
	$60.00

Which said **Lucy** wife and relict, **Benjamin** and **James Tippit**, **A. Gardenhire** and **Solomon Copeland** appear to be all the legatees of said estate, each of which have executed their separate receipts in full, the above specified amounts appearing to be the full received of each legatee given under our hands this 29th day of Jan. 1823.

James L. Green
H. T. Sporing
William Galbreath

Blount County Court Records[14]

Below are the pertinent references that I have found in an available source of the Court records of Blount County for the time period under study, in chronological order[14]. Where court cases are cited, the records did not often show the nature of the case; and where the names of others serving on juries have not seemed relevant to the study at hand, I have not endeavored to list them all. In some cases, where Erastus Tippett is mentioned, the surname was misrepresented as 'Trippett', and I have corrected it. Otherwise, I have given the spelling of names as I found them:

13 June 1796---**Erastus Tippett** appointed and sworn a constable, entered into bond with **William Small** and **David Egleton**, his securites, as by Law directed.

Friday December 1796---Ordered that the Sherriff summon **Erastus Tippett** and **James Martin** constables to attend next court.

Thursday 27 February 1800---**Erastus Tippett** vs **James Greenway**; the jury finds for the pldt. (pleadant?) and assesses damages to sixty dollars and six cents costs.

Friday 27 November 1801---**Erastus Tippett** named on a jury in the case of State vs **Ann Kerr**. Defendant is found guilty and fined $25, $15 of which is remitted.

27 August 1801---**George Rogers** was called (as a juror?) in the case of State vs **Polly Hopkins**, and did not come; he 'forfeits according to Act of Assembly'.

Tuesday 25 May 1802---**Peter Cartrite** (sic) vs **Erastus Tippett**. Finding for the defendant. (There is no indication of what this case was about, but it is is a very interesting record in light of the fact that it

71

gives proof of a Peter Cartwright being present in Blount County, whereas there is no other mention of a Peter Cartwright in the area at all. It seems probable that he was the same Peter who was brother of all the others in Halifax County, North Carolina, for the first indication of said Peter's presence farther along in Wilson County, Tennessee is a deed recorded in 1807---See Chapter Five. But we should also keep in mind the fact that there must have been a brother of Thomas and Jesse Cartwright. In all likelihood he was the Jim Cartwright mentioned earlier, but without proof either way we must simply guess at the identities of both Jim Cartwright and the Peter Cartwright in reference here.)

25 November 1802---**Erastus Tippett** was on a jury in the case of **Putenam Jones** vs **James Rhody**.

Thursday 28 November 1805---**Erastus Tippett** vs **Wm. Lackey**; execution **J. Lowry**. **Joel Wallace** returned that there were no goods and chattles (sic) to be found, and levied on a tract of land on the property of **Wm. Lackey** where he now lives. It is therefore ordered that the same be exposed to sale according to law.

Fourth Monday in November 1806---**George Rogers** called for venire facias and not selected. The next day, Tuesday 25 November 1806, he was selected for a traverse jury.

27 November 1806---**Erastus Tippet** vs **Andrew Miller**. Finding is for the plaintiff, $1.25 and costs.

Monday 28 August 1809---**Thomas Cartwright** was on a traverse jury.

Tuesday 25 March 1815---(pertinent for a description of the location of Jesse Cartwright's home, in realtion to others) Jury of view appointed, finds that the best way for a road leading from Morganton at Lowe's ferry will be from Morganton by **Valentine Mayo's** thence to **Moses Hughes** thence by **Jesse Cartwright's** plantation thence by **Martin's** leaving his plantation all on the left hand thence through **David Walker's** land thence by **Johnston Jones'** field thence across

Gallaher's creek at **Davis** house thence by **James Moore's** thence by **Peter Bowman** thence by **Bain's** Cabin thence to intersect the road now leading to Lowe's Ferry on the **Henderson's** land between **John Gault's** and **James Gillespie's**.

Wednesday 25 September 1816---State vs **Jesse Cartwright**. **John Wilkinson** prosecutes for the state, and the defendant in his own person. Nolle prosequi. The defendant pays costs, and **William Cooke** pays the witnesses. (Evidently this was concerning a dispute of some type between Jesse Cartwright and William Cooke, when taken together with the next excerpt.)

Same date---State vs **William Cooke**. **John Wilkinson** again is the prosecutor for the state, but apparently **Jesse Cartwright** is considered the 'prosecutor' in the case, and a ruling of nolle prosequi is entered. **Jesse Cartwright** to pay costs which have accrued in this case, for which execution may issue.

There were no other references to any of the people under study, in the court records of the county. **William Barnes, Leroy Nobles**, and **Henry Franks** were found mentioned numerous times over the years, usually as jurors or constables, etc., but there is nothing in the records to shed light on any relation to the Cartwrights or Tippetts. A number of others of the surname Rogers are found in the various records of the county, but with nothing to give a clue as to the origins of **George Rogers**.

In Will Book One of Blount County[14] containing records from 1799 to 1858, the only other reference to any of the Cartwrights is a mention of **Polly Cartwright's** land, in the will of **Thomas Noblet**. (It seems likely this name should be Noble or Nobles, and was mistranscribed by the copiers.) The will was written 20 December 1824. He bequeaths a tract of eighty acres 'joining **Polly Cartwright's**' to his son **John Noblet**. There is no indication in the will of a relationship to any of the Cartwrights, but the name itself does indicate that the Leeroy Nobles who is shown in the deed abstracts as a neighbor of Thomas Cartwright's must have been of some relation to this Thomas Noblet. Other children whom Thomas Noblet names are daughters **Sally**,

Catherine, and **Louisa**, son **William**, and daughters **Polly Hardwick**, **Betsy Glass**, and **Peggy Glass**. No wife is mentioned. Executors are **Johnston Jones** and **John Coalson**. Witnesses **Samuel Jones, Elijah Walker, James Jones, Rebecca Jones, Frances Jones**.

I found no other useful references among these early will records of Blount County. But among these and the court records mentioned above, there are numerous familiar surnames which seem to have been found in every place where the Cartwrights and Tippetts are found, all the way from Maryland: Lee, Bond, Gibson, etc.

Cherokee Records[15]

In any examination of the area of Blount County, Tennessee in these early years, it should not be forgotten that the region was most recently Indian territory. Very many of the residents of the area were intermingled with the Cherokee in various ways, whether it be in a friendly and possibly a familial capacity, or simply as opponents in the grab for land. The Cherokee Agency of the times was centered in Blount County, and the records of the Agency contain several surnames which seem relevant to our study. Though there is little to shed light on any possible relationships with persons directly pertinent to our examination, it would seem negligent to leave the investigation of the area without touching upon the brief records concerning the Cherokee.

There are of course many persons of the surname Rogers who are found in the records, because there was a noted family of that name of mixed Cherokee blood. I have not found any reference which connects the George Rogers of our study to the said Rogers in the Cherokee records, and though we still don't know his origins it must be said that there were a number of Rogers present in Blount County who seem *not* to have been connected to the Cherokee.

A **William Barnes** is found in the records in question, and whether he could possibly be the same William Barnes previously examined, or perhaps a son of same, remains unanswered. The clearest reference to him is contained in a list of persons who were allowed claims by the Commissioners for Cherokee Reservations. (Microcopy No. 234, 'Letters received by the Office of Indian Affairs 1824-81'.) Number of decision on docket, 10. 'Heirs of **Wm.**

Barnes; amount allowed $1554.00'; but a notation under the section titled 'remarks' indicates that no payment was made and the claim rejected by the Dept. The heirs are not named.

There are other references among these records in which I suspect the name should be William Barnes, but in which it has been translated otherwise, just as is often found in the other records of Blount County where this surname is concerned. One such instance involves a list of names taken from a detailed statement of 'depredations and wanton spoliations committed on the property of certain Cherokees by the volunteers and militia on the expeditions against the hostile Creeks', October 1813 through February 1814, 'wholly done by the left wing of the army from Tennessee'. (Microcopy 574, 'Special Files of the Office of Indian Affairs 1807-1904'. Roll 17, File 104.) On the list of Cherokees who are placing claims for damages, No. 4 is **William Burns**, residence Chickamaga, claiming $10.50. No further data. Only a few of the other names are given in English, the most being Cherokee names.

On a list giving 'names of tenants on **Doublehead**'s reserve May 25, 1809, number 6 is **William Burney**. (Microcopy No. 208, Roll 4---'Correspondence and Miscellaneous Records 1808-1809'. There is also a James Taylor found on this list.) Since all the names on this list are English names, the indication is that these were whites who had probably intermingled with the Cherokee. The location of 'Doublehead's reserve' is not given.

Another instance in which the name possibly should have been Barnes is the presence of the name '**Wm. Barnes**' on a list of war claims, 'so called to distinguish them from other Indian claims, 1816'. (Microcopy No. 208, Roll 7--Correspondence and Miscellaneous Records 1816-1818.) This 'Wm. Barnes' was claiming $11.00, with no details as to the reason; but other claims on the list were usually for horses used or killed, and supplies provided.

There are other surnames of interest found among these records of the Cherokee Agency, such as Spears or Speers, Taylor, etc., but with none of the given names that seem pertinent and no way to determine whether there is any relation to persons within our study.

For persons who are more closely interested in the Noble (or 'Noblet') family, William Wooten, etc., I have noted these names in various early records of Georgia---particularly John Noblet and

75

William Wooten, so that a search there might bear fruit. (On the other hand, a William Wooten is found still later in other parts of Tennessee where the Cartwrights are found.)

* * * * * * *

In summary of the evidence on the Cartwrights to this point, it must be said again that even without direct proof that the men Thomas and Jesse Cartwright originated among those Cartwrights of Halifax County, North Carolina, it seems indisputable in light of the close connections with the Tippetts. It seems equally clear that it must have been the elder Matthew of Halifax County who was their father. Not only does he appear to be the only one available to have been the father of the men named Thomas and Jesse Cartwright of Blount County, but the numbers in his household on the 1786 census seem to account for them. Although there are also some Tippetts found in connection with the Cartwrights in Wilson County, Tennessee, it is those of Blount County who are found specifically with Erastus and/or Erasmus, the step-sons of the elder Matthew Cartwright, through more than one migration. Further, the children of the Matthew Cartwright of Wilson County, Tennessee are accounted for in his will, and the same holds true for the children of the other sons of John Cartwright of Edgecombe County, North Carolina. Peter and Thomas Notley Cartwright both left wills which will be examined and which name all their children. Though Hezekiah seems not to have left a will, there are numerous other records for the settlement of his estate which name all his heirs. As for John Baptist Cartwright, we have already discussed the probability that he had no children, and that he seems to be still present in the home area of Edgecombe County, North Carolina by the year 1800.

All the evidence points to the conclusion that the Cartwrights of Blount County must have been the sons of the elder Matthew from Halifax County, North Carolina, and thus that they were half-brothers or step-brothers of the Tippett men, Erasmus and Erastus. That they were more likely half-brothers, born of the union of Matthew Cartwright and Jane Lee Tippett, is calculable from the apparent ages of the men in question. There is nothing to directly demonstrate said ages, but the general impression is that neither Thomas Cartwright nor

76

Jesse Cartwright were old enough to have been born before the mid-1770's, when Matthew married Jane Lee Tippett. (Jane's first husband Philip died in 1772, as seen by his will. She was shown in the Halifax County, N.C. deeds as still being Jane Tippett in 1774, but the deed which makes it evident that Matthew Cartwright had married her has a date of 1777, so the marriage took place some time between.) It can be seen from later records that Mary, the wife of Thomas Cartwright, was born in 1779 and their first child was born circa 1801, so it is likely that he was not a great deal older than his wife. He definitely was not an old man when he died in 1814, for as shown he was a soldier during the War of 1812 and it seems probable that he was injured in that conflict, perhaps dying as a result of his wounds. His children were not very old at the time of his death, none of them being over ten years of age, and the youngest being a mere infant, as will be seen from later census records. All the indications are that Thomas Cartwright was most likely a man of under forty years of age when he died, and thus born about 1775 or later.

It is difficult to tell whether Jesse Cartwright was older or younger than Thomas. Judging from all the clues which we are examining, the two men must have been no more than a couple of years apart in age. Jesse's apparent children seem to be about the same age as those of Thomas. From what is known of the age of their presumed father, Matthew Cartwright, it is probable that the latter was married before the union with Jane Lee Tippett. But though Jane herself, as already mentioned, would probably have been in her late thirties when she married Matthew Cartwright, all the evidence seems to point to the probability that she bore Thomas, and perhaps Jesse Cartwright. Again, this is all unproven, but the 'preponderance of evidence' has prompted me to record the data as I have given it in the beginning outline, for this family. As mentioned briefly, however, there is some confusing data to be found concerning a Jesse Cartwright and connections with some others in Virginia, which may be an indication that Jesse Cartwright could have had other origins and possibly was merely a relation of Thomas rather than a brother. For a discussion of the problem, see Chapter Nine. From this point my investigation has led me to concentrate only upon the family of Thomas Cartwright of Blount County, and the next chapter will delineate what is known of them after they left said County.

Bibliography of Sources for Chapter Three

1. 'History of Blount County, Tennessee 1795-1955' compiled by
   Inez E. Burns. Sponsored by Mary Blount Chapter Daughters
   of American Revolution--The Historical Commission, 1957.
2. 1805 Tax list for Blount County as transcribed and published in the
   Blount County Journal May 1988. Blount County
   Genealogical and Historical Society, P.O. Box 4986 Maryville,
   TN.
3. 'Early East Tennessee Marriages', compiled by Byron and Barbara
   Sistler. Byron Sistler and Associates; Nashville,
   Tennessee 1987. (Two-volume set.)
4. Photocopy of will from Blount County, Tennessee, in author's
   collection.
5. 'The Deeds of Halifax County, North Carolina' abstracted by Dr.
   Stephen E. Bradley, Jr.; published (by author) South
   Boston, Va. 1989.
6. 'Early Blount County, Tennessee Deeds' as abstracted by Jane
   Kizer Thomas and published in the Blount County Journal,
   beginning May 1988. Blount County Genealogical and
   Historical Society, P. O. Box 4986, Maryville, TN.
7. 'Blount County, Tennessee Deeds' 1819-1833' by Jane Kiser
   Thomas, Heritage Books, Inc. 1540-E Pointer Ridge Place,
   Bowie Md. 1993.
8. 'Tennessee Tidbits, Vol. I, compiled by Marjorie Hood Fischer
   Southern Historical Press, Inc., P. O. Box 1267, Greeneville,
   S. C. 29602. 1986
9. 1830 Federal census of Tennessee for Blount County, available on
   microfilm from the National Archives, Washington, D. C.; or
   for hourly research at any of the regional branches of same.
10. 'A Compendium of Rhea and Meigs Counties' compiled by Betty
    J. Broyles. No publisher stated.
11. 'Tennessee Cousins' by Worth S. Ray; Genealogical Publishing
    Co., Inc. Baltimore, Md. 1960-1989.
12. 'Tennessee Genealogical Records' by Edythe Rucker Whitley
    (Ibid, 1980)
13. Photocopies of court records from Roane County, Tennessee, in

author's collection.

14. WPA records copied by government-hired workers in the 1930's, collected and printed 1995 by Mountain Press, P.O. Box 400, Signal Mountain, Tennessee 37377-0400.

15. 'Records of the Cherokee Agency in Tennessee 1801-1835' transcribed by Marybelle W. Chase. (No publisher given, but the work is made available Ibid. 1990.) Contains abstracts from 14 rolls of microfilm designated Microcopy No. 208; and lists from Microcopy No. 574 and No. 234. Record Group 75, Bureau of Indian Affairs.

Chapter
Four

Lawrence County, Tennessee
and
Tippah County, Mississippi

The abstract of Erastus Tippett's Revolutionary War pension papers has already been given to show that he was in Lawrence County, Tennessee by 1819. Evidently he died before 1830, for he is not listed on the census for that year; and the only Tippett family which is found, that of a **Jonah** or **Josiah Tippett**, shows no elderly male in the household. Nor do the households of any connected names show such an aged male to account for Erastus. The latest mention of him is a court record of 1822, which see later.

The first indication that I have found of the Cartwrights being present in Lawrence County is their ennumeration on the said 1830 census[1]. The only further indication of when they might have left Blount County is the brief mention of 'Polly Cartwright's' land in the will of Thomas Noblet in that county, as given previously. This is not necessarily proof that she and her family were still there in Blount County at the time of the man's decease, but we may safely assume that the Cartwrights followed Erastus Tippett to Lawrence County, Tennessee by migrating there sometime between 1824 and 1830. That Erastus seems to have died sometime during this period may be an indication of why they traveled there in the first place---either because this elderly relative was ill, or perhaps because he left legacies to them in that area. If it was the latter, however, there seems to be no indication of it in the wills or land records of Lawrence County.

Since it appears also that the census records give the only clues to the Cartwrights' subsequent leaving of Lawrence County, I delineate here the households shown in 1830 which seem pertinent to our examination. These households are not necessarily found next door to each other, since they are extracted from the whole, but they are listed in the order of visitation:

Matthew Cartwright, with one male aged twenty to thirty, one female aged twenty to thirty, two females aged five to ten, and two under age five.

Jonah (probably Josiah) **Tippett** with one male forty to fifty, one fifteen to twenty, one five to ten; one female aged fifty to sixty, three aged fifteen to twenty, two aged ten to fifteen.

George Rogers, with one male aged forty to fifty, two aged fifteen to twenty, one aged ten to fifteen, three aged five to ten, and one under age five. One female aged forty to fifty, one aged ten to fifteen, and one aged five to ten. (These numbers match the children of George Rogers as they are discovered in the later records of Tippah County, Mississippi.)

Amos James (who will be shown to have married Jane, the eldest daughter of George Rogers) with one male aged twenty to thirty, one aged five to ten, and two under age five. One female aged twenty to thirty, one aged ten to fifteen, and one under age five.

Mary Cartwright, with two males aged fifteen to twenty; one female aged fifty to sixty, and two females aged twenty to thirty.

The numbers in the household of **Mary Cartwright** do not account for the son named **Nelson Cartwright**, whose full name appears to be **John Nelson Cartwright**. But it may be that he had married in Blount County and was merely slower in migrating to Lawrence County, or else he had moved around a bit more than the others. There is a **John Cartwright** listed on the 1830 census in Lincoln County, Tennessee, who seems to be unaccounted for among the other Cartwright families of the state and may have been the John Nelson Cartwright in question, since Lincoln County is certainly on the trail between Blount County and Lawrence County. And by 1840,

John N. Cartwright *is* shown in Lawrence County, at a time when the rest of the family had moved on to Mississippi. Yet he must have traveled on to Mississippi at about the same time as the others, and had merely left his family behind or at least maintained both households for a while, for he is found on the 1837 tax list for Tippah County, Mississippi and is also listed *there* on the 1840 Federal census. It was not that great a distance between Lawrence County, Tennessee and Tippah County, Mississippi, and it seems unlikely that these are two separate John N. Cartwrights whom we are discussing. Although various records show that a John Cartwright who was one of those from Wilson County, Tennessee was in Mississippi for a time, it was in connection with a different area of Mississippi. (See Chapter Five.) The name under study here is usually found as John N. Cartwright or as Nelson Cartwright, though never simply as John Cartwright, in the pertinent geographical areas. Neither is there any indication of other Cartwright families in either Lawrence County, Tennessee or Tippah County, Mississippi, to account for an entirely different John N. Cartwright.

Despite the lack of mention of these Cartwrights in any of Lawrence County's records other than the census, it is evident that others connected with them had moved to the area much earlier. **Nathan Spears** (from Halifax, N.C. as well as Blount County, Tennessee) and **George Rogers** were both there among the first settlers of the county as early as 1817---along with **Davy Crockett**. Members of the Franks and James families were also present at an early date. Lawrence County was established in 1818, and in the first court that was held during May of 1819, Davy Crockett was one of the Justices and George Rogers was a juror. The first case resulted in fining a man $1.50 for profane swearing[2]. (I would make a wild guess that Davy Crockett and George Rogers weren't above doing some of that themselves. Davy's reputation is pretty well known, and George is found throughout the court records, alternately serving as a juror and being brought up on charges himself. American justice in the frontier days.)

The court records of Lawrence County indicate some kind of close connection between the family of **Erastus Tippett** and **George Rogers**, for there are several cases in which they sponsored each other. Among these court records also there are numerous instances of George Rogers serving on juries or being paid for wolf scalps, which I have not delineated here. Pertinent abstracts are given below[3]:

August 1818: **George Rogers**, security for **William Tippett**. (No other information.)

October 1820: (for observation of names and at least a general reference to the location of George Roger's residence) ordered that **Robert Chaffin, Moses Penington, David Crockett, William Welch, Sr., William Seahorn, John Ray, George Rogers**, jury to view road. From a proper point near the head of Big Creek on the East Boundary line of this County, thence the nearest and best way of the West Boundary of this County near the head of Indian Creek.

January 1822: The State vs **Josiah Tippett**, charged with assault and battery. The defendant pleads guilty. His security is **George Rogers**.

January 1822: **W. H. Buchanan** vs **George Rogers**. **George** says he doesn't owe $89. 93 and 3/4 cents. The plaintiff recovers.

January 1822: **George Rogers** and **John Edmundson** acknowledge themselves to be indebted to the state of Tennessee for $100. The charge is against **George Rogers** for assault and battery on the body of **William White**. (What may be the same case, below.)

April 1822: State vs **George Rogers**, Assault and Battery. **Rogers'** security is **Erastus Tippett**.

In light of these court records (there are others involving James and John Tippet which I have not delineated here, since they appear to give no useful information, although these were probably sons of Erastus) I would make a guess that the William Tippett and Josiah Tippett named must have been children of Erastus from the first marriage, along with Jenny Tippett as previously mentioned, who married Daniel McKinzey in Blount County. (I have not found signs of these McKinzeys in Lawrence County, although there is a man of the same name found in later Tippah County, Miss. records.) What the connection was between the Tippetts and George Rogers has not

83

been clarified by any records that I have located. It is possible they were merely neighbors who had moved together from Blount County, but it is more likely there was a marriage between members of the two families. It is possible that George Rogers' wife, later shown to be Elizabeth, was another unnamed child of Erastus, since the latter's first wife's name was Elizabeth. George Rogers and his own wife Elizabeth named their eldest daughter Jane, which may be another clue to the Tippett connection.

There seems to be no mention of the Cartwrights in any of the court records of Lawrence County. Neither did I find any reference to them in the wills or deeds of the area. But there are several pertinent references concerning George Rogers and others, to be noted in the deed and land records of the county[3]:

20 June 1823---a land grant (#19337) for 60 acres to **George Rogers**.

2 April 1828---Bill of Sale from **Thomas J. Matthews** to **George Rogers**, for a negro man named **James**, aged about 20 years. Witnesses **J. Boudry**, **D. H. Stockton**. (Stockton was the Sherriff.)

12 May 1828---Deed from **George Rogers** to **John L. McKinney**. **McKinney** is from Blount County. (Could this be the same name as McKinzey?) Witness: **John Franks**.

9 January 1830 (registered 29 October 1831)---Bill of Sale from **G. W. Shackleford** to **George Rogers** for a negro girl named **Felis**, 16 years old. $412.50 paid. Witnesses: **Levi Cunningham**, **W. H. Buchanan**. (Buchanan is a clerk of the Court.)

28 September 1831 (registered 1 June 1832)---**William Wooten** of McNairy County, Tennessee sells six tracts of land in Lawrence County, Tennessee to **Lewis McCane**. Witnesses: **William (X) Patterson, Jane (X) Armstrong**.

28 August 1832 (registered 8 July 1835)---**George Rogers** to **Jesse S. Paine** (no?) acres of land bordering Knob Creek, **Alexander McDonald**. $307.00. Witnesses: **James Kelly, Archibald Munrow** (sic).

22 October 1832 (registered 25 December 1834)---Bill of Sale from **George Rogers** to **R. G. McQuigg**, 'a certain negro girl named **Fillis** (Felis?) about nineteen years of age'. $400. Witnesses: **Amos James**, **Zachariah W. Strickland**.

1 February 1837 (registered 13 February 1837. They're getting better at it.)---Deed from **John Franks** to **Amos James**, both of Lawrence County. $300 for land lying on Knob Creek, corner of tract of **Acton** (or Aston?) **Shaw** and bordering **John Franks'** fence on the north side. Witnesses: **John C. Rogers** and **John W. Franks**.

16 November 1837 (registered 7 December 1837)---Deed from **Amos James** to **Andrew James**. $335.75, for land on Knob Creek (which appears to be the same land bought from John Franks, above). Witnesses: **Wm. R. Bell**, **E. N. Lindsay**.

19 December 1837 (registered 15 January 1838)---Deed of Trust from **John Merritt** to **Washington Franks**. (It is not clear whether Washington Franks is the same as John W. Franks, or whether he may be the George W. Franks as seen in the next transaction. These deeds are included because of the connection of John W. Franks with the Rogers family to be shown later.) For a seventy dollar note due on the first of the next November, conveyed one black man about 6 years (? This must mean either a black child of about six years, or else it must mean to describe a black man of about *sixty* years, though it plainly says 'man', and 'six' rather then sixty), one cow, six sheep. Witnesses: **Wm. A. Edmuston**, **Pearce Floid** (sic).

7 November 1838 (registered 12 November 1838)---Bill of Sale from **Jno. W. Franks** to **Geo. W. Franks**. $1300 for two negroes, **Ned** and **Charlotte**, slaves for life. Ned about 18 years of age and Charlotte about 10 years of age, perfectly sound in body and mind. Witnesses: **John Finy**, **Silas Merrit**.

9 May 1839 (registered 13 May 1839)---Mortgage from **John W. Franks** to **Nathan McClendon**, on the following property: one (blind?) bay mare, 3 sows with pigs and 16 of their shoats, 4 chairs, 1

small trunk, 1 table, 1 iron wedge, 1 copper kettle, 2 other sows with pig and 10 of their shoats, in all 5 sows and 26 shoats, 2 quilts, 3 coverlets, 2 counterpanes. For the purpose of securing to him the sum of thirty-seven dollars due 15th November 1839, the property to remain in Franks' possession, not to make any disposition whatsoever. Witnesses: **F. Buchanan, William Davis**.

Note that **William Wooten** had moved to McNairy County, and had obviously owned land in Lawrence County, while there seems to be no other indication that children or in-laws of Jesse Cartwright had ventured west from Blount County.

As for the previously mentioned reference to a John Cartwright being listed in Lincoln County, Tennessee on the 1830 census, I regret that I have not had a chance to study the records of that county more closely for any other possible references there. I have not done so mainly because of the apparent brevity of the residence of said John Cartwright there, even though it is my belief that he is the same as John Nelson Cartwright who later shows up with the rest of his family in Lawrence County and in Tippah County, Mississippi. For any researchers who are more closely interested in this particular Cartwright, a thorough search of the Lincoln County resources for the time period in question may be in order.

It is interesting, in light of the name John Neslon Cartwright, that there was a John Nelson found in Blount County, Tennessee on the 1801 tax list which was discussed, and a man of the same name is also found in Lawrence County, Tennessee. That he was the same John Nelson in both places seems likely. John Nelson's household in Lawrence County for 1830 showed one male aged sixty to seventy, one aged ten to fifteen, one aged five to ten, and two under age five; with one female aged thirty to forty, one aged ten to fifteen, and one under age five. There are a few deeds and court records concerning him, which I have not included here since there were no recognizable connections to the persons in the current examination. But it could be that Mary Cartwright, the widow of Thomas Cartwright, was a Nelson, and that this John Nelson could have been her brother, seeing that she named a son John Nelson Cartwright. It is also interesting to note, however, that there were Hendersons both in Blount County,

86

Tennessee and in Lawrence County, Tennessee. Considering the fact that the name William Henderson Cartwright shows up in later generations of this Cartwright family, it could be relevant that there was a William Henderson evident in the Blount County court records, and a person named **R.G. Henderson** was Mary Cartwright's next door neighbor in Lawrence County on the 1830 census. The usage of such names as John Nelson and William Henderson for Cartwright males is at least some indication that females in the family may have originated in those families. But we must not forget the possible Barnes connection, for there is a Polly Barnes (perhaps the same Mary Barnes who was wife of the William Barnes mentioned both in Halifax County, North Carolina and in Blount County, Tennessee) who is found on the 1840 census of Lawrence County, Tennessee. (Though not on the 1830 census). Thus, we have several possibilities for the maiden name of Mary Cartwright, the wife of Thomas. There seem to be equal clues that she could have been a Barnes, a Nelson, or a Henderson.

The John Franks mentioned in the deed records above was found on the 1830 Lawrence County census, and it appears that he may have been the father of **John W. Franks,** who is later shown to have married a daughter of George Rogers.

By the time of the 1840 census for Lawrence county, we find a couple of other Franks households, but not John W. Franks. Nor do we find George Rogers himself, nor any of the Tippetts. Neither Mary Cartwright nor Matthew Cartwright is there, although as mentioned, John Nelson Cartwright seems to be listed both in Lawrence County, Tennessee and Tippah County, Mississippi in the year 1840. He is shown in Lawrence County as John N. Cartwright, and in Tippah County, Mississippi as Nelson Cartwright. A **Bennett James** is listed on the 1840 census of Lawrence County, and since he was present both in Halifax County, North Carolina and in Blount County, Tennessee, this is a good indication that he may have been the father of the man named Amos James who married Jane Rogers, the eldest daughter of George.

Tippah County, Mississippi

The Cartwright family as well as most of the Rogers family had all moved south and west across the line into Mississippi, some time before 1840. But for the first time since the exodus from Maryland, I find no Tippetts in the same county. On the 1837 tax list for Tippah County[4], Mississippi we find **Thomas**, **John N.**, and **James Cartwright**. This John N. Cartwright must certainly be **John Nelson Cartwright**. The 1840 Federal census[1] for Tippah County shows the household of **Matthew Cartwright** with one male 30-40, one female 20-30, 8 females 15-20, 6 females 10-15, 4 females 5-10, and 1 female under age 5! (Unless he was running a female boarding school, or the census figures were simply a mistake, this huge number of females in Matthew's household must have included some of his wife's relatives.) The same census shows the household of **Nelson Cartwright**, with one male 30-40, 3 males 5-10, 2 males under 5; and one female 20-30, 1 5-10, and 1 under 5. **James Cartwright** is shown with his own household on this 1840 Federal census, with one male 20-30, one male 5-10; one female 20-30, and one under 5. There is a household headed by **Thomas Cartwright** (Jr.), although it doesn't appear that he is married as of yet. The numbers show one male 20-30, one under 5; one female 60-70, and 2 females 20-30. It is obvious that the females listed are his mother Mary and the two sisters, Nancy and Polly, who remain unmarried throughout. The male child listed is apparently the boy named **James T. Asbury Cartwright** who is found in the household with the Cartwright women on the later 1850 census. (To be demonstrated hereafter.)

On the state census of 1841 for Tippah County, Mississippi, **Thomas Cartwright** (Jr.) does not seem to have his own household. We have the household of **Matthew Cartwright** with one male and nine females (is this a mistake for *nineteen* females, as shown one year previously, were the earlier numbers a mistake, or had he lost ten females in such a short time?). **James Cartwright** is again listed, with two males and one female; and **John N. Cartwright**, with six males and four females. This is a large enough number of persons shown in the household of John N. Cartwright to possibly account for his widowed mother **Mary**, and the two sisters **Nancy** and **Polly**, as well as John's own wife at that time. Later records show that he had no daughters old enough to have been born at the time of this census, but he did have five sons who were apparently all born by 1841, and along with John N. himself this accounts for the six males. It leaves the question, however, of where the youngest brother, **Thomas Cartwright, Jr.**, might have been at the time of this 1841 state census. He does not appear as head of his own household in any of the surrounding Mississippi counties, but since he is found to be still in residence in Tippah later, it isn't likely that he had moved elsewhere. He married **Lavinia Rogers** at about this time, as will be seen, and they may have simply been missed by the census if they did not yet have their own household. (The sister of these Cartwright men who was named Sarah is not found after the mention of her in the will of her father Thomas Cartwright, Sr. in Blount County. As stated, perhaps she had married so that we cannot identify her from the available records; or else it is possible that she died young.) Also in Tippah County, Mississippi in 1841 we find the households of **William R. Rogers** (who is the eldest son of George Rogers, with many household numbers indicating that perhaps the parents were there with possibly some of his younger siblings as well). **James Rogers**, another son of George, is found on this 1841 state census; and **Amos James** is also there by this time. William R. Rogers and Amos James are next door to John N. Cartwright., with both Matthew Cartwright and James Cartwright some distance away and having neighbors whose names are unrecognizable as far as our study is concerned. (Although it might be guessed that their neighbors could be relations of their wives.) There are a number of other Rogers families in the county, some of whom had been present in Lawrence County, Tennessee previously, indicating that they may have been brothers or other relatives of George. Yet again, we find some surnames that have been noted along the trail all the way from Maryland and/or Halifax County, North Carolina---Lee, Merritt, Hobson, Good, Ayres, Barnes, Gibson, Hobson or Hopson, etc. There are Hendersons, including a William Henderson; and several Nelson families are listed, but not John Nelson. Again, I have found no definite indication of what became of the Tippetts who were clearly relatives, perhaps children, of Erastus. There is, however, a James Tippet listed on the 1830 census of Hardeman County, Tennessee, adjoining Tippah County, Mississippi. William R. Rogers was listed there at that time as well, and since that is where his marriage occured, it is probably not amiss to assume that the James Tippet residing there is the same as the son of Erastus who seemed to be present in Lawrence County for a time.

At this point I will interject the brief genealogy that I have compiled on the Rogers family, since the numerous references to them may have become too confusing without the prior knowledge of the relationships. Records referencing the information in the outline will follow:

George Rogers
b. ca 1785-88 (probably in North Carolina or Virginia)
m. ca 1800-1805 **Elizabeth** _____ (possibly **Tippett?**) b. 1788 (the
    state of birth given for her on the 1850 census appears
    definitely to be Ga., based on the enumerator's peculiar
    formation of the letter 'G' in other places; although other
    researchers have identified it as Va.) d. Dec. 1854 or Jan.
    1855, Tippah County, Mississippi.
d. July 1845
Children:
1. **Jane Rogers**, m. **Amos James**
2. **William R. Rogers**, m. **Nancy Robinson** (7 May 1828, Hardeman County, Tn. marriage records[5])
3. **James M. Rogers**, m. **Elizabeth** _____
4. **George W. Rogers**, m. **Mary Ann Medford** (3 February 1840, Hardeman County, Tn. marriage records[5].)
5. **Hiram K. Rogers**, m. Elizabeth ___; Sarah ___.
6. **Catherine Rogers**, m. (Washington?) **Wray** (see later discussions of confusing data concerning this daughter.)
7. **John Cornelius Rogers**, m.
8. **Lavinia Rogers**, b. 21 July 1820[6] in Lawrence County, Tennessee, m. **Thomas Cartwright**. She d. 17 July 1893 in Hardeman County, Tennessee.
9. **Jefferson C. Rogers**, m. ?
10. **Elizabeth Rogers**, m. **John W. Franks**

The following abstracted records[4] provide most of the above information, all taken from the same collective source of transcriptions. Photocopies of the originals of some of these records are available for a fee by contacting the Mississippi State Archives in Jackson, Mississippi; but some of the records are not available at all at this point. Thus, with gratitude to the compiler, I have chosen to reproduce all the different bits of data from the source footnoted above:

Tippah County Death Notices from Ripley newspapers: **George Rogers**, dec. 7-26-1845. Administrator **William. R. Rogers**.

Probate records: **Rogers, George**, 1848-1854. (The latter date is apparently due to his wife Elizabeth's death in the latter part of 1854, which required further resolution of George's estate.) **William R. Rogers**, adm. Heirs are **Jane James** & husband **Amos**; **H. R. Rogers**; **George W. Rogers**; **Serena Cartwright** (certainly this is just a mistranslation of Lavinia, or Levina, as her name is sometimes found); **James R. Rogers**; **Cornelius Rogers**; **Catherine Wray** and husband **Washington Wray**; **Elizabeth Rogers**.

Deed to settle estate: **Elizabeth Rogers, Amos & Jane James, H.K. & Elizabeth Rogers, Thomas & Levinia Cartwright, James M. Rogers, George W. & Mary Rogers, Jefferson C. Rogers, Cornelius & Mary Rogers, John W. Franks** and wife **Eliza**---to **Wm. R. Rogers**, 30 September 1847. Heirs of **G. Rogers**. (Another version of what is apparently the same deed, though transcribed in the same collective source, shows the wife of Hiram Rogers as Mary, rather than Elizabeth; it also gives Cornelius Rogers the middle initial 'A.', when he should most probably be John Cornelius Rogers as shown in other sources.)

Probate Fee Book: **Elizabeth Rogers**, dec., **Washington Wray** adm. First claim made 1 January 1855.

From an unnumbered probate packet: **Rogers, Elizabeth**, dec. Admin. bond 17 January 1855. **Washington Wray**, adm. **Joseph Wray**, surety. Will, written 28 October 1854, filed 5 April 1855. (I

91

have not been able to obtain a copy of said will) leaves bequests to **Emily C. Wray; Lavinia Cartwright**, dau.; **William R. Rogers**, son; **James M. Rogers**, son; **J. C. Rogers**, son; **John C. Rogers**, son; **Catherine Wray**, dau.; and **Rachel C. Wray**. Witnesses: **G.W. Carter, Joseph Wray**. In the same packet, a final account names heirs as **W.R. Rogers, Hiram K. Rogers, George Rogers, James Rogers, Jefferson Rogers, Comdus Rogers, Jane James, Eliza Franks**, and **John Rogers**.

The fact that the actual sons and daughters of Elizabeth are distinguished here with those designations is important, for it will be seen from the census records given later that it is difficult to tell just exactly who Emily C. Wray was, in relation to Elizabeth. The previous records clearly show Washington Wray as the husband of the daughter Catherine Wray who is mentioned, and yet the 1850 census (see later) shows the wife of Washington Wray as Emily C. Wray. Emily C. and Catherine seem to have been shown as distinctly different people in the will of Elizabeth as mentioned above. (There were Wrays/Rays in Blount County, Tennessee and in Lawrence County, Tennessee, the name evidently deriving from the spelling 'Rhea'; although the census shows these Wrays as having come from Kentucky.) Also, there is some confusion about the name of the wife of Hiram K. Rogers, shown here as both Elizabeth and Mary. Most of the records here and later show her as Elizabeth. But to confuse matters even more, see the 1850 census abstracts below, where a Hiram Rogers who is apparently the same man is found with a wife named Sarah A Not only that, but he is listed twice on the same census, in different areas of the county, and yet clearly being the same man. There are some indications from unverified sources that Hiram married more than once, which may account for the wife on the 1850 census being shown as Sarah.

Lavinia Cartwright is not mentioned in the final settlement of Elizabeth Rogers' estate, despite the fact that bequests had been left to her in the mentioned will. Although Catherine Wray is not mentioned in the final settlement either, the reason for Lavinia's absence at that point may be the fact that she was missing and presumed dead herself at the time of her mother's death. That presumption was in error, and the mystery surrounding the lives of Thomas Cartwright, Jr. and his wife Lavinia seems to require a full discussion, hereafter. First, however, I will delineate here the other deed abstracts which have been found as relates to Tippah County and the persons under study. (Again, these abstracts do not always give an adequate amount of information, but they seemed the most readily available source for the information. Photocopies of the originals of these deeds can usually be acquired by contacting the Mississippi State Archives at Jackson, Mississippi. It is the policy of the staff to do minimal research in securing copies for the inquirer, for a fee.):

Deed Book B, pg. 381---7 January 1839, **Edgar C. Spears** to **James R. Cartwright**. Witnesses: **H.W. Strickland, Geo. N. Green**.

Deed Book D, pg. 506---19 March 1842, **James R. & Elizabeth Cartwright** to **John Medlin**.

Deed Book E, pg. 42---3 October 1832, **Thomas & Laura Cartwright** to **Henson Purnell**, to **Wm. Norton**. (? It is my opinion that there are several mistakes in this abstract. First, presuming that this should be Thomas and *Lavinia* Cartwright, not Laura. There were no other persons of similar names present in the county during the time period in question, so the record must refer to same. If so, then the year given for this deed must certainly be wrong, since other records indicate that Thomas and Lavinia did not marry until ca 1840-41. In 1832, Thomas would only have been eighteen years old, and Lavinia only twelve! Evidence for presuming that the wrong year has been given is the fact that this deed occurs in a book which otherwise records only those deeds for the time period of the 1840's. The correct year for this deed must be 18<u>4</u>2, not 1832.)

Deed Book E, pg. 400---9 February 1844, **Absolem & Jane Stewart** to **James R. Cartwright**. Witnesses: **Thos. Moore, Robert White.**

Deed Book F, pg. 191---13 May 1845, **Charles P. & Sarah Miller** to **Thomas Cartwright**.

Deed Book F, pg. 461---24 January 1846, **James R. & Elizabeth Cartwright** to **Hiram K. Rogers**.

Deed Book F, pg. 462---24 January 1846, **John K. & Elizabeth Rogers** to **James R. Cartwright**. (John K. Rogers must be a mistake. It apparently should be either John C. or Hiram K.)

Deed Book G, pg. 264---2 January 1847, **James R. & Elizabeth Cartwright** to **Anderson Street**.

Deed Book G, pg. 612---21 August 1847, **Thomas & Lavina Cartwright** to **Joseph Hines**.

Deed Book H, pg. 546---1 March 1849, **Matthew Cartwright** to **Elias Crum**.

Deed Book I, pg. 363---5 January 1850, **Hiram K. & Elizabeth Rogers** to **James R. Cartwright**. Witness: **B.M. Singleton**.

Deed Book I, pg. 380---20 February 1850, **Hiram K. Rogers** to **John W. Thompson**.

Deed Book J, pg. 15---18 April 1850, **John N. & Mary Cartwright** to **H.W. Strickland**.

Deed Book J, pg. 26---5 December 1849, **William & Nancy Rogers** to **Archibald L. & James H. McNeil**.

Deed Book K, pg. 341---3 October 1842---**James O. & Angerona M. Nelson** to **Thomas Cartwright**.

Deed Book K, pg. 437---26 February 1852, **Jane James**, wife of **Amos James**, schedule. (What kind of schedule?)

Deed Book K, pg. 447---6 March 1852, **Mary & Nancy Cartwright** to **Elizabeth Rogers**.

Deed Book L, pg. 106---20 July 1852, **Wm. R. Rogers** to **J.Y. Murry**.

Deed Book L, pg. 473---23 January 1850, **Thomas & Levina Cartwright** to **R.W. Roberson**.

Deed Book N, pg. 112---23 February 1854, **James M. & Elizabeth Rogers** to **Amos James**.

Deed Book N, pg. 113---31 January 1848, **Matthew & Sarah Cartwright** to **Amos James**.

Deed Book N, pg. 271---3 July 1854, by probate order of May 1854, **Hardy W. Strickland**, admin. of **Thomas Cartwright**, dec. to **Wm. R. Cole**.

It will be seen that the last deed given above comes into play rather importantly, along with other records, in the mystery alluded to earlier concerning Thomas and Lavinia Cartwright. With numerous descendants of this couple and their close relations being in evidence at the present time, the story bears repeating in full along with the details of the search which has made it so interesting. It began, as is often the case, with a 'family tale'. Any genealogist with a little experience knows that such family traditions are usually somewhat inacurrate, if not entirely fabricated. But this one seems to have been covering a truth that is more indicative of the 'wild west' than the original tale. The long search has not only uncovered a great deal, but has opened up more questions than those with which I began.

At the time that I began the search, there was no apparent knowledge that the family of William Lavert Cartwright had lived across the line in Mississippi in *earlier* years, for as far back as the remembrances went, the Cartwrights of my branch of the family had been living in Hardeman County, Tennessee. The family tale as passed down to me was that my great-grandfather William Lavert Cartwright had a father who had left to travel to California during the Gold Rush era (no one could even remember the man's name) and that he had departed on this trip before William was born, leaving his family behind. It was said that he had written letters home saying that he'd made a rich strike of gold and was returning with 'bags of gold' for the rest of the family. But he was then never heard from again. It was further said that his wife, having waited for the required seven years, finally had her husband declared dead and married again to 'a man named Jones'. No one seemed to remember any other details, including Lavinia's name. But there were a number of Jones half-siblings in evidence, whom my father had known well as a child. He frequently mentioned 'Uncle Dick and Uncle George' Jones, along with an 'Uncle Dude'; but concerning the latter, he could not readily recall the family origins.

The numerous debacles and errors that were uncovered in the search are typical of the kinds of stumbling blocks which must be overcome in order to be successful in the field of genealogy. There were a number of wild goose chases before the real trail was discovered. One of the errors involved the fact that William Lavert Cartwright's tombstone[6] gives the wrong years for birth and death, making it difficult to find a death certificate even though he died well after the time when such records were being kept. (The tombstone records the dates as b. 23 May 1851, d. 1 April 1927. The family bible gives William Lavert Cartwright's birth date the same way, having been recorded by one of the later generation rather than by William himself; though the Bible does not record his death date. The actual dates, according to the death certificate, are b. 23 May 1852, d. 1 April 1928.)

Finally obtaining the said death certificate for 1928[7], I found that it gave the information that William's parents were 'Tom and Lave' Cartwright; but it was stated that the entire family had come from Illinois. A great deal of time and energy went into a search among the records of Illinois, with some further confusion because there were indeed some Cartwrights to be found there. There was nothing whatsoever on the *pertinent* Cartwrights, however. Acting on a mere hunch, I began searching diligently among the records just south of the Tennessee line in Mississippi. Voila, the correct Cartwrights were there on the 1850 census[1], and it showed that Thomas and Lavinia Cartwright had both been born in Tennessee. There was nothing about Illinois. It appears that the basis of the erroneous 'Illinois' data was the simple fact that Lavinia and her second husband, John Jacob Jones, had moved there for just a few years, and had then returned to the Hardeman County, Tennessee--- Tippah County, Mississippi area where their families still resided.

Further complicating the matter was the testimony of an elderly Jones relative (her name being unknown to me and the reports circulating from other researchers as hearsay, after her death). She had been old enough to know Lavinia Jones, and had related that the latter had borne a number of illegitimate children before her marriage to John Jones. Among the illegitimate children, the relative named William Lavert Cartwright, 'Dude' Pool, William Riley Russell, and Logue Russell. This of course elicited a more frantic scramble for information, since I had a whole family of Cartwrights awaiting reports, only to possibly find out that they were not Cartwrights at all!

I found no concrete data concerning the reputed children William Riley Russell and Logue Russell, though I gleaned hints that there were descendants of these men engaged in searches of their own. The two were not found on the censuses with Lavinia and John Jones in 1860 or 1870. But neither was 'Dude' Pool, and yet it seemed obvious that the latter was somehow a member of the family, per my father's memories. It turned out that the relative who had made the report concerning illegitimate children had been totally unaware that Lavinia had been married to a Cartwright before the Jones marriage, and thus her own recollections were probably only partially correct. It was for that lack of knowledge, most likely, that she had named the son William Lavert Cartwright among the other apparently illegitimate children of Lavinia Jones. As for the others, William Riley was the full name of Lavinia's own elder brother, William 'R.' Rogers; which might be an indication that the William Riley Russell named was indeed Lavinia's natural son and had been named after her brother. The 'Uncle George' whom my father remembered clearly as a Jones was evidently one of the children borne to John J. Jones from a previous marriage, for he is shown as being seven years old on the 1860 census (given later). There were evidently other previous Jones children, and Lavinia herself had children by John Jones named Richard, Callie, and Frank. But there is much to discuss concerning Thomas Cartwright and Lavinia in the years before she married John Jones.

The Thomas Cartwright family is found on the 1850 census of Tippah County, Mississippi, although William Lavert Cartwright was not listed since he was not yet born at that time. The census was taken on the first day of October, 1850. Pertinent information concerning all the parties involved in this study is given below. (Again, these households are not necessarily next door to each other but are given in order of visitation without ennumerating the intervening households):

Name	Age	Born
Wm. R. Rogers	45	TN
Nancy	41	SC
Wm. C.	21	TN
Caroline	19	TN
John W.	17	TN
Angeline	15	TN
William P.	13	TN
Beloved H.	12	MS
Augustine P.	10	MS
Sylvanus	8	MS
Elizabeth	6	MS
Robert C.	4	MS
Geo. W. F.	2	MS
Matthew Cartwright	49	TN
Sarah	49	TN
Martha A.	20	TN
Sarah C.	16	TN
Rachel E.	16	TN
Maria J.	14	MS
Elvina F.	8	MS
Polly A. Cartwright	22	TN
Mary E. J.	1	MS

(I have not been able to identify this Cartwright at all. Since all the brothers in the main family under study are accounted for here, it is obvious she is not the widow of one of them.)

Hiram Rogers	37	TN
Sarah A.	23	ALA
Wm.	7	MS

Jas. M.	5	MS
Geo. W.	3	MS
Cornelius A.	1/12	MS
Geo. W. Rogers	35	TN
Mary	23	GA
Sarah E.	8	MS
Geo. J.	4	MS
Jesse T.	2	MS
Wash. Wray	25	KY
Emily C.	19	TN
James M.	9/12	MS
Joseph Wray	50	KY
Rachel	49	KY
Eliz. F.	20	KY
Sarah A. M.	19	KY
Mary	13	TN
Charlotte	10	MS
Manza(? Male)	8	MS
Matilda C.	6	MS
Joseph E.	2	MS
Abram Rossin	14	TN
Cornelius Rogers	23	TN
Mary J.	20	VA
Harriet C.	5	MS
Lavinia E.	2	MS
Thomas Cartwright	36	TN
Lavinia	29	TN
Mary E.	7	MS
James H.	5	MS
General Taylor	3	MS
Thomas R.	1/12	MS
Mary Cartwright	71	NC

Nancy	42	TN
Polly	37	TN
James T.A.	12	MS
Nancy A.	2.	MS
Nelson Cartwright	41	TN
Mary	45	NC
James H.	19	TN
William F.	17	TN
Thomas F.	15	MS
John J.	13	MS
Benjamin M.	11	MS
Theresa J.	9	MS
James Cartwright	37	TN
Elizabeth	34	TN
Thomas O.	12	MS
Mary P.	9	MS
Sarah J.	8	MS
Samuel C.	6	MS
John H.	4	MS
James M.	1	MS
William S.	1/12	MS
Amos James	47	TN
Jane N.	42	TN
Franklin	20	TN
Elizabeth	22	TN
Francis M.	18	TN
Amanda C.	14	TN
Newton J.	9	MS
(Indecipherable)	7	MS
Jefferson H.	5	MS
Amos	3/12	MS
Eliz. Rogers	62	GA

Jefferson C.	20	TN

(It is here that, oddly, Hiram Rogers is recorded again, a few households away from Elizabeth. Clearly the same man, with the same family.)

John B. Wallace	44	TN
Delilah	34	TN
Margaret E.	17	TN
Thomas J.	15	TN
Henderson C.	10	MS
Samuel A.	8	MS
James A.	6	MS
Esther A.	5	MS
Amanda J.	2	MS
John P.	6 days	MS

(This household is recorded here because it is the family of Amanda J. Wallace, the first wife of William Lavert Cartwright. There was an elder Henderson C. Wallace found earlier on this census, and he was a man in his sixties; thus he may have been the father of John B., shown here.)

I did not find on this 1850 census a John W. Franks household, or any other to account for the daughter of George and Elizabeth Rogers named who was named Eliza, and who married John W. Franks. It is possible they were living in one of the surrounding counties, for which I have not checked the censuses. Where the Wray family is concerned, it is a frustrating matter to try to work out the correct relationships. Apparently the Rachel Wray who was named with a bequest in Elizabeth Roger's will was the mother of the Wray family shown, wife of Joseph. Washington must have been the son of Joseph and Rachel Wray. But I have not spent a great deal of time in trying to find other tidbits to compare, concerning this problem. The scope of this investigation makes it necessary to return to the story of Thomas and Lavinia Cartwright.

Since the family of Thomas Cartwright was intact on the 1850 census, it is evident that if he had gone west it was after that date.

And according to the family tale, it was before his son William Lavert Cartwright was born. There is difficulty there because the errors in the latter's birth and death dates, and the fact that the child Thomas R. Cartwright was shown as being one month old on the first of October 1850. This made it highly unlikely that William Lavert could have then been born in May of 1851, quite aside from the other indications that his birthdate as given on the tombstone is incorrect. At the very least he would have had to be a premature baby, which children rarely survived in those days. Apparently, then, we must presume that William was indeed born 23 May 1852, not 1851. *Where* he was actually born is another question.

The first surprise was the discovery of probate records concerning Thomas Cartwright, beginning in 1852 in Tippah County. (Same collective source from which the records pertaining to the Rogers were taken, earlier.) An exact date was not given on the copied record, but it seemed at first to be an indication that the family tale must have been concocted, even though the date coincided with the claim that Thomas had disappeared just before William was born, per my reasoning concerning the latter's birthdate. Clearly, however, Thomas Cartwright did not disappear at all, if someone knew well enough that he was dead to have entered the probate proceedings in court by 1852. It certainly had not been long enough at that point for a wife to have the man declared dead, even if he *had* gone missing. Nor even in 1854, when the probate came into court again. I did find the marriage record of Lavinia Cartwright to John J. Jones, 26 August 1858 in Tippah County, Mississippi, which made the seven-year theory stand up. But there was no denying the probate records for Thomas Cartwright. *Someone* had known that he was dead, not missing; and with enough certainty to convince the courts of it.

The records, however, aroused even more of a mystery. The court had declared the children Mary E. Cartwright, James H. Cartwright, and General Taylor Cartwright 'orphans', and gave custody to Thomas's unmarried sisters, Nancy and Polly Cartwright. I threw up my hands. *Where was Lavinia?* I knew full well that she was not dead at that time, and that her children were not orphans. She was certainly in evidence later to marry John Jones and to bear more children, living to a decently ripe age of seventy-two and having died on 17 July 1893. She was buried in the State Line Cemetery in

Hardeman County, Tennessee, alongside John Jones and near her son William Lavert Cartwright. She was on the 1860 census of Tippah County with John Jones, and with the children James H. Cartwright, General Taylor Cartwright, and William Lavert, along with some of the Jones children. (Alas, William L. was called a Jones on that 1860 census, while the other two Cartwright boys were distinguished as such, rousing the controversy once again. Still, the final conclusion is necessarily that the census is in error, for William Lavert could not have been a Jones, being listed as nine years old and with no sign that Lavinia and John Jones had ever been together at such an early point.) Given here is the abstract of the first probate record:

(PR 1852) **Cartwright, James H.**, Minor, et. al. **James H. Cartwright**, age 8; **Mary Elizabeth Cartwright**, age 10; & **General Taylor Cartwright**, age 5; orphans. **Nancy & Polly Cartwright**, guardians. **James R. Cartwright**, surety. Heirs of **Thomas Cartwright**, dec.

The probate case on Thomas Cartwright came up again in 1854, when the custody of the 'orphaned' Cartwright children was changed and they were given to Evaline Cartwright and David Hunt. Why this was done is not clear, and neither do I have any clue as to the relationship with either Evaline Cartwright or David Hunt. (Though Evaline may possibly have been the 'Elvina F.' Cartwright listed as one of the children of Matthew, Thomas's brother, on the 1850 census.) But the far greater question still seemed to be *where was Lavinia*? There was the further evidence of her mother's will, which named her in a bequest but with Lavinia not being in evidence among the final heirs of the estate, indicating that she was still missing as late as the beginning of 1855. And where was William Lavert Cartwright and the other child, Thomas R. Cartwright, who was listed on the 1850 census with Thomas and Lavinia at one month of age? Neither of those sons were named in the probate with the others, as 'orphans', so it seemed evident that wherever Thomas and Lavinia had gone, they must have taken the youngest children with them. Perhaps William L. was not born in Mississippi, as indicated by the later censuses.
Further pertinent census abstracts[1]:

1860, Tippah County, Mississippi

Name	Age	Born
John J. Jones	30	TN
Lavina Jones	39	TN
J. H. Cartwright	16	MS
Gen. Taylor "	13	MS
Wm. L. Jones	10	MS
G. W. Jones	7	MS
W. A. Jones	5	MS
J. R. Jones	2	MS

(Next door are G. W. Wray and Emily C.)

1870, Hardeman County, Tennessee

Name	Age	Born
Jones, J. J.	40	TN
" Levina	48	TN
" W. L.	19	MS
" G. W.	17	MS
"W. A.	15	MS
" J. R.	12	MS
" F. J.	8	MS
" M. C.	5	IL

1900, Hardeman County, Tennessee

Name	Relation	Birthdate	Place
Cartwright, W. L.	Head	May 1851	MS
" Harriet	Wife	Oct. 1848	MS
" William	Son	Sept. 1874	MS
" Jim J.	Son	Aug. 1882	TN
" Josh. B.	Son	Oct 1885	TN
" Ed. L.	Son	Mar. 1887	TN
" John A.	Son	Sept. 1888	TN
Dowty, Sarah	Sis.-in-law	May 1858	MS

(next door)

Name	Relation	Birthdate	Place
Jones, J. J.	Head	Jan. 1831	TN
" Narcissus	Wife	Jan. 1859	TN
" Tom	Nephew	Feb. 1883	TN

It can be seen from the above data that William Lavert himself evidently believed his birthdate to be 1851. It can also be seen that John Jacob Jones had acquired yet a third wife sometime after Lavinia's death. Notwithstanding the rumors and confusion about William L.'s surname, it seems that the children G. W. Jones and W. A. Jones must have both been children of John Jones from a previous marriage, since they were born well before the marriage between Lavinia and John Jones, and it was hardly likely that Lavinia was producing children by three or four different men all within a couple of years, no matter what the technical possibilities. An attempt to trace John Jones prior to the records in question, in order to clarify the matter, has come to naught. Other researchers are in possession of information which indicates his prior marriage and the names of his parents, etc., although it is unverified by me and thus I will avoid complicating the matter by giving that information here.

At the point of the previously-mentioned discoveries per Thomas Cartwright's probate records, I was assuming that he and Lavinia must have gone west together, taking the two youngest children and leaving only the older ones behind with their relatives. I could not but assume that some tradgedy such as an Indian attack had befallen them along the way. There were indications of a party of persons who had left Tippah County for the Gold Rush and had been attacked by Indians, and my natural conclusion was that Thomas and Lavinia must have been among them. It was not far-fetched to assume that this must have been why Thomas and Lavinia were presumed dead, but with Lavinia surviving despite the reports and managing to return after a number of years to dispell the illusion of her own death. It seemed the best theory to account for all the conflicting facts of the other records.

At one point, however, there came word through the grapevine of other researchers that there is a Cartwright presently residing in one of the southwestern states who seems to be descended from this same 'missing' Thomas Cartwright! He certainly believes his own ancestor to be the same man, and the data he provided as having come from the traditions of his own family history gives some strong evidence. There have also been some reports from descendants of one of Thomas Cartwright's brothers in Arkansas, that Thomas had actually 'disappeared' on purpose. According to their version of the 'family tale', he had shot and killed a man in Arkansas on the way west and refused to come back to Mississippi, in order to avoid the repercussions. As with the story told by my own branch of the family, there must be elements of truth in the second version. I can only say that the evidence of the various records seem to support the story, but with so little information concerning Lavinia's whereabouts or activities during the 'missing' years, a further investigation is in order, perhaps among the records of Arkansas. There are still many questions. Who were the parents or fathers of 'Dude' Pool, William Riley Russell, and Logue Russell? What happened to the baby Thomas R. Cartwright? Where, exactly, was William Lavert Cartwright born?

Below I have reproduced the data from a family bible record which lists the family of William Lavert Cartwright. As mentioned, the Bible record was apparently kept by William Lavert's son John Allen Cartwright rather than by William himself, and thus it contains several errors, which will be explained in my commentary afterwards. At one time the original of the Bible record was in the posession of my father, but unfortunately it disappeared from his home shortly before his death, and I have been unable to determine what became of it. A photocopy was made, however, and it is in my own possession along with some remaining original Bible pages which contain only the records of a few of the marriages in the family. No title pages or other materials from the Bible were preserved, but this Bible record as well as the entire story laid out here certainly shows the dangers of accepting detailed information as 'remembered' and recorded by later generations.

Family Bible record of William Lavert Cartwright:

W. L. Cartwright was born May 23 1851
A. J. Cartwright was born (left blank)
H. A. Cartwright was born (left blank)
W. H. Cartwright was born Sept. 28 1874
Roxanna Cartwright was born June 24 1877
C. C. Cartwright was born Nov. 7 1879
J. J. Cartwright was born Aug. 6 1882

J. B. Cartwright was born Feb. 23 1884
E. L. Cartwright was born Mar. 7 1886
J. A. Cartwright was born Nov. 21 1887
M. N. Cartwright was born Jan. 16 1890
C. O. Cartwright was born April 13 1913
W. J. Cartwright was born Feb. 7 1915
Laurene Cartwright was born Feb. 13 1917
Lillian Cartwright was born April 16 1919
Ronald Earl Cartwright was born Feb. 19 1923
J. W. Cartwright was born Dec. 12 1925

W. L. Cartwright of Pocohontas, Tenn. and **A. J. Wallace** of
Pocohontas Tennessee, (married) April 10, 1873 at
Pocohontas,   Tenn. by **Thos. Wilson**.
W. L. Cartwright of Pocohontas, Tenn. and **Harriet A.**
Dowty of   Pocohontas, Tenn. (married) 17 July 1881 at
Pocohontas, Tenn. by **A. C. Nelms**.
Johnnie Cartwright and **Manie Mellon** was married Feb. the
26 1912 by **D. S. Nelms** at Essery Springs

A. J. Cartwright was Amanda J. Wallace, the first wife of
William Lavert Cartwright; and the marriage date is correct; but the
record is in Tippah County, Mississippi rather than in Pocohontas,
Tennessee. (Although it is possible they obtained the marriage license
in Mississippi and the ceremony occured across the line in Tennessee.)
Amanda died 15 November 1879, shortly after the birth of their third
child, Christopher Columbus Cartwright. The child himself died a few
months later on 5 February 1880, according to tombstones[6]. The
information concerning the second marriage of William Lavert
Cartwright is correct[8], although obviously neither of the parties were
born and raised in Pocohontas, Tennessee. The birth date of the
second wife, Harriet A. Dowty, is 12 December, recorded as 1844 on
her tombstone in the State Line Cemetery; but probably it should have
been 1848, as shown by her age given on various censuses from the
time when she was a child in Tippah County, Mississippi. She was the
daughter of **Edward Dowty** and **Sarah Norvelle**, who were married 1
January 1838 in Madison County, Alabama[9]; and Harriett had several
brothers and sisters.

The places named in the Bible record---Pocohontas, Tennessee and Essery Springs---are sites in Hardeman County, Tennessee near the Mississippi line. The town of Pocohontas became a ghost town during the Depression era, and since I have not visited the area in some time I cannot say if it still exists at all. Essery Springs, as I last saw it, was merely a crosssroads area with an old abandoned church and a small spring, the water of which contained heavy deposits of iron and thus was reputed to be a health enhancer. As far as I could tell when visiting the site as a child, the water was completely undrinkable and would turn any container a bright orange color, from the iron content.

W. H. Cartwright, in the Bible record, was William Henderson Cartwright, the eldest son of William Lavert by his first wife Amanda. William Henderson Cartwright was known as 'Uncle Hen' in our branch of the family, and produced a number of descendants, many of whom who still live in the general area of West Tennessee. The children J. J. Cartwright, J. B. Cartwright, E. L. Cartwright, and J. A. Cartwright, were James Cartwright, Joshua Benton Cartwright, Edward Leon Cartwright, and John Allen Cartwright, respectively; sons of William Lavert and his second wife Harriet A. Dowty. M. N. Cartwright in the Bible record was Manie Noonie Mellon, the wife of John Allen Cartwright. She was born in Alcorn County, Mississippi, and was the daughter of Jonathan Mellon and Temperance A. Overton. The remainder of the names with birth dates on the Bible record are the children of John Allen and Manie, all of whom are now deceased save for Lauren Cartwright, who married Charles Bridges and is currently a widow residing in Memphis, Tennessee.

Bibliography of Sources for Chapter Four

1. Federal Census records 1830 through 1900 for Tennessee; 1840 through 1870 for Mississippi. Available on microfilm from the National Archives in Washington, D. C., or for hourly research at any of the regional branches of same.
2. 'History of Tennessee, Illustrated'. The Goodspeed Publishing Co., Nashville, Tennessee 1886. Reprinted in 1979 with new material by Southern Historical Press, P. O. Box 1267, Greeneville, S. C. 29604
3. Author's personal collection of microfilmed records of Lawrence County, Tennessee, obtained from the Tennessee State Library and Archives, Nashville, Tennessee.
4. 'Tippah County Death Notices', Vols. I thru III. Compiled by Don Martini. Old Timer Press, P. O. Box 572, Ripley, MS. 38663. (The title of this compilation is deceptive, since it contains a great deal of material other than death notices from the area's early newspapers, such as abstracts of court and probate records, military lists, etc.)
5. 'Early West Tennessee Marriages', by Byron & Barbara Sistler, Nashville, Tennessee. Published by Byron Sistler & Associates, 1712 Natchez Trace, P. O. Box 120934, Nashville, TN. 37212.
6. Tombstone data from the State Line Cemetery of Hardeman County, Tennessee---Tippah County, Mississippi.
7. Certified copy of original death certificate, Hardeman County, Tennessee, in author's collection.
8. Certified copy of original marriage certificate, Hardeman County, Tennessee, in author's collection.
9. Photocopy of original marriage record, Madison County, Alabama, in author's collection.

Chapter
Five

The Wilson County, Tennessee Cartwrights

We have come so far in following the Cartwrights who traveled from North Carolina to Blount County, Tennessee and beyond that a few things might bear reiterating before delving into the study of those who settled in Wilson County, Tennessee. We have seen that the patriarch of this family, **John Cartwright**, died in Edgecombe County, North Carolina in 1780. Of his five sons, we have shown to a reasonable degree of certainty that the son named **John Baptist Cartwright** had no male issue and seems to have stayed in North Carolina. Of the other sons, **Thomas Notley Cartwright** and **Hezekiah Cartwright** were still in Edgecombe County, North Carolina as of the census of 1790, and a **Matthew Cartwright** who appears to have been the son of that name in the same family was residing in Pitt County, North Carolina that same census year. **Peter Cartwright** was not found in North Carolina, and I have stated my guess that he had gone on to Tennessee before the others. As seen in the previous chapter, he may have been the **Peter Cartwright** whose presence in Blount County was indicated at least for a time, by some type of dispute with **Erastus Tippett** in 1802.

The data to be found in the area of Wilson County, Tennessee makes it evident enough that the Cartwright families who are detailed in many of the records there are the same Cartwrights from Edgecombe County, North Carolina. Though some of the records make it easy to confuse these Cartwrights with the family of Robert Cartwright of the Nashville area, there are certain details which allow them to be distinguished.

But without unnecessary discussion of such details, I will proceed with the records and provide commentary afterwards, where it seems necessary. The earliest mention that I have found of any of the pertinent Cartwrights in the Wilson County area are contained in abstracts of land and deed records of the County:

(From Deed Book #1, 1793-1797, Sumner County. Both Wilson and Smith were taken from Sumner 26 October 1799. Other Cartwright transactions not mentioned here but listed in the same source are covered in Part II of this work)[1]: **Cartwright, Matthew**, from **Stephen Cantrell**. No details given in abstract.

(From Wilson County Deeds)[2,3]:

18 November 1805---**Micajah Barrow** of Davidson County, Tennessee to **Mathew Cartwright**, a tract of land on Round Lick Creek. (Deed Book B, Pp. 78-79)

9 November 1807---**Joel Payne** of Rutherford County to **Matthew Cartwright**, a tract of land on Hickman's Creek. Bounded by **James Hill**. Witness: **Pettes Raglin** (sic) (Deed Book C, Pg. 85).

2 November 1807---**Isaac Moore** to **Peter Cartwright**, 100 acres on Hickman's Creek. Witnesses: **Lewis Burk, William Moore**, and **Henry Moore**. (Deed Book C, Pg. 214)

It seems likely that the dates of the first deed abstracts to be found dealing with each man, Matthew Cartwright and Peter Cartwright, may indicate the approximate time of their respective arrivals in Wilson County. Since I have postulated that the Peter Cartwright in Blount County, Tennessee is likely this same Peter, it appears that his brother Matthew may have passed him up and arrived in Middle Tennessee first, while Peter lingered in Blount County for a time. There are more deed abstracts to be examined, but since the latter abstract is the only Wilson County reference to be found concerning **Peter Cartwright** before his death in 1808, I prefer to interject here the records pertaining to said death of Peter. Various indices show a will on record, but several attempts to obtain a copy of said will have resulted only in the receipt of a copy of the inventory, from both the state archives and the local court personnel. Evidently, they were unable to find the will which is indexed, although I have received no such explanation. Clearly the will existed at one time, per the abstract given below. (With much gratitude due the compiler of the source.) My account of the attempt to obtain a copy of the will should not deter anyone else who is interested from submitting the request. It may be that I was simply having a string of bad luck, and the will was overlooked by those responding to my own requests for it. The page numbers given in the abstract source indicate that it must have been a fairly long will, and there is always the possibility that there were useful details contained in it which were not abstracted.

Peter Cartwright will[3]: Heirs are wife **Ann Cartwright**; daughter **Sousannah** (sic) to receive two hundred dollars when collected from **William Green**, Esquire, of the State of Georgia; three sons **John, Joshua,** and **Jonas Cartwright** to receive the land to be drawn for in Georgia; other son **William**. My eight children **Sarah, John, Elener** (sic), **Joshua, Jonas, Peter, Ann,** and **Elizabeth**. Witnesses: **William Neil, Pallis Neil,** and **Samuel Bucks**. Executors: wife **Ann Cartwright** and son **John Cartwright**. Recorded 18 March 1808. (Will Book #5,   Pp. 150-152.)

With the name of his wife being the same and the presence of his brothers in the same county, there is little doubt that this is the **Peter Cartwright** of Edgecombe County, North Carolina. This appears to be the only record which names his children, and I have had little luck in tracing them after this date. However, I have made only a somewhat cursory check of Georgia resources to find out whether the sons named as inheriting 'land to be drawn for' in that state may have returned to that area and remained there. A closer look by interested researchers would be advised.

It seems possible, at least, that the **Polly Cartwright** who was shown on the 1850 census of Tippah County, Mississippi, and who

112

was unaccounted for among the Cartwrights under study there, may have been the widow of one of the sons of Peter---possibly of Peter, Jr. An abstract of records dealing with land claims in the Mississippi Territory[4] certainly shows that a Peter Cartwright had been living in Mississippi since before the date of 3 March 1803, a time when the sons of Peter, Sr. certainly could have been adults with families of their own:

Peter Cartwright's case, No. 122 on the docket of the Board, and No. 157 on the books of the Register---Claim: A right of pre-emption of one hundred and fifty-nine acres, one rood, and thirty poles, under the first section of the act. (Act of Congress passed 3 March 1803 for receiving and adjusting claims to lands south of the Tennessee, and east of the Pearl River.) The claimant presented his case together with a surveyor's plot of the land claimed. (The land is described, situated on the west side of the Tombigbee, Washington County, Mississippi; bounded on the southeast by Mimm's line and otherwise by vacant land). Chain carriers were **John Wamack** and **John Walker**. (Said chain carriers in these cases were often neighbors and/or other claimants.) Entered in record of claims, Vol. 1, pg. 487 by **Edward Lloyd Wailes** for **Joseph Chambers**, Register. Chain carriers were sworn in before **William Pierce**, Justice of Peace. **Raleigh Green** was presented as a witness: deposed that he was not interested in this claim; that **Peter Cartwright** inhabited and cultivated the land on the 3rd of March 1803 and before that time and ever since. That said **Cartwright** was on the 3rd day of March 1803 the head of a family. **Thomas Malone**, surveyor, was produced as a witness and deposed that he surveyed the land in question; that there were no other lines that interfere with the said claim that he knew of; that it lies on the west side of Tombigbee river, and below the old Indian boundary. Postponed for consideration.

The Board later allowed the claim and ordered that a certificate be granted to Peter Cartwright. However, another entry shows that the surveyor Thomas Malone made another statement to the effect that part of Peter Cartwright's claim and most of that of a **John Pickering** interfered with a claim of **Robert Farmer's** heirs---a claim of one thousand acres granted by the British Government of West Florida to **Farmer** on 6 August 1778.

I found no further reference to this case, but it serves to show that there had been a Peter Cartwright and family in Mississippi at the beginning of the nineteenth century. The time frame certainly makes it possible that he could have been the son of Peter Cartwright of Wilson County, Tennessee. The fact that the area described in the land claim is in southeastern Mississippi rather than the general region of Tippah County would seem to argue against the presumption that the Polly Cartwright mentioned in the latter area could have been connected with the Peter Cartwright of the early land claim. But if her husband had died it might be presumed that she would have wanted to move back to an area where some relatives were living, and the indication that the claim was eventually disallowed might also explain the changed location. Without more data, however, there is little use in belaboring the point. There is evidence of other Cartwrights in southern Mississippi, about whom I have determined little but who also may have been of the Peter Cartwright family mentioned in the above land claims..

There is an inventory of the estate of **Peter Cartwright** of Wilson County, Tennessee[5] which was not recorded until 1810. (Will Book #5, Pp. 216-217.) The date of nearly two years after Peter's death leads me to wonder if the inventory may have arisen when his wife died, although there is nothing in the record to attest to that. It may have been only that other matters kept the case open until that time Aside from a fairly large number of household and farm items which I will not delineate here, the inventory names '3 negroes, **Robbin**, **Rose**, and **Leala**', with no indication of their dispostion.

Notes listed in the inventory:

Will Green---one for nine hundred dollars due the 25th December 1807; also two containing eight hundred and thirty dollars due the 25th of December 1808.

William Heard---one for fifty-six dollars, six and a fourth cents, due the 25th of December 1807.

William King---one for $5.26 due the 25th of December 1807.

114

Thomas Dawson---$28 due the 25th of December 1807.
George (Naughwood, or Vaughwood?)---$5.68 3/4 cents due
'as before mentioned'.
Sarah Tippet---$10.22 due ditto.
William Oliver---$28.43 3/4 cents due ditto.
Hardy Phillips---$16.78 due ditto.
John Cartwright---$11.43 3/4 cents due ditto.
Charles Burk, Jr.---judgement against him for $42.

John Cartwright, executor of the
estate of Peter Cartwright, dec'd.

Recorded by **John Allcorn**, clerk, 1 January 1810.

Judging from the dates on the notes listed above, it may be that
the record had been submitted at the time of Peter's death and simply
was not recorded until much later. As for the Sarah Tippet mentioned,
I have found no indication of her further identity. As will be seen,
there were other Tippetts in Wilson County, but nothing to show her
connection.

There are more deed abstracts[6] of this time frame, referring to
the several Cartwright brothers:

13 November 1807---**Robert Baker** of Smith County to **Matthew
Cartwright** a tract of land on Hickman's Creek. (Deed Book C, pg.
93)

4 February 1809---This indenture made this 4th day of February in the
year of our Lord 1809 between **Bennet H. Henderson**, acting
executor of the last will and testament of **William Henderson**
deceased and **William T. Henderson** of the one part, and **Matthew
Cartwright** of the other part, 640 acres on Hickman's Creek. (Deed
Book D, pg. 29)

March 1809---**Matthew Cartwright** to **Thomas Bonner** 60 acres on
Cedar Creek. (Deed Book G, Pp. 229-230. This deed must have been

discovered very late and recorded likewise, for it is given in a deed book which otherwise holds records of a period ten years later.)

30 August 1809---**John G. Blount** of Beauford County, North Carolina to **Hezekiah Cartwright** a tract of land on Jennings' Fork. (Deed Book D, pg 351)

30 March 1810---**Willie Barrow** of Davidson County to **John Cartwright** 696 acres on Jennings' Fork. (Deed Book D, pg. 368-369)

20 August 1811---**Mathew** (sic) **Cartwright** to **Richard Hankins** 150 acres on Round Lick Creek. (Deed Book D, pg. 459)

20 August 1811---**Mathew Cartwright** to **Pettus Ragland** 320 acres on Hickman's Creek. (Deed Book D, pg. 460)

20 August 1811---**Mathew Cartwright** to **James Edwards** 320 acres on Hickman's Creek. (Deed Book D, pg. 461)

28 January 1812---**James McNairy** and **Nathaniel A. McNairy** of Davidson County to **Thomas N. Cartwright** 420 acres on Round Lick Creek. (Deed Book D, pg. 533)

January 18__ ---**James Vinson** of Sumner County, Tennessee to **Thomas N. Cartwright** 69 acres near the land of **John Bass**. Witnesses: **Benjamin Chapman** and **James Vinson**. (Deed Book D, pg. 535)

1 November 1810---**Jordan Bass** to **Hezekiah Cartwright** 253 acres on Round Lick Creek. (Deed Book E, pg. 171)

Note the connection between Cartwrights and Hendersons here, just as there were some type of connections in Blount County and other areas where the previous branch of the family was examined. There almost certainly must have been some type of intermarriage between the two families, at some point. The deed above which is made between the executors and/or heirs of **William Henderson** and

Matthew Cartwright may or may not imply some type of familial relationship at that point.

Also from the above deed abstracts, it again seems probable that the first findings of Hezekiah and Thomas N. are the indications of when those two Cartwrights first arrived in Wilson County, following their brothers Matthew and Peter, although the latter was deceased by the time Thomas and Hezekiah appear in the records. Another important point to be noted is the three transactions of **Matthew Cartwright**, all on the same day, in deeding land to his sons-in-law. That they are his sons-in-law becomes obvious from his will, given shortly. The marriage of **Elizabeth Cartwright**, daughter of **Matthew**, to **James Edwards** is found among the records of Sumner County, Tennessee, dated 19 June 1800. The marriage of **Sally Cartwright** to **Richard Hankins** is found in the same county, 7 February 1800. I have found no marriage record for another daughter, **Polly**, who married **Pettus Ragland**; but that marriage is made clear in Matthew's will. Neither have I found a marriage record for the daughter **Susannah** to **John Hallum**, though that marriage is also obvious from her father's will and other records. Why there is no similar deed to the above for the son-in-law **John Hallum** seems to be explained also by the will, in which the other daughters are given only money and slaves, while land is left to Susannah.

As for the John Cartwright who is mentioned in one of the above deed abstracts, he was probably the son of Matthew, since the John Cartwright who was the son of Hezekiah, seems to have come to adult age at a slightly later date. As can be seen from the various records still to come, Matthew had only the one son, and Thomas N. Cartwright had no sons named Matthew, Peter, or John. Hezekiah had a large number of children, and had sons of all the names that were in use in use in the family---except for the name Jesse, which seems to have been used only by those Cartwrights of Blount County.

There are still further deed records to be examined, but in chronological order, the records concerning the death of **Matthew Cartwright** are found next. The inventory is recorded first by the court, but since Matthew's will was written nearly a year earlier, I will begin with it, reproduced here in full[5]:

In the name of God, Amen. I **Matthew Cartwright** of Wilson County & State of Tennessee being in a low state of health but of perfect mind and memory, knowing the certainty of death and that all men are born to die, do make this my last will and Testament revoking all others in manner and form following.

First I recommend my soul to Almighty God.

2nd I request all my just debts to be paid.

3rd I give and bequeath to my daughter **Elizabeth** one negro boy named **Emanuel**, also the sum of two hundred dollars.

4th I give and bequeath unto my daughter **Sally G.** one negro girl named **Lidia**.

5th I give and bequeath unto my daughter **Bethany** one negro boy named **Lewis** and one girl named **Chaney**, also two hundred & fifty dollars.

6th I give and bequeath unto my son **John Cartwright** two negro boys **Harry & Tom**, also two stills with their appurtenances.

7th I give and bequeath unto my daughter **Polly** one negro girl named **Judah**, also two hundred and fifty dollars, which money together with the sums above named to be paid out of such monies as may arise from sales made by my executors, or such debts as may be due me at my decease, and is not to be demanded in less than eighteen months after my death.

8th I give and bequeath unto my daughter **Susanah** one hundred and twenty acres of land on Hickman's Creek, deeded to me by **Jack Paine** and **Robert Baker**. Also one negro girl named **Jinny** and one boy named **Charles**.

9th I give and bequeath unto my grandson **Mathew Cartwright** son of **John Cartwright** & **Polly** his wife (at the death of his grandmother) all the land lying east of my spring branch beginning on my south boundary line on the road at a cedar stake running then through the spring and down said spring branch to my north boundary line (it being part of the tract of land I now live on with the appurtenances).

10th I give and bequeath unto my grandson **Matthew Cartwright Hankins** son of **Richard Hankins** and **Sally G.** his wife, all the land lying west of my spring branch (at his grandmother's death) beginning on my south boundary line on the road at a cedar

118

stake then running through said spring and down said spring branch to my north boundary line, it being part of the tract of land I now live on.

11th I lend unto my wife **Polly Cartwright** during her life the whole of my plantation tract of land I now live on with the appurtenances, also such part of my stock & furniture as she may think proper to keep for her own use, also one negro boy named **Leaven**, one girl named **Alsey**, which said negroes, stock & furniture I wish to be equally divided among my children at her death.

It is my wish that the following negroes, **David, Periden, Patience, Ben, Crawford**, and **George** together with such other part of my estate as has not been herein bequeathed be equally divided among all my children, viz. **Elizabeth Edwards, Sally G. Hankins, Bethany Jarney, John Cartwright, Polly Ragland**, and **Susanah Hallum**.

Lastly I do hereby constitute and appoint my son **John Cartwright, Richard Hankins**, and **Pettes Ragland** my sole executors of this my last will and Testament given under my hand and seal the eleventh day of February one thousand eight hundred and eleven.

Signed, sealed, and acknowledged before us **Samuel Harris**
                                                    Samuel Hogg
                                                    Hezk. Cartwright
Recorded the 3rd of June 1812 by **John Allcorn**, clerk
of Wilson County Court

The inventory of Matthew's estate[5] is dated 28 February 1812 (recorded 3 June 1812.)   The discrepancies in names of persons between the will and the inventory are reproduced as found.   Along with a very long list of household and farm items and livestock, the inventory names the following persons:

1st---one Negro boy named **Emanuel** willed to **Elizabeth Edwards**.
2nd---one Negro girl named **Lydia**, (willed to) **Sally Hankins**.
3rd---Two Negroes to **Bethany Joiner**, named **Lewis & Chaney**.
4th---Two Negroes to **John Cartwright**, named **Harry** and

Tom.

5th---One Negro girl named **Judy**, to **Polly Ragland**.

6th---Two negroes to **Susanah Hallum** named **Jinney** &
        Charles.

Six negroes to be equally amongst 'hrs' and children, by the
        names of **David, Pander, Patience, Benjamin,
        Crawford, George**.

Two Negros lent to his wife during her life, named **Levin** and
        Alsey.

Recorded by **John Allcorn**, clerk.

A memorandum to the inventory was recorded 6 June 1812 (it states that Matthew Cartwright was deceased 'this 24 February 1812', apparently referring to the exact day that Matthew died.) The memorandum lists all those person who were indebted to the estate for either goods or monetary notes. Since the list is so voluminous, I will not attempt to record all the details here but will merely show the names, for their inherent value. (Some persons were listed for more than one account. Names which were uncertain or partially illegible are shown with a question mark after my interpretation):

Edward Calwell	**Stephen Rogers**	**Andrew Johnson**
Shadrack Greggs	**Widow Smith**	**Roley Stone** (yes)
Joseph Tippet	**Benj. Hudson**	**James Fulton**
Arthur Hankins	**Samuel Cartwright**	**William R. Bradley**
John Telford	**Peter Steele**	**Joseph Bradley**
Wilson Bradley	**James Davidson**	**James Wilson**
Charles Lambert	**Alexander Baird**	**William Jones**
James McCown	**James Crutchfield**	**John Boon**
Evan Tracy	**Thomas Cartwright**	**Frederick Wadkins**
John Jones	**Joseph Weir**	**Anderson Tucker**
William Cox	**William Prim**	**Thomas Bonner**
James Jones	**Samuel Patterson**	**Henry Carson**
William Petway	**Neil Thompson**	**James Cropper** (?)
William Weir (?) **Jr.**	**Aaron Lambert**	**Jesse Hicks** (?)
John Bradley	**John Baker**	**Jonathan Bean**
Meshack Baker	**William Telford**	**John Marshall**
James Roach	**John Lawrence**	**John L. Davis**

Parks Goodall	John (Weab?)	William Edwards
Aaron Freeman	Meredith Heag (?)	James Bell
Robert Fullerton	James A. Rawlings	William Stone
Edmund Barker	Daniel Miles	William Bartlett
Baley Taylor	John Berkley	Levi Rogers
James Boyd	J. Reeves	Edwin Perry
James Perry	Andrew Smith	William Draper
Joseph Adicar (?)	Willie Adams	Benjamin Hubbard
John Nicks	Jonah Jones	Koley Organ

Recorded by **John Allcorn**, clerk.

More deed abstracts[6] are in order next, involving **Hezekiah Cartwright** and **Thomas N. Cartwright**, and various of the children of the set of brothers. Some of these deeds, as in the one instance of those previously given, were far out of place in chronological order of the deed books. For the purpose of keeping a better grasp on the timeline of events, I have rearranged them in chronological order, but with the references to the proper deed books intact:

1 November 1810---**Jordan Bass** to **Hezekiah Cartwright** 253 acres on Round Lick Creek. (Deed Book E, pg. 171)

13 November 1810---**James Taylor** to **Hezekiah Cartwright** 67 and 1/2 acres on Round Lick Creek. Deed Book H, pg. 252)

10 March 1813---**John Cartwright** to **John Bradley** 200 acres on Jennings Fork. (Deed Book E, pg. 65)

20 September 1813---**John Cartwright** to **William Howard** 116 acres on Round Lick Creek. (Deed Book E, pg. 231)

9 November 1814---**John Cartwright** to **William Harrison** 207 acres on Round Lick. (Deed Book E, pg. 522)

17 March 1815---**Ezekiel Cartwright** to **William Webb** 100 acres in Wilson County. (Deed Book E, pg. 474. This name Ezekiel almost

121

certainly must be a mistranslation of the name Hezekiah, for there is no other sign of an Ezekiel Cartwright in the area.)

25 January 1816---**Joseph Tippitt** to **Robert Cartwright** 16 acres on Round Lick Creek. (Deed Book H, pg. 99)

5 February 1816---**Thomas M. Cartwright** to **Samuel Cartwright** 135 acres on Round Lick Creek for one cent. (Deed Book H, pg. 42. These were evidently sons of Thomas N. Cartwright, or else the initial 'M.' is a mistranslation of 'N.", in which case this may have been a deed from father to son.)

20 May 1816---**John Allcorn** to **John Cartwright** a tract of land on Barton's Creek. (Deed Book F, pg. 516)

29 December 1816---Sheriff **Thomas Bradley** to **Hezekiah Cartwright** 50 acres in Wilson County. (Deed Book H, Pp. 263-264)

15 September 1817---**Martin Tally** to **William Cartwright** 150 acres on Round Lick Creek. (Deed Book F, pg. 435)

15 December 1817---**Morris Hallum** to **John Cartwright** ten acres on Barton's Creek. (Deed Book F, pg. 499)

4 December 1817---**John Hallum** to **John Cartwright** 108 acres on Barton's Creek. (Deed Book F, pg. 514)

2 May 1818---**William Cartwright** to **Richard Belcher** 100 acres on Hickman's Creek. (Deed Book G, pg. 96)

8 June 1818---**Robert Cartwright** to **Ezekiel Bass** 214 acres on Round Lick Creek. (Deed Book G, pg. 251.)

19 May 1818---**John Cartwright** to **John H. Spencer** 111 acres on round Lick Creek. (Deed Book G, pg. 291)

19 May 1819---Division of **Hezekiah Cartwright** estate. Heirs: **Richard Cartwright, Peter A. Cartwright, Benjamin Cartwright,**

Matthew T. Cartwright, John Cartwright, Elizabeth Lambert, Penelope Cartwright minor, James N. Cartwright minor, Hezekiah Cartwright, Hannah Cartwright, William Cartwright, Edward W. Cartwright, Polly P Pool, Nancy McIntosh, Sally McIntosh, and Lucinda Cartwright. (Deed Book G, Pp. 413-415)

8 December 1819---John Cartwright to John Davidson, Sr. 130 acres in Wilson County. (Deed Book H, pg. 141)

9 December 1819---Thomas Griffin to John Cartwright a tract of land in Wilson County. (Deed Book H, pg. 105)

9 December 1819---John Cartwright to Harry L. Douglass a tract of land in Wilson County. (Deed Book H, pg. 443)

25 January 1820---John Edwards to Robert Cartwright 50 acres on Round Lick Creek. (Deed Book H, pg. 111)

25 January 1820---Robert Cartwright to Joseph Tippett 20 acres in Wilson County. (Deed Book H, pg. 133)

13 November 1820---John Cartwright of Wilkerson County, Mississippi to Hezekiah Cartwright and Benajah Cartwright two town lots in the town of Lebanon. (Deed Book I, pg. 217. This John Cartwright is apparently the son of Matthew, who went to Texas but spent some time in Mississippi and Louisiana along the way.)

5 February 1820---John Cartwright, George Clark, and Elizabeth Cartwright, administrators of Hezekiah Cartwright deceased, to John Maholland 150 acres on Jennings' Fork. (Deed Book I, pg. 277)

7 February 1821---John Afflack to John Cartwright 138 acres on Cedar Lick Creek. (Deed Book M, pg. 259)

4 July 1822---Hezekiah Cartwright and Benajah Cartwright to Henry Smith two town lots in the town of Lebanon. (Deed Book I, pg. 317)

16 October 1826---**John Cartwright** of Louisiana to **John S. Tapp** and **Albert H. Wynne** a town lot in the town of Lebanon. (Deed Book L, Pp. 461-462)

22 September 1828---**Joseph Phillips** to **Richard Cartwright** 185 acres on Round Lick Creek. (Deed Book M, pg. 253)

14 April 1828---**Thomas Cartwright** of the Province of Texas to **Hezekiah Cartwright** 130 acres on Round Lick Creek. (Deed Book M, pg. 415)

8 June 1829---**Hezekiah Cartwright** to **Shelah Waters**, **Jr.** 22 acres on Round Lick Creek. (Deed Book M, pg. 445)

23 June 1828---**Hez. L. Cartwright** to **D. A. McEachern** of Smith County a town lot in the town of Lebanon. (Deed Book M, pg. 464)

29 September 1829---**Matthew Cartwright** of the Province of Texas to **Reuben Satterfield** 222 acres, it being the land willed to him by his grandfather. (Deed Book M, pg. 510)

      In relation to all the records thus far presented, note the familiar names which were connected with the Cartwrights earlier along the trail---Edwards, Tippett, Taylor, etc. Aside from those, there are many other surnames present in Wilson County which are either well-known from earlier parts of the study or, interestingly, are the same surnames as those which are closely connected with the Cartwrights who moved through Blount County, Lawrence County, and into Tippah County, Mississippi. Rogers, Wrays, Jones', and Hendersons are present in Wilson County, Tennessee, just as there were persons named Joiner and Hallum in Tippah County, Mississippi. At this point, all of these familiar names found in the same areas as the Cartwrights may mean nothing more than an illustration of the migration patterns typical of the times; but in many cases it was definitely due to the fact that the people tended to intermarry with those whom they knew well, and to travel to places where other relatives were already present. Regardless, the observations have done little to help us work out family relationships, and so we must continue to concentrate only on the records themselves and what they can tell us.

Although many of the same given names for the Cartwright sons are found in the families of the different brothers, it is usually possible to distinguish them. The **Matthew Cartwright** of the Province of Texas who was mentioned as selling 'the land willed to him by his grandfather', was of course the son of **John Cartwright** who was son of **Matthew**. The **John Cartwright** who is mentioned in the earlier deeds and who is described as being of Mississippi in one instance and of Louisiana in another is apparently the same John, son of Matthew. It seems likely that the **John Cartwright** who was mentioned as being in Alabama was the son of Hezekiah. **Thomas N. Cartwright** was the only one who had a son named Thomas, as we are about to see from his will, so it is probable that the **Thomas Cartwright** 'of the Province of Texas' was the son of Thomas N.. (Selling land to Hezekiah, who was probably his brother rather than the Hezekiah who was son of the *elder* Hezekiah.)

Before getting into a greater discussion of other records which will help to identify certain of the children of these men, we should explore the will of the final brother of the original North Carolina Cartwright family, **Thomas N. Cartwright**. The fact that he died later than his brothers and that his children seem to have married later than those of his brothers is a fair indication that he was probably the youngest son in the family of John Cartwright of Edgecombe County, North Carolina. His will is reproduced here in full[5]:

Will of Thomas N. Cartwright

In the name of God Amen. I **Thomas Cartwright** of the state of Tennessee and county of Wilson being in perfect health, mind and memory calling to mind the mortality of my body and knowing that is (sic) appointed for all men once to die first of all I recommend my soul into the hands of Almighty God, who gave it, nothing doubting but I shall receive the same again by the mighty hand of God. My body I recommend to the earth to be buried in decent christian burial at the discretion of my executors. Calling to mind the worldly goods wherewith it hath pleased God to bless me with in this life I dispose of the same in the following manner and form towit,

Item 1st My desire is that my lawful debts be paid.

Item 2nd I give and bequeath unto my son **Samuel Cartwright** one negro boy called **Harry** together with the rest of the property I have given him hertofore.

Item 3rd I give and bequeath to my daughter **Sally** one negro girl named **Pammey** with the rest of the I have (sic) given her heretofore.

Item 4th I give and bequeath to my son **Thomas Cartwright** one half of the land whereon I now live after the death of my wife **Martha** also one negro boy called **Dave** with the rest of the property I have given him heretofore.

Item 5th I give and bequeath unto my son **Hezekiah Cartwright** the other half of my land whereon I now live after the death of my wife **Martha** also one negro boy called **George** and one hundred and fifty dollars in money. Also one bed and furniture also a certain bay mare colt a little upward of a year old.

Item 6th I give and bequeath unto my daughter **Patsy Stafford** one negro girl called **Ansey** together with the other property she had heretofore received.

Item 7th I give and bequeath to my daughter **Susannah Davidson** one negro girl called **Malissa** together with other property which she has heretofore received.

Item 8th I lend my wife **Martha** the plantation and land whereon I now live which contains two hundred and seventy acres with the following negroes towit one negro man called **Edmund** once negro woman called (Edo?) Also one negro girl called **Dice** together with all the plantation utensils and stock of every discription also my household and kitchen furniture during her natural life or widowhood. And after her death my desire is that the property above lent to my wife **Martha** except the land which I have given to my two sons **Thomas** and **Hezekiah** be equally divided amond all my surviving heirs.

Item 9th I lend my wife **Martha** three negro girls called **Esther, Lucy** and **Junitha** (or Jintha?) during her natural life or widowhood at her death to be divided as follows between my three daughters **Sally, Patsy** and **Susannah**. **Sally** is to have **Esther**, **Patsey** is to have **Juntha**, and **Susannah** is to have **Lucy**.

Lastly I consititute my wife **Martha** and son **Hezekiah** my sole executrix and executor of this my last will and testament ratifying and confirming this and no other to be my last will and testament.

In testimony whereof I have hereunto set my hand and affixed my seal this 21st day of June A.D. 1820.

Thomas N. Cartwright

(Seal)

Signed, sealed, and delivered in presence of: **Edward Sweat**

George Waters
William Sweat

Entered December Term 1822, recorded by **Jno. Allcorn**, clerk.

Thomas N. Cartwright, Inventory

The following is an inventory of all the goods and chattles rights and credits of the estate of **Thomas N. Cartwright**, dec'd., except what was left by his last will and testament to certain legatees Decr. term of Wilson County court 1822. One still and nine tubs. Tobacco quantity not known, fodder and oats quantity not known, one note on **William Harris** for four dollars, one note on **Hugh** (Henry?) for three dollars and seventy five cents (bad) One note on **John Jone** (sic) for seven dollars (bad) One note on **James Jones** for five dollars (bad) one note on **Moses Ellis** for ten dollars sixty eight cents and three fourths of a cent. One note on **William Sweat** for three dollars twelve cents and a half and some accounts amt. not known.
December term Wilson County Court 1822. Recorded by **Jno Allcorn**, clk.

Also concerning this estate:

'Pursuant to an order (-------) at December Term 1824 appointing **Thomas B. Reese** & **John W. Payton** commissioners to settle with **Hezekiah Cartwright** Executor of the estate of **Thomas**

Cartwright dec'd. & to report to next court We the above named do report as follows (Towit,

We find in the hands of the executor amount of sale $252.25 and notes

Vouchers as follows account by **James Frazer**		15.25
One note	do	26.37
Note by (Yerger?) **Hollady**		35.81
Account by	do	8.00
Note by **William Maholland**		109.69
Account by **Shela Waters** note **Sally Harris** (?)		116.00
Account by **James Shelton Shela Waters** (?)		10.58 3/4
Note by **John Hall** acct **James Shelton** (?)		7.50
Note by **John Hall** Attorney		10.00
Clerks & actioners fees (auctioners?)		3.87
Commisioners fees 200 this report (acc'ts?)		2.60

A true report from the papers presented to us Given under our hands this 8th January 1825 **Thomas B. Reese**

Jno. W. Payton

Commissioners

Recorded the 15th June 1825, **John Allcorn**, Clk.

Aside from the foregoing wills and inventories, there is a record in the Wilson County will books of a Power of Attorney from a **John Cartwright** to a **Matthew Cartwright** which has been abstracted in several sources. Though the document is hard to decipher, there is no punctuation whatsoever, and in at least one area the meaning or intent is very difficult to grasp, I prefer to transcribe it here in full, following the original as closely as I can manage[5]:

Know all men by these presents that I **John Cartwright** of the parish of Natchetoches and state of Lousiana have and by these presents do nominate, constitute, and appoint **Matthew Cartwright** my free and lawful attorney for me and in my name and state to sell three hundred acres and one quarter of land in the county of Madison and state of Tennessee partly lying in the Town of Jackson on the (---?---) having the same purchase of **Stephen Sypert** also to execute a good and sufficient title to the purchaser for me in my name the same when sold apply to his own benefit also to sell my interest in the estate of **Matthew Cartwright** deceased of the County of Wilson and state of Tennessee also the interest of **Susannah Hallum** and **John Hallum** which I purchased of them in said estate and the same when sold apply to his own benefit also to collect a note on **Littleton Joyner** and **Stephen Sypert** for about seven hundred dollars both of the state of Tennessee and when collected or sold apply to his own benefit also to transfer certificates of any lands belonging to me in Pike County and state of Mississippi or convey land belonging to me in any wise lying in the county of Pike and state of Mississippi and the benefit of the same when conveyed apply to his own benefit or my own as he may think proper hereby agreeing to (rectify? --It certainly does not appear to be 'ratify') and confirm every act. and thing which my said attorney may do In testimony whereof I **John Cartwright** have hereunto set my hand and affixed my seal this 4th day of June 1825.

John Cartwright (Seal)

State of Louisiana
Parish of Nachitoches: Personally appeared before me **John C. Carr** parish Judge of the parish of Nachitoches and notary public ex officio the above named **John Cartwright** who acknowledged that he had signed sealed and delivered the above power of Attorney to the above named **Matthew Cartwright** on the day and year thereon named as his act. and deed for the purpose therein expressed In testimony whereof I have hereunto subscribed my name and affixed my seal of office as Parish Judge in and for the parish of Nachitoches & notary publick ex officio at the town of Nachatoches this fourth day of June in the year of our lord one thousand eight hundred and twenty five.

John C. Carr, Parish

Judge
Rec. 5th Oct. 1826 (in Wilson County)   Teste **Jno Allcorn**, Clk.

The deceased **Matthew Cartwright** who is mentioned is clearly the one whose will has been given heretofore, with **John Cartwright** being his son and the **Susannah Hallum** mentioned is his daughter, as named in said will. The further implication, though without direct statement, is that the second **Matthew Cartwright** to whom the Power of Attorney was given is the son of John, also mentioned in the elder Matthew's will. This family has been delineated in other sources, naming **John Cartwright** as having wife **Mary Crutchfield** and with the couple having moved to Texas, their son **Matthew** being a noted man of that name who resided in San Antonio. Several of the records to be examined throughout the rest of this chapter provide the basis for that genealogy. I have not personally seen adequate proof of the fact that Mary or Polly, the wife of the John Cartwright in question, was a Crutchfield, but there may well be other sources for that information that I have not examined. Apparently a record which may be part of the basis for naming John Cartwright's wife as Polly Crutchfield is the will of **George Crutchfield** of Smith County, Tennessee, 1823, in which he names a daughter as Polly Cartwright. I have not been able to examine a copy of the will in question; the only reference which I have seen being a query in a genealogical journal and therefore completely unverified by me. It does not mention the husband of Polly Crutchfield Cartwright. Since some of the data that has heretofore been published on the family in question can be shown to be in error[7,8], I must reserve judgement as regards data shown in sources not closely verified. It might be noted that there was another family of Cartwrights who were more directly located in Smith County, evidently spearheaded by a **Joseph Cartwright** who may have been connected with those thus far examined, and thus they will be examined in the latter part of this chapter.

The next relevant record of Wilson County to be explored is the second accounting of the estate of **Matthew Cartwright** (the elder) at the time when his widow died[5]. This second inventory, along with a detailed list of the buyers at the estate sale, is seven pages long. Thus I will not attempt to reproduce the document in full, but again I will list the names for the value of those connections:

'An account of the property belonging to the Estate of **Matthew Cartwright** deceased at the death of his widow':

Thomas Vaughn	**John Mitchel**	**Robert Furgerson**
Gregory D. Johnson	**James McCown**	**Phillip Johnson**

William Buchanan

Littleton Joiner-his list includes 'negro boy **Bartlett**'

Thomas B. Reese

James Hearn

William (illegible)

John Jonas

James Guthery

Eligah Williams

Thomas Hearn, Sr.

Samuel Cartwright

Richard Hankins--his list includes 'negro girl **Sarah**'

Joshua Dallas

Ephraim J. Harris

James Bundy

Alpha Phelps

John Cox

Thos. Delap

Richard Cartwright

Jeremiah Owens

John Hern

Benjamin Billings

Robert Long

Ebenezar Hern

William Dackings

John Wier

Brice D. Callings

James Turner--his list includes 'hire of negro **Jove**

Nathan Ellis

David Billings--his list includes 'negro **Levin**'

David McMurry

William Newt

Robert Thomas

Robert Daniel

Lemuel Loyd

Robert Turner

James Crutchfield

Isham Morris

RollyOrgan (actually a person's name, and not a reference to a musical instrument)

John McSpadden

Benejah Cartwright

Joshua Joiner

Joseph B. Chance

James Tally

Nathan Bundy

James Baker

William F. Bennett

Elijah Jones

John Hankins

Robert Standfield

Mary Allen

Sutton Belcher

Reuben Dackings

Francis Palmer

Pettus Ragland-his list includes 'negro boy **Spencer**'

Robert Williams

William McIntire--his list includes 'hire of boy **Spencer**'

Adam Trout

John T. Goodall

Henry D. Lester

Moses Ellis

Michel Jones

Robert Delles

Robert Hallum

James D. Johnson

Edward D. Trailor--his list includes '**Bartlett**'s hire'

Edward Sweat

William Allen

John Rains

Littleton Benthal

William Cox

James Motheral

William Palmer

Benjamin Standley

Gabriel Barton

Benja. T. (Malley?)

David Standly

Thomas Hern, Jr.

John Palmer

Arthur Hankins

William Carlen

James Edwards--list includes 'negro girl **Emily**'; note on **Allen Dackens**; note on John **Cartwright**; note on **Anderson Seat** (Street?); act. on

Wm. Dacking; acct. on (**Crim?**); acct. on **John Bradley, Jr.**

Richard Hankins and **Pettus Ragland**, executors.
March Term 1825; recorded 4 June 1825, **Jno Allcorn**, clk.

Out of all the references thus far given, we may derive well enough the basic outlines of the families of Cartwrights who settled in Wilson County, Tennessee. At this point we don't know the specific relationships between these Cartwrights and the Tippetts who are also found in the county in the same time frame, but since we have studied the latter family almost as closely as the Cartwrights until now, it seems appropriate to give the data that is to be found concerning them. The only pertinent will or inventory data that I have located is given below[5]:

Inventory of the estate of **Joseph Tippett** dec'd., taken the 25th of May 1821. Two hundred and thirty acres of land, five negroes towit **Molly, Squire, Morrison, King, Milas** (or possibly Milly?); one note on **Hezekiah Cartwright** for $17.50. Account sale on the 28th of August 1821 (names only are listed, some were repeated several times):

Reuben Phelps	**Widow**	**William F. Bennett**
John C. Tippett	**Robert Cartwright**	**Thomas B. Reese**
John Edwards	**Ezekiel Bass**	**Gabriel Barton**
James Turner	**Benajah Cartwright**	**John Cox**
John W. Gregory	**Daniel Shaw**	**Bazel Davis**
John Foster	**Charles Seay**	**John Maholland**
Thomas Griffin	**Simpson Organ**	**John Beard**
Isham Jones	**Richard Phelps**	**Isaac Moore**
Christopher Brooks	**David Beard**	**Richard Cartwright**
John Cartwright	**Joseph Morley**	**Willie Dackings**
Hezekiah Cartwright	**Isham Palmer**	

Exhibited at November term 1821, recorded 26 November 1821.

John Allcorn, clerk.

Next, there is an inventory for a woman who appears to have been Joseph Tippett's widow:

'A true return of sale of the property of **Anne Tippet** dec'd. the 17th January 1822' (names only are listed):

John C. Tippett	**Benjamin Coats**	**Benajah Cartwright**
John Edwards	**Anderson Cock**	**William F. Bennett**
John Boone	**Gabriel Barton**	**Anne Barton**
James Turner	**Benjamin Bartley**	**Jonathan Baker**
John (L.?) Foster		

Exhibeted March term 1822, recorded 29 March 1822. **John Allcorn,** clk.

Note that many of the names listed in the above inventories are the same people whose names were present in similar records concerning the Cartwrights, and that many Cartwrights themselves are present on the Tippett lists. The Cartwrights shown---Richard, Benajah, John, Hezekiah---are evidently the children of Hezekiah, Sr. (who was already deceased at this time), and this may indicate that Joseph Tippet was somehow closer to them than to the other Cartwrights, if only in geographical proximity. That Anne Tippet of the second inventory was the wife of Joseph Tippett seems likely, and we will see presently from the marriage records that are examined that there is a marriage record for a Joseph Tippett to Anne Ragsdale. But if this was the couple whose inventories are given above, they must have married quite late in life or else there was a notable tragedy, for the marriage occured on 3 January 1821, just months before Joseph died, and with Anne dying only a year later. It is possible that the couple shown in the marriage record may have been of a younger generation, and a closer examination of the original records may shed light on the matter.

Deed abstracts concerning persons of the surname Tippett, other than those already given, are meager but contain some important information[6]:

28 March 1810---**John Dabney** of Williamson County, Tennessee to **Joseph Tippett** 211 acres on Round Lick. (Deed Book G, pg. 392)

3 September 1817---This indenture made this 3rd day of September 1817 between **John Jones, William Davis**, and **John Tippitt**, executors of **William Hale** of the one part to **Gregory Johnson** 50 acres on Spring Creek. (Deed Book G, pg. 140)

The information shown in the latter deed abstract may be a significant indication that the John Tippitt or Tippett in question had married a daughter of the deceased William Hale, for when several different men are named as executors thus in a will, it often is because the men were sons-in-law.

The remaining data to be gleaned on the Tippetts in Wilson County will be included with abstracts concerning the Cartwrights. There is much information in Wilson County resources which can allow some of the Cartwright descendants of the original brothers to be traced all the way up to the Twentieth Century, but the scope of this work precludes any attempt to go beyond a general stopping-place of the 1830's. As can be seen from most of the data being examined in this chapter, the children of Peter seem to have gone elsewhere; the only son of Matthew went west to Texas; and only those of Hezekiah seem to have remained in the area of Wilson County. It can be seen from the examination of some of the records of Smith County, Tennessee (given later) that at least two of the children of Thomas N. Cartwright had connections in that county.

A few further deed abstracts are listed below, all of them seeming to involve Hezekiah's children[6,9]:

4 August 1823---**William Cartwright** to **John Cox** 84 acres on Round Lick Creek. (Deed Book Q, pg. 22)

8 December 1826---**Nathaniel Williams** to **Richard Cartwright** 88 acres on Round Lick Creek. (Deed Book N, pg. 3)

1 December 1827---**Richard Cartwright** to **William Maholland** a tract of land on Round Lick Creek. (Deed Book O, pg. 19)

29 June 1830---**John Cartwright** of Madison County, Alabama to **John Palmer** 154 acres on Round Lick Creek. (Deed Book N, Pp. 199-200)

30 July 1830---**Robert W. P Pool** and **Mary P Pool** his wife of Calaway County, Kentucky to **James B. Taylor** seven acres on Round Lick Creek, it being the same tract that the said **Mary P Pool** drew as heir of **H. Cartwright** deceased. (Deed Book N, Pp. 212-213)

10 March 1832---**Matthew T. Cartwright** to **Levi Donnell** 37 acres on Round Lick Creek. (Deed Book O, pg. 184)

5 August 1833---**John Rains** to **M. T. Cartwright** two town lots in the town of Commerce. (Deed Book P, pg. 139)

11 February 1835---**Edward W. Cartwright** to **Wilson T. Waters** 45 acres on Round Lick Creek, it being lot number 12 in the division of **Hezekiah Cartwright** deceased. (Deed Book P, pg. 540)

Records relating to the deaths of the various Cartwrights, which have not already been given, are shown below[3,10]:

Hezekiah Cartwright, settlement: Minor heirs are **Matthew, Elizabeth, Edward, William H., Penelope S., Peter A.,** and **James N. Cartwright. William Maholland**, guardian.   Recorded 14 May 1823. (----Pp. 380-382)

Matthew Hankins income: 31 March 1827, **Richard Hankins** reported on money received on behalf of **Matthew Hankins**, the heir of **Matthew Cartwright**. (Wills and Inventories, 1824-1827)

James Motheral, Guardian: Guardian of **Sedector, Elizabeth, Mariah, William, John, Malinda, (Matlock), Lasy,** and **Edward**, minor heirs of **Matthew Cartwright**. Recorded 9 May 1827. (I have a vague hunch that this abstracted record may be in error somehow. If not, then this Cartwright family is completely unidentified insofar as my own search has gone. I find no other evidence whatever of any Cartwrights with names such as those listed here.)

Court records which are relevant to the study[10,11,12]:

Robert Cartwright Relinquishment. January 1813. I sell my interest in my father's estate to **Jesse Cartwright** of (?Pa....couper) Parrish, Louisiana. I relinquish all my rights to my brother, the above-mentioned. My mother has a life estate. Recorded 29 November 1817.

Richard and **John Cartwright** versus **Robert W. P Pool** and wife **Mary**. **Hezekiah Cartwright**, father of complainant, settled **John Cartwright** on a tract of land bounded by **Robert W. P Pool**. **Mary P Pool** is one of the children of **Hezekiah Cartwright** deceased. 1822. (Circuit Court records 1821-1825, Pp. 27-28)

John Tippett charged with an affray. He was found guilty and fined seven dollars and a half. Recorded 22 June 1822. (Quarterly Court Minutes 1822-1824, pg. 29)

Benajah Cartright charged with an affray. Recorded 22 June 1822. (Quarterly Court Minutes 1822-1824, pg. 29)

Hallum Power of Attorney. 19 November 1824. **John** and **Susannah Hallum** of Pike County, Mississippi, and heirs of **Matthew Cartwright** of Wilson County, gave their power of attorney to **Matthew Cartwright** of Pike County. Recorded 11 May 1825. (Wilson County Court Minutes 1814-1829, pg. 354)

Matthew T. Cartwright versus the heirs of **William H. Cartwright** 2 May 1832. (Circuit Court records 1830-1833, pg. 235)

John B. Barton and **Joseph Tippitt** charged with arson. 2 May 1834. (Circuit Court records 1833-1836, pg. 55. There is a repetition of this case, and then the same once more, dated 4 May 1835 with the added names of James Dodson and Jefferson Dodson, also charged.)

The Grand Jury brought into court a bill of indictment against **John C. Tippitt, Samuel Brown, Thomas Brown**, and **Alfred Woollard** marked with the name **William Goodall**, prosecutor for an affray. Endorsed a true bill. Recorded 23 September 1834. (County Court Minutes 1833-1836, pg. 133)

Richard W. Cartwright, guardian. Guardian for the minor heirs of **William F. Bennett**, to wit, **Micajah, William, Nancy**, and **Oliver**. Recorded 12 May 1836. (Guardian Settlements, 1836-1841, Pp. 4-5. See later the marriage records wherein it is shown that the wife of William F. Bennett was a Tippett.)

M. T. Cartright Guardian. Guardian for **James N. Cartright** and **Thomas Atwood**, minor heirs of **Hezekiah Cartright**. Recorded 15 February 1837. (Guardian Settlements 1836-1841, pg. 71. The inclusion of both boys as heirs of Hezekiah Cartright might be a mistake, for see below.)

Matthew T. Cartright Guardian. Guardian for **James W. Cartright** who is the minor heir of **Hezekiah Cartright**. Recorded 18 January 1839. (Guardian Settlements 1836-1841, pg. 123)

Matthew T. Cartright Guardian. Guardian for **Thomas Atwood**, minor heir of **Edwin Atwood**. Recorded 18 January 1838. (Guardian Settlements 1836-1841, pg. 123)

Marriage Records

The marriage records for many of the Cartwrights of Wilson County can be found abstracted or reproduced in many different sources[13,14,15]. I have collated the data concerning said marriages and have listed them here. (All those listed are Wilson County marriages):

Luke Tippet to **Jenney Cooksey**, 12 March 1808. Witness **John Allcorn**; surety **Henry Carson**.
Hezekiah Cartwright to **Elizabeth Maholland** 2 September 1808. Witness **John Allcorn**; surety **M. W.Cartwright**.
Sally Cartwright to **John Harris**, 7 February 1809. Witness
137

Samuel Merrets; surety Samuel Cartwright.

William Cartwright to Patsy Fuller, 3 June 1809. Surety William Draper.

John Cartwright to Polly Dillard, 16 March 1810. Surety Robert W. P'Pool.

Samuel Cartwright to Letty Moore, 20 March 1810. Witness Samuel Meredith; surety John Harris.

Polly Cartwright to Robert W. P'Pool, 16 March 1811. Surety John Cartwright.

John C. Tippet to Caty Hart, 14 March 1812. Witness John Allcorn; surety Stephen Barton. (One source says Caty Hail.)

Elly Tippet to William Bennett, 31 January 1814. Witness John Allcorn; surety John C. Johnson.

Richard Cartwright to Ann Waters, 6 November 1815. Surety Wilson T. Waters.

Martha Cartwright to William Stafford, 28 May 1818. Surety John Jones.

Hannah S. Cartwright to Samuel Justice, 30 August 1818. Surety Michael Yerger.

Susan Cartwright to William Davidson, 1 November 1818. Executed by John Peyton, J.P.; surety George Swann.

Thomas Cartwright to Patsy Davidson, 2 November 1818. Executed by Wm. Steele, J.P.; surety Alexander Braden. (Another source says 1 November 1819.)

Joseph Tippit to Ann Ragsdale, 3 January 1821. Surety Isaac Moore.

Hezekiah Cartwright to Mary Brown, 7 January 1823

Penny Cartwright to John A. Nettles, 15 May 1824. Surety Jas. Dodds. (One source shows the given name of this bride as 'Pemmy', but it probably should be Penny Cartwright, as given here. The name Pemmy was used in the Robert Cartwright family of Nashville, whereas Penny was clearly a Wilson County name. It is entirely possible, however, that one of the Davidson-Sumner area Cartwrights could have married in Wilson County.)

Lucinda Cartwright to John Rains, 23 August 1824. Surety

William Maholland. m. by John Smith.

Hezekiah Cartwright to **Sally Mallan**, 16 October 1827. Surety
  Wm. Davidson. (One source says Sally <u>McHollan</u>. Probably
  it should be 'Maholland'.)

Hezekiah L. Cartwright to **Delila Searcy**, 6 June 1828. Surety
  John Cox.

Jane M. Cartwright to **Francis Davidson**, 22 March 1830

Penelope Cartwright to **Thomas Turner**, 28 April 1831

Edward W. Cartwright to **Dicy H. Crutchfield**, 19 February 1833

Julia Ann Cartwright to **Purnell Hearn**, 4 January 1834

Susan Tippett to **James Davis**, 4 September 1834

Hezekiah Cartwright to **Nancy H. Grissim**, 6 October 1834

Joseph Tippet to **Tempy Harrison**, 31 December 1835. m. by M. T.
  Cartwright, J. P. Bondsman Joseph Manning.

Mary Tipet to **James Spears**, 24 October 1836. m. by A. Bass.

Susannah M. Cartwright to **Robert L. Pulley**, 26 October 1836. m.
  by Solomon Caplinger.

Thomas Cartwright to **Mary Fisher**, 3 January 1838

James Cartwright to **Martha Ann Coleman**, 18 June 1838

Wilson T. Cartwright to **Elizabeth Tracy**, 10 December 1839

Aside from the above marriages, **Thomas Cartwright** was the surety
on the marriages of **John T. Goodall** and **Elizabeth Aken**, 7 January
1818; and **Benjamin T. Bell** and **Charlotte** _____, 30 January 1818.
A **Hezekiah Cartwright** was the surety on the marriage of **Alphy
Philips** (Phelps?) to **Elizabeth Edwards**, 23 September 1826; and on
the marriage of **Wm. Maholland** to **Sally Hopson**, 20 December
1827. **Matthew T. Cartwright** was the surety on the marriage of
Elisha Dowell to **Elizabeth Barbee**, 5 February 1827.

In addition, I believe that the following Sumner County, Tennessee
marriages may relate to Cartwrights who originated among the Wilson
County group, although one or more of them may actually be
descendants of Robert of Nashville. I am basing the presumption of
Wilson County connections merely on the fact that the surnames of the
spouses are found in the Wilson County data:

William Cartwright to **Elizabeth Goodall**, 13 February 1811.
Thomas W. Cartwright to **Elizabeth Cook**, 14 July 1825.
Mary Cartwright to **James McGowan**, 23 May 1827.

     Although I have stated the wish to circumscribe the scope of this work by confining the collected data to the time period of the 1830's and earlier, I am making every effort during this investigation to aid those researching African-American genealogy; and thus I will include the following marriage record[13], also from Wilson County, Tennessee: '**King Tippett** to **Harriett Cartwright**, 17 September 1865'; recorded as a black couple. Note that the groom is listed previously in the household of **Joseph Tippett** (inventory, given earlier). We also saw that there was the name of a 'negro girl **Harriett**' listed in the household of Erasmus L. Tippett who died in Blount County in 1822. If, as seems to be implied, the girl named **Harriett** was a young child at that time, she may be the same as the bride in the marriage record cited above. Although she would have been perhaps in her fifties by the time of the marriage record in 1865, many of those who were formerly slaves did not have the opportunity to become officially married until after emancipation. It is entirely possible that **King Tippett** and **Harriet Cartwright** were actually a couple, perhaps with children having been born to them, long before the time of the marriage record.) Unfortunately, many of the compilations from which I have taken the abstracts cited in this volume did not include data concerning slaves. Yet, judging from the information which I have reproduced from original records myself, it is clear that there must be many such references to slaves in the many wills, inventories, and court records of the times.
     Thanks to the works of **Jeanette Tillotson Acklen** (detailed in Bibliography) we have a ready means of further data on some of the Cartwrights of Wilson County. In her volume titled 'Bible Records and Marriage Bonds' we find the Bible record of **Thomas Turner**, who married **Penelope Cartwright** (The Bible record was copied for the collection by Mrs. W. P. Bouton, Lebanon, Tennessee, 1933 or earlier; the Bible was then in the possession of Horace E. Turner of Lebanon, Tennessee, a grandson.) I will not try to reproduce the

entirety of the Thomas family record from the source stated, since the works are readily available in many large library collections and/or from the publisher. The Bible records shows the marriage of **Thomas Turner** and **Penelope S. Cartwright**, 28 April 1831; It gives the birth date of Thomas Turner as 15 July 1809, and the birth date of his wife Penelope as 30 September 1813. Thomas Turner died 14 October 1871, and Penelope died 9 August 1888. Presumably the rest of the names for which births and deaths are given are the couple's children, or possibly spouses of some of them. (There are fourteen other names for whom birth dates are given, and death dates of the same.) For anyone descended from this family, the works of Mrs. Acklen would be a tremendously helpful resource. The companion volume entitled 'Tombstone Inscriptions and Manuscripts', contains the cemetery inscriptions for the same Turner family. (Location of cemetery described as 'Eleventh District, near Zion Methodist Church'.) This record gives the added information of the birth and death dates of Penelope Cartwright's mother **Elizabeth (Maholland) Cartwright**, who was the second wife of **Hezekiah Cartwright, Sr.**. The inscription reads, according to the transcription, 'Sacred to the memory of **Elizabeth Cartwright**, Dec. 10, 1786--Oct. 23, 1851'. The list of cemetery inscriptions for this family gives the death dates of those already mentioned above in reference to the Bible record, along with those for a number of others, including a Cartwright child of a later generation who died very young.

Also in the same source, we find some important data concerning two of Hezekiah Cartwright's sons, from a list of the Cedar Grove Cemetery, Lebanon, Wilson County, Tennessee. (Copied for the volume by Mrs. W. P. Bouton.) The pertinent inscriptions are: **James Nesbet Cartwright**, Mar. 28, 1818--Oct. 16, 1895; **Nancy Jane Goodner**, his wife, April 12, 1827--July 12, 1894; and **Matthew Thomas Cartwright**, June 13, 1809--Jan. 28, 1848; **Martha Harris Goodner**, his wife, May 7, 1818--Nov. 23, 1854. Next on the same list is an inscription for **Ophelia Cartwright**, wife of W. P. Turner, Mar. 25, 1837--Oct. 23, 1878. (I do not know the identity of this Cartwright, or the Turner mentioned. She may have been a child of Matthew T. Cartwright and wife Martha.)

Further, the latter volume contains data on another of Hezekiah's sons, **Richard Cartwright**. He and his wife are found

141

buried in the cemetery of Gregory D. Johnson, Nineteenth District, Wilson County, Tennessee. (The location is described as 'east of Tater-Peeler Road on Hankins Hill, five and one-half miles from Lebanon'.) The relevant inscriptions are '**Richard Cartwright**, 1795--Jan. 11, 1842. **Annie Cartwright**, April 10, 1793--May 15, 1865; joined the M. E. Church 1829. There is a notation by the transcriber, 'Box tomb down'. The list of data here includes a number of other names, particularly some members of the Hankins family, though not Richard Hankins and wife Sally G. who was daughter of Matthew Cartwright.

Miscellaneous data from various sources:

      Thomas Cartwright was listed among the heirs of **Martha P. Davidson**, who was deceased before 2 February 1825[16]. Other heirs were **John Donnell, William B. Gill, Benjamin Davidson, William P. Davidson, Francis P. Davidson, Wilson Z. Davidson, & Polly Bloodworth**. Sold to **Alfred Bloodworth** a 'negro woman named **Amy** & her children'. Wil. Co. TN. Reg. Bk, pg. 338. (See the marriages previously given. Thomas Cartwright had married Martha 'Patsy' Davidson, obviously the daughter of the above deceased. Susan or Susannah Cartwright, Thomas's sister, had married William Davidson. These were children of Thomas N. Cartwright, per his will. The brother Samuel Cartwright married Letty Moore, but it is difficult to tell which of the many 'Hezekiah' marriages might have been that of the other brother in the family of Thomas N. Cartwright.)

Some data related to the above, from Smith County, Tennessee[17]:

10 December 1819---**William Patterson** to his nephews and nieces, to wit, **Benjamin Davidson, William Davidson, Patsy Cartwright, Polly Davidson, Frances P. Davidson, Wilson Y. Davidson, Catherine Davidson, Elizabeth Donnell,** and **Anne Gill**, children of **James** and **Martha Davidson**, a tract of land. (Deed Book I, pg. 478.)

      The above abstracts obviously give a great deal of information concerning the Davidson family, into which family two of the children of Thomas N. Cartwright married. In light of the fact that said children of Thomas N. are found in Smith County records, it seems that the other Cartwright data found in Smith County could be extremely relevant to the study of those Cartwrights in Wilson County, and thus it is detailed here.

Other data from Smith County, Tennessee[17]:

12 August 1815---**Null Thompson** to **James Cartwright**, ten acres. (Deed Book E, pg. 176.)

14 March 1815---State of Tennessee Grant, No. 6721. 20 Acres to **James Cartwright**. (Deed Book E, Pp. 526-527.)

11 October 1817---**James Cartwright** to **Charles Cornwell** a tract of land on Defeated Creek. (Deed Book F, pg. 118.)

11 May 1815---State of Tennessee Grant No. 6999. 20 acres to **James Cartwright**. (Deed Book F, pg. 296.)

27 May 1818---**James Cartwright** to **James Williams** 20 acres. (Deed Book F, pg. 299.)

4 July 1818---**John Goad** to **James Cartwright** 160 acres. (Deed Book F, Pp. 307-308.)

13 February 1820---**Admiral White** to **James Cartwright** a tract of land. (Deed Book G, Pp. 407-408.)

29 December 1820---**James Cartwright** to **Demps Sutton** a tract of 21 acres. (Deed Book H, Pp. 181-182.)

24 May 1824---**George Sutton** to **James Cartwright** 160 acres. (Deed Book I, Pp. 2-3.)

7 October 1826---**Samuel D. McMurry** to **Joseph Cartwright** a tract of land. (Deed Book I, pg. 328.)

10 August 1825---**James Cartwright** to **Joseph Cartwright** a tract of land on Payton's Creek. (Deed Book I, pg. 337.)

July 1832---**Demsey Sutton** to **James Cartwright** 154 acres on Defeated Creek. (Deed Book L, pg. 81.)

6 December 1832---**Willis Dean** to **Asberry Cartwright** 24 acres. (Deed Book L, Pp. 165-166.)

6 January 1834---**James Sutton** to **James Cartwright** 40 acres. (Deed Book M, pg. 278.)

Smith County Will Book 1814-1816, pg. 16[1]: Will of **John Corder** made 28 September 1815, proved Feb. 1815; Names wife **Gracy**, son **Joel**, dec., his heirs; dau. **Elizabeth Cartwright**; **Lewis Corder** and **Jannett Cowell** executors.

There are some Cartwrights found among the records of Franklin County, Tennessee, and because of the similarity of some of the names and the fact that Franklin County eventually descended in part from Smith and White Counties, it seems likely that the Cartwrights found in Franklin County are related to those under study here, rather than to those of the Nashville area. On the other hand, many of the names in this Franklin County group are similar to those used among the Pasquotank Cartwrights, as will be seen later. Nonetheless, I have decided to include the Franklin County abstracts in this section[18]:

20 April 1808---State of Tennessee Grant No. 130, 200 acres in White County to **Jacob**, **Abraham**, and **James Cartwright**.

22 July 1809---**Joseph Cartwright** in behalf of **Jacob Cartwright**, **James Cartwright**, and **Abram Cartwright** to **James Brandon** 200 acres. Said **Joseph, Sr.** is father to the said Cartwrights.

8 October 1824---The heirs of **Daniel Morris**, to wit, Widow **Rosannah Morris**, **Nancy Jackson**, formerly **Nancy Morris**, **Isaac Cartwright** and wife **Sally**, formerly **Sally Morris**, **William Draper**

and wife **Susannah**, formerly **Susan Morris, Graves Morris,** and **Phebe Morris** to **Daniel Morris**, son of **Graves Morris**.

25 March 1826---**Groves Morris, Isaac Cartwright** and wife, formerly **Sally Morris, William Harper** and wife, formerly **Phebe Morris** to **Nancy Jackson** a tract of land for $400.

24 May 1819---**Nathaniel Hunt** to **Isaac Cartwright** a tract of land on the Elk River.

20 September 1829---**Abraham Cartwright** to **James Brandon** a tract of land granted to **Joseph Cartwright** and **James Cartwright**.

23 August 1830---**Isaac Cartwright** to **James Cargyle** 120 acres.

19 February 1824---**James Cartwright** of **Alabama** to **James Brandon** a tract of land.

It does not seem likely that the **Joseph Cartwright, Sr.** who is mentioned in the above records could be the same as a **Joseph Cartwright** to whom a North Carolina grant of land was made in Tennessee in 1786---#527, Joseph Cartwright, 640 acres on Halfpone Creek.[19] (In what was then Davidson County, with most of Middle Tennessee being that county at the time.) From a fuller version, or perhaps a later renewal, of the land grant[20] it can be seen that the Joseph Cartwright of the grant was of Pasquotank County, but he seems not to have come to Tennessee to take possession of the land; or at least, his family was still in Pasquotank and the land was transferred to another person, though it was at an early date. On the back of the original paper there is an assignment, thus: 'Assignment to **Frederick Davis**, viz. we, **Mary Sawyers, Thomas Britt, Keziah Cartwright**, and **Sarah Cartwright** of the State of North Carolina and County of Pasquotank dor for ourselves as heirs and assigns of the State and County aforesaid for the consideration of the full and just sum of six pounds currency of said State. Witness and signed this 6 June 1788. (Though it says witnessed, there are no witnesses listed in the abstract.) This does not prove, of course, that the Joseph Cartwright of the land grant never came to Tennessee; only that he did not retain the land in question. It also gives at least the appearance that he may have been deceased at the time of the assignment, and had only daughters as heirs, which would eliminate him as the Joseph Cartwright in Franklin County, Tennessee.

It cannot be shown to a satisfactory extent that the Cartwrights of Smith and Franklin are either the same or are closely related, and the mention of James Cartwright of Franklin being 'of Alabama' in 1824 while the man of the same name in Smith County is still there in 1834 would seem to nullify the idea. But the similarity of the names makes it a possibility worth a closer investigation than I have been able to conduct thus far. (Franklin County was established 3 December 1807 from a part of Warren County and a part of Bedford County. Warren County, in turn, came from White, which came from Smith, which came from Sumner. Sumner County was taken from Davidson County and the Cumberland settlement. A closer analysis of the land records would probably establish with even more certainty whether the Franklin County Cartwrights are the same as those mentioned in Smith County.) Whether the two groups of Smith and Franklin Counties are connected or not, it is easy enough to distinguish them from those of the Robert Cartwright family of the Nashville area. The names Joseph, Abraham, Isaac, etc. were not used in that family, and the only James who was son of Robert and would have been of an age similar to the one in question above is shown to have remained in Sumner County, apparently for the length of his life. (See Part II.)

To conclude the study in this chapter, I might add a few bits of commentary to clarify some of the data which may not be clear where relationships are concerned. The fact that there is a Robert Cartwright found in several references among the Wilson County records can be confusing, since there is no Robert Cartwright among the children of the original Cartwright brothers who were from Edgecombe County, North Carolina. It seems that he was probably the son of the noted Robert Cartwright of Nashville, judging from the fact that said son Robert was left land in or close to that area by his father's will. (See Chapter Seven.) On the other hand, there was actually a 'second' Robert Cartwright of the Davidson County area, who originated among the Pasquotank, North Carolina group, and it may have been he who is seen in Wilson County. That he was somewhat closely intertwined with *all* the others will be seen, making it difficult to separate the Roberts, and those of the name David Cartwright as well, since both Roberts had sons by that name. The data concerning the two Roberts themselves, however will be shown clearly enough to leave little doubt of their separation.

Bibliography of Sources for Chapter Five

1. 'Tennessee Genealogical Records' by Edythe Rucker Whitley. Genealogical Publishing Co., Inc. Baltimore, MD. 1980.
2. 'Wilson County, Tennessee Deeds, Marriages, and Wills 1800-1902' by Thomas E. Partlow. Southern Historical Press, Inc., P. O. Box 1267, Greeneville, S. C.29602. 1987.
3. 'Wilson County, Tennessee Wills, Books 1-13, 1802-1850' by Thomas E. Partlow. Ibid. 1981.
4. 'American State Papers--Documents, Legislative and Executive, of the Congress of the United States' selected and edited under the authority of Congress by Walter Lowrie, Secretary of the Senate, and Matthew St. Clair Clarke, Clerk of the House of Representatives. Published by Gales and Seaton, Washington, D. C. 1832; reprinted 1994 by Southern Historical Press, Easley, S. C.
5. Photocopies of original records in author's collection.
6. 'Wilson County, Tennessee, Deed Books C--M, 1793-1829' by Thomas E. Partlow. Southern Historical Press, Greeneville, S. C. 1984.
7. 'DAR Roster of Members and Soldiers, Vol. II' by the National Society of the Daughters of the American Revolution, Washington, D. C.
8. 'The Compendium of American Genealogy', compiled by Frederick A. Virkus. Originally published 1925-1942; Reprinted by Genealogical Publishing Co., Inc., Baltimore, MD 1968 and 1987.
9. 'Wilson County , Tennessee Deed Books N-Z 1829-1853' by Thomas E. Partlow. Southern Historical Press, Greeneville, S. C.
10. 'Wilson County, Tennessee Miscellaneous Records 1800-1875', Ibid. 1982.
11. 'The People of Wilson County, Tennessee 1800-1899', Ibid 1983.
12. 'Wilson County, Tennessee Circuit Court Records 1810-1855' Ibid. 1988.
13. 'Early Middle Tennesse Marriages' by Byron and Barbara Sistler,

Nashville, Tennessee. Byron Sistler & Associates, Inc.
Nashville, TN. 37212. 1988.

14. '35,000 Tennessee Marriage Records and Bonds 1783-1870' by
The Rev. Silas Emmett Lucas, Jr. and Mrs. Ella Lee Sheffield.
Southern Historical Press, Greeneville, S. C.

15. 'Bible Records and Marriage Bonds', and 'Tombstone
Inscriptions and Manuscripts', compiled by Jeanette Tillotson
Acklen. Originally published Nashville, 1933. Reprinted
Genealogical Publishing Co., Inc. Baltimore, MD. 1967, 1976,
and by same for Clearfield Company, Inc., Baltimore, MD.
1992.

16. 'Tennessee Tidbits, Volume II', by Marjorie Hood Fischer and
Ruth Blake Burns. Ram Press, 1239 Coventry Road, Vista,
CA. 92084. 1988.

17. 'Smith County, Tennessee Deed Books B-M 1800-1835', by
Thomas E. Partlow. Southern Historical Press, Greeneville,
S. C. 1993.

18. 'Franklin County, Tennessee Wills 1808-1876 & Deeds 1801-
1840', by Thoms E. Partlow. Ibid. 1991.

19. 'North Carolina Land Grants in Tennessee, 1778-1791' compiled
by Goldene Fillers Burgner. Ibid. 1981.

20. 'Land Deed Genealogy of Davidson County, Tennessee 1783-
1792' by Helen C. & Timothy R. Marsh. Ibid. 1992.

Part II

The

Princess Anne
and
Pasquotank
Cartwrights

(Virginia and North Carolina)

Chapter
Six

The Progenitor John Cartwright

The listing of **John Cartwright** as a transportee to Virginia in 1623[1] appears to be one of the earliest references to the man of our study in this chapter, or indeed to any Cartwright whose destination was the colony of Virginia. That John Cartwright was in the area even earlier than the year 1623 is shown by another record which will be examined presently. There are other Cartwrights who came to Virginia in the seventeenth century, but for whom there is little accounting beyond the point of their apparent arrival, save for references to persons who may have been children of the John in question. As mentioned in Part I of this work, there was a **Henry Cartwright** whose destination was given as Maryland but who appears to have resided in Virginia; and for him there are a few records to attest to his existence during the further years of the same era, with perhaps some evidence of offspring. But with no indication of connections, the said references concerning Henry Cartwright and others of early arrival will be given in a later chapter as miscellaneous data. The main focus of the examination in this half of the volume will be the descendants of John Cartwright, who are numerous and have spread far and wide.

The noted authority on the Lower Norfolk County and Princess Anne County area of Virginia, Alice Granberry Walter, has done much work and published much data in the form of charts, concerning John Cartwright and several generations of his descendants.[2] I cannot hope to improve upon her data, particularly when working without her type of knowledge and personal access to the geographical area in question. Instead I have used her work as a reference in giving the first part of the genealogical outline below, and have continued it with the results of my own observations concerning the later generations of his lines.

I. John Cartwright
b. (probably ca 1600)
m.
d. ca 1666

Children: II-A.   **Thomas Cartwright**, see further.

                      II-B.   possibly **Robert Cartwright**, of Surry Co., Va. will 1676, Surry Co.. Had a son **Robert**, who left a will 1699.

II-A.   Thomas Cartwright
b. by 1618
m. **Mary** _____ (signed a deed, 1673, Lower Norfold Co., Va.).
d. by 1680; probably earlier. He may not have been alive when his father d. ca 1666, since Thomas, Jr. adm. estate of John.

Children: III-A.   **Thomas Cartwright** (called Jr. when adm. estate of John, 1666). See further.

III-A. Thomas Cartwright
b. before 1650
m. 1st. **Alice** _____; she was tried for witchcraft, 15 September 1687. (Whether this resulted in her death is unclear, but she seems to have died about this time.)
m. 2nd. **Grace Trueblood** (widow). She d. 1728, Pasquotank Co., N.C.
d. 1707, Pasquotank County, N. C.

Children: IV-A.   **John Cartwright**; exec. of father's will; appears to have d. 1714, naming only

brothers and sisters. (though the will
was never proved.)

IV-B. **Mary Cartwright**, (m. **Jeremiah Murden**?)

IV-C. **Catherine Cartwright** (called 'Catren' in
father's will.)

IV-D. **William Cartwright**, see further

IV-E. **Robert Cartwright**, m. **Anne Shipp**; see
further

IV-F. **Job Cartwright**, m. **Lydia (Avery?)**
children: **Job, Jr., Thomas**, possibly
Isaac.

IV-G. **Elizabeth Cartwright**, m. **Amos Trueblood**

IV-H. **Joseph Cartwright**, m. **'Ele'?**_____; children:
Benjamin, Elizabeth, Christopher.

IV-I. **Thomas Cartwright**, m. **Mary (Jackson?)**
children: **Thomas, Jr.; Moses.**

IV-D. William Cartwright
b.
m. **Sarah** _____.
d. 1733; Pasquotank County, N. C.
Children: V-Da. **Tamer Cartwright**
              V-Db. **Mary Cartwright**, m. **Owen Reese**
              V-Dc. **Hannah Cartwright**, m. _____
                    Stafford.
              V-Dd. **William Cartwright**, d. 1731; apparently had
                    no children.
              V-De. **Thomas Cartwright**
              V-Df. **Robert Cartwright**, m. **Martha** _____;
                    children: **Hezekiah; Josiah;**
                    Ezekiel; David; Martha; m.
                    Zachariah Jones; John; Sarah, m.
                    Robert Palmer.
              V-Dg. **Joseph Cartwright**
              V-Dh. **Caleb Cartwright** (to Tennessee?)
              V-Di. **David Cartwright**
              V-Dj. **John Cartwright**, d. before father; had

dau. **Elizabeth**.

IV-E. Robert Cartwright
b.
m. **Anne Shipp**, daughter of **Francis Shipp**
d. 1719/20 Princess Anne County, Va.
Children: V-Ea. **William Cartwright**, see further
               V-Eb. **John Cartwright**, d. 1733 Princess
                         Anne Co., Va.; issue, but
                         unknown--perhaps **Lemuel** (See
                         Chapter Seven.)
               V-Ec. **Katherine Cartwright**, m. **James**
                         Cotten
               V-Ed. **Sarah Cartwright**, m. **Adam Keeling**
               V-Ee. **Thomas Cartwright** (seen only briefly as
                         signing on a deed; otherwise no data.
                         Probably had issue.)
               V-Ef. **Anne Cartwright**, m. **John Keeling**
               V-Eg. **Frances Cartwright**, m. _____
                         Clayden.

V-Ea. William Cartwright
b.
m. **Mary Keeling**, daughter of **Thomas Keeling** and **Elizabeth**
     Lovett
d. 1753 Princess Anne Co., Va.
Children: VI-A. **Robert Cartwright**, see further
               VI-B. **Elizabeth Cartwright**, m. _____**Harper**
               VI-C. **Margaret**, m. **John Dudley**; ____ **Dunn**
               VI-D. **Martha Cartwright**, m. **Carraway**; **Nimmo**.
               VI-E. **Frances Cartwright**, m. _____**Holmes**.
               VI-F. **Anne Cartwright**, m. **James Carraway**.
               VI-G. **Sarah Cartwright**
               VI-H. **Amy Cartwright**
               VI-I. ? **Mary Cartwright**, m. **William Gaston** or
                         Gaskin. (Neither William Cartwright's
                         will nor that of his wife Mary show this

daughter named Mary; but she is evidenced in a deed which names her father as William Cartwright. There may have been another William Cartwright who was her father, since there are others shown by inventories listed for the time frame.)

VI-A. Robert Cartwright (see Chapter Seven for greater
  detail on this family)
b. 22 February 1722 Princess Anne County, Va.
m. 1st: **Anne Hugins** (Huggins), dau. of Robert and Mary Huggins.
m. 2nd: **Mary Hunter**, dau. of John and Jacamine Hunter.
m. 3rd: **Pembroke Hunter** ('Pemmy', sister of Mary).
d. 24 December 1809
Children: VII-A. **William Cartwright** (son of first wife Anne; all accounts of this family to date have shown this son as d. in infancy; but see later discussions and evidence. He did *not* die young. He perhaps was the William Cartwright of Sullivan County, Tennessee, who had numerous descendants.)
           VII-B. **Martha Cartwright** (did *not* die young.)
           VII-C. **Mary Cartwright**, (m. James H. Wallace?)
           VII-D. **Anne Cartwright**, (m. Thomas Nelson?)
           VII-E. **Susannah Cartwright** (d. Aug. 1759?)
           VII-F. **Robert Cartwright**, d. 23 March 1776.
           VII-G. **John Hunter Cartwright** (d. young?)
           VII-H. **Thomas Cartwright**, m. **Agnes Christian**
           VII-I. **Pemmy Cartwright** (d. young?)
           VII-J. **Jacob Cartwright**, m. **Patience Hobdy**; children: **Lizette, Alexander Cotton, John Hunter., Harriett, Tabitha, Robert, Marcus D. Lafayette.**
           VII-K. **James Cartwright**, m. _____; m. **Mary** (Kittrell?); children: **Polly**, others?.

VII-L. **William Hunter Cartwright**, (d. young?)
VII-M. **Elizabeth Cartwright**, m. **James Rutherford**;
   children: **Pembroke**, others?
VII-N. **David Cartwright**, m. **Elizabeth Powell**;
   children: **Jacomine, Albert,**
   Pembroke, Emily, Eliza, Sally.
VII-O. **Robert Cartwright**, m. **Elizabeth** (Lawson?);
   children: **Pembroke**, others?
VII-P. **Jesse Hunter Cartwright**, m. **Patsy Rawlings**.

****

Sources and Commentary

The data that is known concerning the progenitor **John Cartwright** is detailed in the works of Ms. Walter, as stated, but for much of it there are also other sources readily available in published form. Mentioned earlier was the fact that John Cartwright is shown to be in the colony of Virginia even before the year 1623 when his name first appears on the extant immigrant lists. The record attesting this is the will of **John Rolfe** of Virginia (who married Pocohontas, as his second wife), on which **John Cartwright** signed as a witness.[3] The will was drawn up in Jamestown 10 March 1621 and proved in London 21 May 1630. While the body of said will does not mention John Cartwright and is not relevant here, the presence of the latter's signature as a witness is proof enough that he was present in Virginia at an earlier date than the immigration lists would show. Other witnesses to the will were **John Milwarde, Robert Davys, Lady Temperance Yeardley** (wife of Sir George), and **Richard Bucke**, the minister who had earlier performed the marriage ceremony for **John Rolfe** to **Pocohontas**.

Aside from the said record, there is very little other than certain punctuating occurences to attest to the life of John Cartwright. He was listed among those living at James City in 1624.[4] There are several records involving his transport to Virginia[1,5], indicating that he traveled back and forth from England a number of times over the years, with little doubt that the transport records refer to the same

John Cartwright. Other than his transport at those early dates, there is the record of a patent to **Stephen Gill** of 1,000 acres, 24 April 1642, received for the transport of twenty persons, among whom is named **Jon. Cartright**. The next reference to John that is found is a patent of his own, dated 14 July 1664, for 100 acres on the south side in east branch of Elizabeth River, bounding on the east side of **Henry Nicholls**. (Lower Norfolk County, Va.) Received for the transport of two persons, who are not named in the record. Later on the persons *are* named, in a renewal of the patent dated 27 September 1665-- transport of two persons, **Mary Williams** and **Anthony Coates**. What is apparently another renewal for the same patent is recorded 1671.

Though I have not personally examined the sources, Ms. Walter's chart[2] indicates that there is a record showing the administration of John Cartwright's estate in 1666 by **Thomas Cartwright, Jr.**, evidently John's grandson. **Thomas, Jr.** also executed a deed 14 January 1670/71 as the administrator of the estate, for what is apparently the same 100 acres received by John Cartwright earlier, being sold to **John Sammons**. There seems to be no concrete indication of other children of John Cartwright, though Ms. Walters indicates the belief that possibly a **Robert Cartwright** of Surry Co., Virginia may have been his son. According to her chart, this Robert Cartwright was of Droitwich, County Worcester, England and sailed ca. 1654 from Bristol, England with a destination of Virginia. Died 1676, will Surry County. (I must interject at this point the comment that there is at least some degree of possibility that some of the Cartwrights attributed to the family of the progenitor John could have been of those Cartwrights of Maryland. There are a few cases where the records do not precisely show the parentage of some of the Cartwrights who are presumed to be of the John Cartwright line; and since there is evidence of interaction with some of the same connected families of Maryland such as Burroughs, Lees, etc,, we must not completely rule out the possibility that one or more of the Cartwrights in Princess Anne County, Virginia and/or Pasquotank County, North Carolina may have been of the Matthew Cartwright line.)

The references to John Cartwright's son, **Thomas Cartwright, Sr.** are also rather meager while yet being enough to establish his existence and verify that he was the son of John. There are several transport and patent records for him found in the same sources as given above; and the fact that his wife's name was Mary is established by a deed indicated on Ms. Walter's chart, on which **Mary Cartwright** signed, 1673 in Lower Norfolk County. The indication of Mary Cartwright, wife of Thomas, signing on said deed may be that Thomas was deceased by that time; and in fact he may have been deceased by 1666 when his father John died, a possible explanation of why his own son Thomas Cartwright, Jr. would have been the administrator of John Cartwright's estate.

Aside from the data on Ms. Walters' charts, there are a couple of tidbits in her volume of Lower Norfolk County records[6]:

15 February 1649/50: (Book 'B', pg. 133a) **Jno. Carraway** hath given unto **John Cartwright** eldest sonne unto **Tho. Cartwright** of Lower Norfolk County one heifer of two yeares old. (There may be some indication here of a familial relationship with Jno. Carraway. Possibly Thomas's first wife, Mary, was a Carraway.)

17 November 1646: (Book 'B', pg. 10a) Upon the petition of **Thomas Cartwright** against **Ellis Browne** concerning a parcell of hoggs in the (..........) thereof. It is ordered that the said hoggs bee equally divided betwixt them and to bee so shared by (...........) in different men/ theire neighbors/ and the said **Ellis Browne** to pay Court Charges als execucion.

The bits of data of course are referring to **Thomas Cartwright, Jr.** (I refer to him thus at this point, although later he is seen as 'Sr.', since he had a son of his own named Thomas). There is much further information concerning him, and it will be examined fully in a later chapter, since he is found in the records of Pasquotank County, North Carolina at the time of his death. For now, it is imperative to note that his children are divided between Princess Anne County, Virginia (which was taken from Lower Norfolk 1691) and the neighboring Pasquotank County, North Carolina, certainly not truly divided in actual space. It is due to that division of counties and states that I discuss them in different chapters, as well as for the expediency of separating the numerous descendants. Thomas Cartwright, Jr.'s son

John Cartwright, who was evidently the eldest, is little known. Aside from the tidbit above and the evidence of his being the executor of his father's will, there is no data concerning him, although it may be he who is evidenced briefly in Perquimans County, to be shown later. For some of Thomas's daughters, however, there will be data found in Pasquotank County, North Carolina, along with much information relating to several of his other sons. The son **Robert Cartwright** and his descendants are found among the records of Princess Anne County, Virginia; and the records there are very intriguing considering that there are a number of connected surnames which are highly reminiscent of those found in conjunction with the Maryland Cartwrights. Shown in the Princess Anne deeds to be examined shortly, there are close connections to a **Burroughs** family, and a **John Edwards** is evident in connnection as well. All along there are such vague indications that there might have been a relationship between the Maryland Cartwrights and those who were descended from John Cartwright of Virginia, with only the breadth of the bay separating them in any case. But there is simply no data which seems to shed light on the question of whether they were actually related or not. With John Cartwright apparently having originated in England, and the Matthew Cartwright of Maryland being shown to have been born in Holland, it is still not difficult to imagine that the latter's origins may have been due to a father or other earlier ancestor who was engaged in a maritime career. Cartwright is certainly an English name, rather than a Dutch one. Further, as stated in Chapter One, the town Middlebourgh of the Province of Zealand where Matthew Cartwright was born was a very active trading center during Medeival times, and no doubt there were many English residents.

With so little to go on concerning those very early generations of Cartwrights, I prefer to concentrate here upon the examination of the later generations, about whom there is much to discuss. There are a number of misconceptions concerning the family of the later **Robert Cartwright** who was a descendant of the Princess Anne County Cartwrights, which confusion appears to have remained unchallenged to this point for the simple lack of any work done on the lines. The problem needs to be addressed, since it may have resulted in various Cartwrights of other areas remaining 'unidentified' as to origins. While some of my own postulations remain theoretical, there is

159

considerable evidence available for the correction of some of the errors in earlier accounts. Thus, notwithstanding the brevity of this first chapter, I will move on to the study of Princess Anne County, Virginia and the sources of data relating to that area.

Bibliography of Sources for Chapter Six

1. 'Passenger and Immigration Lists Index' by P. William Filby with Mary K. Meyer. Gale Research, Book Tower, Detroit, MI. 1981.
2. 'Cartwright and Shipp Families of Lower Norfolk, Princess Anne, & Surry Counties, Va. & North Carolina', Chart, researched & compiled by Alice Granberry Walter. 1968. (Now available through Genealogical Publishing Co., Inc., Baltimore, MD.)
3. 'Virginia Will Records, from the Virginia Magazine of History and Biography, the William and Mary College Quarterly, and Tyler's Quarterly' indexed by Judith McGhan. Genealogical Publishing Co., Inc., Baltimore, MD. 1993.
4. 'The Complete Book of Emigrants 1607-1660' by Peter Wilson Coldham. Ibid. 1988.
5. 'Cavaliers and Pioneers, Volume One' by Nell Marion Nugent. Ibid. 1963-1991.
6. 'Lower Norfolk County, Virginia Court Records, Book A 1637-1646 & Book B 1646-1651/2' by Alice Granberry Walter. Clearfield Co., Inc. (Reprinted for Clearfield by Genealogical Publishing Co., Inc. Baltimore, MD. 1994, 1995.)

Chapter
Seven

Princess Anne County, Virginia and the Robert Cartwright Family of Nashville, Tennessee

I have grouped the data of this chapter in such a way because the Robert Cartwright family of the Nashville, Tennessee area seems to have been the only readily-visible male Cartwright line which originated in Princess Anne County, Virginia and can be traced for some time and distance afterward. As regards this subject, we must go back and forth a bit between the two distant places. In order to investigate and deal with the mentioned errors, we must examine both the Princess Anne County records and the data to be found in Davidson County, Tennessee at the same time.

Robert Cartwright was a noted figure in the early history of the Middle Tennessee area, being one of those who made the very rough and perilous journey by boat from Fort Patrick Henry near the Watauga settlement, to begin the new outpost which was first called 'Nashborough' and later became Nashville, Tennessee. Consequently, as such a prominent pioneer and member of the group of founding fathers of Nashville, he and his children have been one of the few Cartwright families about which there has been any published information at all, to this date. It is for that reason that I wish to begin with him and then do a bit of backtracking to examine the sources of earlier data in Princess Anne County, Virginia, before we move on to the rest of the Cartwrights in the same group. The records in Princess Anne County can help to clear up questions and add to the information concerning Robert Cartwright, his wives, and his children.

There is a valuable set of data concerning the Robert Cartwright family to be found in the works of Jeanette Tillotson Acklen[1], which volumes have already been mentioned in Part I of this work. They contain transcripts of the Robert Cartwright Bible records as well as tombstone data for the some members of the family. Reproduced here is the Bible record in question (sent to the collection by Mrs. E. E. Pearson of Nashville, along with many other bible records, in 1933). Whether it is a direct, verbatim reproduction with all the original punctuation, I cannot say, but it seems to be fairly direct. The source volume contains a heading which refers to the group of bible records in which this one is found as 'Exact Copies', although one or two comments have clearly been inserted by the copier. This could make it difficult to tell precisely what was the writing in the Bible and what may have been added; although the comments in themselves, made at a time that is now quite long ago, are valuable tidbits. I have noted from various lists of source materials an indication that the Bible record should be on file at the Tennessee State Archives, but a closer look at the contents list of one such source proved not to contain the actual record in question, but rather a transcription similar to the one shown here; and I have not pursued it further. Therefore, I cannot say if a microfilm or other copy of the acutal Bible record itself still exists.

'Record in **Robert Cartwright** Bible (in the possession of John Beasley of Goodlettsville, Tennessee at the time of the original publication of the source volume, 1933):
Robt. Cartwright and **Anne**, his wife, married Aug. 15, 1745.
Wm. Cartwright, son of **Robert Cartwright** and **Anne**, his wife, born July 4, 1746.
Robert Cartwright and **Anne**, his wife, daughter of **Robert Hugins** and **Mary**, his wife, married Aug. 15, 1745; as it was God's pleasure to take this loving _____(note says 'marked out') March 17, **Anne Cartwright** died March 17, 1747.
Robert Cartwright and **Mary**, married April 20, 1749.

163

Martha Cartwright, daughter of **Robert Cartwright** and **Mary**, born May 14, 1750.

Mary Cartwright, daughter of **Robert** and **Mary**, born Aug. 11, 1753.

Anne Cartwright, daughter of **Robert** and **Mary**, his wife, was born June 2, 1755.

Susannah, daughter of **Robert Cartwright** and **Mary**, his wife, born Sept. 4, 1757.

Robert Cartwright, son of **Robert** and **Mary Cartwright**, born Dec. 17, 1759; died March 23, 1776.

Aug. 11, 1760, found a pin betwixt the skin and his ribs, which remained to Oct. 20, and then was cut out by **Doctor Wright**, out of my son, **Robert Cartwright's**, side. Written by, father of the child.

John Hunter Cartwright, son of **Robert** and **Mary Cartwright**, born Feb. 26, 1762.

Mary Cartwright, wife of **Robert Cartwright** and daughter of Mr. **John Hunter** and **Jacamine**, his wife, died Jan. 22, 1764.

Thomas Cartwright, son of **Robert** and **Pemmy Cartwright**, born Nov. 20, 1763 or 68 (?).

Pemmy Cartwright, daughter of **Robert** and **Pemmy**, his wife, born Feb. 28, 1765.

Jacob Cartwright, son of **Robert** and **Pemmy**, his wife, born Feb. 21, 1767.

James Cartwright, son of **Robert** and **Pemmy**, his wife, born Feb. 14, 1770.

William Hunter Cartwright, son of **Robert** and **Pemmy**, born Oct. 4, 1772.

Elizabeth Cartwright, daughter of **Robert** and **Pemmy**, born Sept. 2, 1776.'

A note by the copier is added, in parenthesis: '(Here the record ends, although there were more children in this family, viz: **David**, born 1782. **Robert**, born 178_. **Jesse Hunter**, born 1778.)' The existence of these sons is verified by various other records, to be explored later.

As seen, there is the addition of 'or 68' and a question mark in parenthises, after the birthdate of the son Thomas Cartwright. There are reasons for this which are clearly not a matter of legibility. It seems apparent that Thomas, the son of Robert's third wife Pemmy, was

164

born illegitimately to her at least two months before Robert's second wife Mary died. Since this is verified by a reference in Robert's own will, to be explored later, there is little reason to avoid a forthright discussion of the matter here. For the record at this point, I will comment that this reference of 'or 68' would hardly have been contained in the original Bible record, so that it is obviously an insertion by the copier; and yet the date of 1763 must not have been illegible, else the copier would have merely noted same. The birth is recorded before that of the daughter named Pemmy, born 1765, and Jacob, born 1767, and for Thomas's birthdate to have been 1768, it would have required the insertion of the data concerning him in the wrong place in the Bible record. I note this reasoning here merely to clarify the Bible record as it must have genuinely been found without the copier's notations. It may be understandable why a copier of the era in quesiton may have been hesitant to let the date stand as it was clearly found, but any descendant directly concerned with the facts of this Thomas Cartwright's birthdate would find these details very important. Otherwise there arises a confusion not only as to the actual year of Thomas's birth but perhaps as to the actual mother of the man.

The second son named Robert, shown among the additions made by the copier, was of course a different child from the first of that name who is described as having a pin stuck in his side and then removed. The first Robert's death at the age of sixteen is the only indication in the Bible record of any child of the family who died in youth, and this is an important point for consideration as regards the errors in some published material, which create confusion concerning this family. Notably, various DAR records[2] which have long ago been circulated not only contain a number of inconsistencies in names and other data as concerns the various children of Robert Cartwright, but said records name several of the children who died in infancy or died young. Some of those statements are shown definitely to be in error through a close examination of other records. The DAR material clearly has been used as a source for other published material, and so there has been perpetuated an illusion of factuality concerning the data. The accounts in question show certain children of **Robert Cartwright** thus: the eldest son **William**, stated to have died in infancy; the daughter **Martha**, stated to have died in infancy; the daughter **Susannah**, stated to have died in August of 1759; the son **Robert**, died 1776 (which death date of course is verified by the Bible record); **John Hunter**, stated to have been 'killed by Indians', with one such record giving no further details and another giving a year of 1780 for his death; the daughter '**Pembrooke**' (Pemmy), stated to have died young; **William Hunter**, stated to have died young.

As mentioned, there is ample evidence to show that at least two of the children named above did not die in infancy or at any young age, and thus it leaves a necessity to question the other data as well, though much of it may very well be correct. The issue must be cleared up for the sake of helping to trace further Cartwright lines, whether by identifying families descended from the children who did not actually die young, or simply for the purpose of eliminating them as a source with more clarity. One important point to note at this time is the obvious fact that Robert Cartwright was very scrupulous in recording the birth and death data of his family, for he did it with great detail. This of course does not always mean that all relevant data would have been recorded. But since he records the deaths of his first two wives and of the son who died in 1776, and since all the recordings of data in the Bible seem to be in correct chronological order, it does not seem likely that he would have neglected to record the death of any other child who died young. I must add, conversely, that the seeming absence of any later data concerning the children **Susannah**, **Pemmy**, **John Hunter Cartwright** and **William Hunter Cartwright** may be an indication that the references could be correct where they are concerned. All the same, the appearance of an absence of data certainly is not proof of a death in youth, and it was apparently such precipitous presumptions which led to erroneous statements in the first place.

Before moving on to a further discussion of the problem, I will give here the tombstone data concerning Robert Cartwright which is also transcribed in the above-mentioned volumes of Ms. Acklen. The Robert Cartwright burial ground is described as being located about ten miles from Nashville on Dickinson Road, 'overlooking the old road and about a quarter mile from the new highway on Dry Creek':

Robert Cartwright, Feb. 22, 1722-Dec. 24, 1809. (Tombstone bears the following inscription): 'A wit's a feather,
A chief's a rod;

But an honest man
Is the noblest work of God.'
Also there:
David Cartwright, 1782-Jan. 25, 1814.
Elizabeth Powell Cartwright, Oct. 26, 1786-Mar. 8, 1856.

Elizabeth Powell must certainly have been the wife of David, and various records concerning their deaths will also be examined. There are other Bible and tombstone records concerning other members of this Cartwright family, as well. Those records will be shown presently. At this time I would like to continue with the effort to clarify the children of Robert Cartwright who lived to adulthood.

The chronology of events in the life of Robert could be important for the attempt to trace his children's lives, and we must begin with the data in Princess Anne County, Virginia, where Robert himself is first found mentioned. It can be seen from the records below that he did not leave the area until sometime after 1768, and we know from numerous historical accounts that he was in the party of Col. John Donelson which left from the site of Fort Patrick Henry on the Holston River (Tennessee) in December of 1779. How long he was there in the area of that frontier settlement before the latter date could be a pertinent question, but there seems to be little to shed light on that matter. For now, given here are the abstracted records containing any and all mentions of Cartwrights, as found in the Deed Books[3,4] of Princess Anne County, Virginia:

8 August 1693: (Deed Book 1, pg 43.) **Randolph Lovett** to **Robert Cartwright**--whereas father **Lancaster Lovett** bequeathed 800 acres to my brothers **Lancaster, John** and **Thomas**; brother **John** died without issue and so sells his portion for 6000 lbs. pork. Witnesses: **Benoni Burrough, Malachy Thruston**. (This Robert Cartwright was the elder, apparently son of Thomas Cartwright, Jr. His own son William married Mary Keeling, daughter of Thomas Keeling and his wife Elizabeth Lovett; see the demonstration in part of such connections, below.)

25 October 1700/03: (Deed Book 1, pg. 360, clearly a will, rather than a deed. The first date is when the will was written, the second is

the date of probate) **Lancaster Lovett**--sons **Lancaster, Thomas, Adam, William** and **John**; daughters **Sarah** and **Elizabeth** wife of **Thomas Keeling.** Executor, wife **Mary.** Overseers, **Adam Thorowgood,** son-in-law **Thomas Keeling, Thomas Harrison** and son **William.** Witnesses: **Thomas Herison** (sic), **Henry Walstone, Robert Cartwright, John Edwards.**

1 December 1705, 1 May 1706: (Deed Book 1, pg. 467; will) **Mary Lovitt**--sons **Lancaster, Thomas, Adam, John** and **William**; daughter **Elizabeth Keeling** wife of **Thomas,** and their children **Mary** and **Thomas**; **William's** son **William** and daughter **Mary**; granddaughter **Ann Kemp**; daughter **Sarah Richason** wife of **Thomas.** Executor, son **William.** Overseers, **Col. Adam Thorowgood, John Carroway, Jr.,** and **Robert Fountain.** Witnesses: **Robert Cartwright, Katherine Cartwright, M. Boush.**

28 March 1719, 6 May 1719: (Deed Book 3, pg. 228, will) **John Pallett**--son **Mathew,** daughter **Elizabeth.** Executors, two brothers-in-law **William Ellegood** and **John Cockroft.** Witnesses: **Christopher Burrough, Robert Cartwright, Adam Lovett.**

15 October 1719, 6 January 1719: (Deed Book 3, pg. 296, will) **Robert Cartwright**--sons **William, Thomas,** and **John** (land in Nuce River), wife, grandson **William Cotten**: daughters **Sarah Keeling, Ann,** and **Frances.** Executors, sons **William** and **John.** Witnesses: **Benedict Horsington, John Cartwright, John Turner.** (Whether the John Cartwright who signed as a witness was a different one than Robert's son, I cannot say. Recall that Robert had a *brother* named John, about whom little is known.)

23 October 1730, 3 December 1730: (Deed Book 4, pg. 311, will) **Ann Cartwright** (wife of Robert, above)--son **William,** son-in-law **James Cotton,** daughter **Katherine,** daughters **Sarah Keeling, Frances Clayder** (or Clayden) and **Ann Keeling,** son **John's** children, son **Thomas.** Executors, sons **William** and **Thomas.** Witnesses: **William Poole, James Guarill.** (Note the reference to son John's children, proving that he had issue; but there do not seem

168

to be any other records to give information on him or his family. See, however, further abstracts below concerning a Lemuel Cartwright, who may possibly have been one of the said John's children; or else of Thomas, Robert's brother.)

9 August 1734, 4 September 1734: (Deed Book 4, pg. 517, will) **William Ackiss**--brother **John**, sons **Francis** and **Nathaniel**, daughters **Sarah** and **Frances**. Executor, **William Cartwright**. Witnesses: **Francis Ackiss, William Poole**.

2 November 1741, 2 October 1741 (?): (Deed Book 6, pg. 99, will) **John Norris**--sons **John, Charles**, and **George**; daughters **Sarah** and **Ann**; wife **Ann**. Executors, **William Cartwright** and **James Carroway**. Witnesses: **Arthur Sayer, Thomas Cartwright**.

14 September 1747: (Deed Book 6, pg. 687, deed) **William Gaston** and wife **Mary** to **John Turner** for 15 lbs. half of plantation **William Cartwright** father of **Mary** lived on. Witness: **Arthur Sayer**. (This is no indication that William Cartwright was deceased at this time. He did not die until 1753, as per further abstracts below, unless this is referring to a different William Cartwright. As stated in the outline, the wills of William Cartwright and his wife Mary do not mention a daughter named Mary; but there seems to be no other William in this area who could have been the one named as father of Mary in this deed.)

23 March 1747/8: (Deed Book 7, pg. 8, deed) **John Brinson** to **James Carroway** for 52 lbs. 10 shillings 70 acres on the Eastern Shore which his father **Thomas** bought of **John Raney**. Witnesses: **William Cartwright, William Moye, Charles Malbone**.

6 April 1740, 15 May 1750: (Deed Book 7, pg. 168, will) **John Turner**--**Lemuel Cartwright, Thomas Turner, William Salmons, Lewis Price, Job Gasking, John** son of **Tully Williamson, Francis** (?--added by transcriber; perhaps the name was illegible) son of **Tully Williamson, Mary** daughter of **Tully Williamson**, her brother **Henry, Sarah Cartwright** daughter of **Mary Barrot, Anthony**

169

Williamson, child **Elizabeth Price** goes with, **Mary Barrot**. Executors, _____ **Gasking, Jr., Lemuel Cartwright**. Witnesses: **James Carraway, Mary Cartwright**.

17 March 1752: (Deed Book 7, pg. 307, deed) **William Keeling, Jr.** and wife **Mary** and **Cornelius Calvert** and wife **Elizabeth** to **Lemuel Cartwright** for 5 shillings 50 acres--same land **John Thorowgood** father of **Mary** and **Elizabeth** died seized of. Witnesses: **Adam Keeling, Jr., James Carraway, Robert Cartwright, William Carroway**.

19 December 1752: (Deed Book 7, pg. 393, deed) **George Wishart** to **Moses Fentriss** son of **John Fentriss, Sr.** dec. for 5 shillings 50 acres. Witnesses: **Thomas Walke, Lemuel Cartwright, Benjamin Moseley**.

28 February 1753, 17 April 1753: (Deed Book 7, pg. 439, will) **John Hunter, Sr.**---wife **Jacomine**; sons **Jacob, John, Thomas** and **James**; daughters **Margaret Harper, Mary Cartwright, Jacomine, Pemmy**, and **Joyce**. Executrix: wife. Witnesses: **Dinah Williamson, Amy Barrot, Arthur Sayer**. (Here is the family of the second and third wives of Robert Cartwright who later pioneered his way to Middle Tennessee. This record shows that the third wife, Pemmy, was the sister of the second wife, Mary.)

8 April 1753, 17 April 1753: (Deed Book 7, pg. 455, will) **John Dudley**--son **Richard**, brother **Daniel**, father-in-law **William Cartwright**, wife **Margret**. Executor, father-in-law. Witnesses: **John Flinch, Daniel Dudley, Robert Burrough**.

20 May 1753, 19 June 1753: (Deed Book 7, pg. 474, will) **William Cartwright**--wife **Mary**; **Robert**; grandson **William**; daughters **Elizabeth Harper, Margaret Dudley, Martha Carraway, Frances, Anne, Sarah,** and **Amy**. Executors, wife and son **Robert**. Witnesses: **James Carraway, Lewis Price, William Holmes**. (Note that William's will names his *grandson William Cartwright*. The child

William, son of Robert, is certainly not dead here. Neither is he precisely an infant. He would have been seven years old at this time.)

15 January 1754: (Deed Book 7, pg. 555, appraisal) Appraisal of the estate of **William Cartwright** by **Francis T. Land, John Biddle, Adam Lovett.**

21 August 1753, 16 April 1754: (Deed Book 7, pg. 587, will) **Robert Huggins**--sons **Robert, Natt,** and **Markham**; daughters **Olive, Argent,** and **Mary,** grandson **William Cartwright,** wife **Mary.** Executrix, wife. Witnesses: **John Shipp, Thomas Grainger, Dinah Grainger.** (This is the family of Anne Huggins who was the first wife of Robert Cartwright of Nashville, TN., and who was at the time of this will already deceased. Here again, Robert Huggins who is the other grandfather of Robert Cartwright's son William, names *grandson William Cartwright.*)

17 December 1754: (Deed Book 7, pg. 664, audit) Audit of the estate of **William Cartwright** by **Charles Gaskings, John Biddle, Andrew Stewart.**

19 August 1755: (Deed Book 8, pg. 19, Inventory) Inventory and appraisal of **Robert Huggins** by **Francis Thorowgood Land, Alexander Poole, Robert Cartwright.**

19 January 1756: (Deed Book 8, pg. 37, deed) **Edward Hack Moseley** to **Robert Cartwright** for 5 shillings 220 acres called the Ashen Swamp which **Robert Harper** sold to **Joshua Nicholson.** Witnesses: **Christopher Wright, Tully Moseley, William Godfrey.**

20 February 1756: (Deed Book 8, pg. 59, deed) **Adam Keeling, Sr.** deed of gift to son **Adam** of 400 acres. Witnesses: **Thorowgood Keeling, Edward Cannon, Robert Cartwright, William Godfrey.**

23 February 1756: (Deed Book 8, pg. 77, Inventory) Inventory and appraisement of **Henry Burgess** by **Francis Thorowgood Land, Robert Huggins,** (Jr., apparently). **Robert Cartwright.**

20 June 1757: (Deed Book 8, pg. 191, deed) **Henry** and **Anne Gasking** to **Henry Lamount** for 100 lbs. 150 acres at Rodee Creek--same land **Adam Hayes** gave in his will to **Gasking**. Witnesses: **Gershom Nimmo, Charles Gasking, Robert Cartwright**.

18 September 1759: (Deed Book 8, pg. 402, appraisal) Appraisal of the estate of **Adam Lovett** by **Francis T. Land, Robert Cartwright, John Biddle**.

17 February 1761: (Deed Book 8, pg. 557, deed) **Mary Lovett** deed of gift to children **Sarah** and **Frances**. Witnesses: **Robert Cartwright, John Norris, Charles Gasking**.

17 March 1761: (Deed Book 8, pg. 573, audit) Audit of the estate of **Adam Lovett** by **John Biddle, William Moseley, Robert Cartwright**.

16 March 1762: (Deed Book 9, pg. 50, will) **Mary Cartwright**--daughter **Sarah**, grandson **William Cartwright**, daughters **Frances Holmes, Martha Nimmo, Margarett Dunn** and **Ann Carraway**, grandsons **Robert** and **John Harper**, son **Robert**. Executor, son. Witnesses: **Charles Gasking, George Wishart, John Williams**. (Here the grandmother of William Cartwright, son of Robert, also names him in her will. The boy William is now sixteen years old, at this date.)

15 March 1763: (Deed Book 9, pg. 151, deed) **Reuben Lovett** to **Lemuel Cornick, Sr.** for 50 lbs. 133 acres--part of a patent granted to **John Cornick** father of **Lemuel**. Witnesses: **William Nimmo, Jr., Peter Singleton, Robert Cartwright**.

18 October 1763: (Deed Book 9, pg. 259, audit) Audit of the estate of **Mary Cartwright** by **John Biddle, William Haynes, William Moseley**.

7 August 1766: (Deed Book 9, pg. 599, deed) **Robert Cartwright** and wife **Pemmy** to Capt. **James Kempe** for 5 shillings 179 acres left him by his father **William**. Witnesses: **John Ackiss, Andrew Stewart, Tully Moseley**.

24 April 1766: (Deed Book 9, pg. 613, will) **Peter Harbut**---sons **Willoughby** and **William**, daughters **Betty** and **Mary**, wife. Executors, wife and **William Wiggins**. Witnesses: **Qualla Suggs, Betty Cartwright, James Tooley**. (Whether the daughter Betty is the same as the Betty Cartwright who signed as a witnesses is uncertain. I have not been able to determine the identitiy of this Betty Cartwright. She was probably the wife of one of the chidren of John Cartwright, mentioned earlier and not named; or else was of the family of Thomas Cartwright, son of the elder Robert, who is seen only briefly as signing on a deed.)

8 April 1768: (Deed Book 10, pg. 247, deed) **Robert Cartwright** to son **William Cartwright** for 5 lbs. 100 acres heired from his father **William**. Witnesses: **W. R. Curle, John Hancock, Daniel Richardson, Walter Lyon**.

As seen, we have in the above set of abstracts some irrefutable evidence to correct one of the mentioned errors in the accounts of the Robert Cartwright family of Middle Tennessee. William, the eldest son of Robert, is named in the wills of both his grandfathers, William Cartwright and Robert Huggins, in the year 1753 when he would have been age seven; and in the will of his grandmother in the year 1762, when he would have been age sixteen. And then there is the last quoted deed abstract in which we see that Robert Cartwright transferred land inherited from his own father William to his *son* William. At the time of the latter transaction, Robert's son William would have been nearly twenty-two years old. This certainly erases altogether the notion that he died as an infant. Although it is still not full proof that he lived to an even older age, there is indeed further evidence to clinch the matter, at a much later date. To that end, even though there are a few further bits of data to discuss as relates to Virginia, I move directly to an examination of other abstracted records concerning the death of Robert Cartwright, at a date of 1809/10, in Tennessee.

Will records of Davidson County, Tennessee[5]:

Will of **Robert Cartwright**, deceased. (proved) Feb. 19, 1810. To my beloved son **Thomas Cartwright** alias **Hunter** 270 acres of land it being the plantation and tract of land whereon I now live. To my beloved son **Jacob Cartwright** 200 acres of land it being the plantation and tract of land whereon he now lives. To my son **James Cartwright** $500.00 it being in obligation on sundry persons in Natchez whenever collected to him. To my beloved daughter **Elizabeth Rutherford** 200 acres of land whereon she now lives by Deed of Gift formerly made to her. To my beloved son **Robert Cartwright** 300 acres of land be (sic) the plantation and tract of land whereon he now lives near the Black Fox Camp on the east end in Rutherford County, TN. To my beloved son **David Cartwright** all that part of two tracts of land that I purchased of **Nathaniel Overall** and **Thomas Hobby** (Hobdy?) that lies south of the Public Creek Road that he now lives on supposed to be 215 acres. To my beloved wife **Prim**(illegible, notes the transcriber. The name, of course, is Pemmy or Pembroke) Cartwright the plantation and tract of land whereon I now live with the use of seven negroes also household furniture etc. To my beloved son **Jesse Cartwright** the balance of the money due me on obligations on sundry people in natchez after deducting the $500.00 for my son **James**, also $600.00 at the death of my wife. At death of my wife, my plantation be sold and divided among my sons, **Thomas, Jacob, James, Robert, David,** and **Jesse** and my daughter **Elizabeth Rutherford**. Also at death of my wife, negroes are to be sold and divided equally among my children **William, Martha, Mary** and **Anne** each $1.00 (sic; there must be a lack of proper punctuation here.) Also **Aquilla Carmack** $1.00. I appoint my sons **Thomas, Jacob** and **David** executors. This 24 October 1809. Witnesses: **Thomas Fawlkes, William Trotter,** and **Shadrack Nye.**

174

Here we see *two* of the children who supposedly died in infancy named in their father's will in 1809---William and Martha. There is no question, of course, that they must have been alive at the time of the writing of the will; and the grouping is clearly of the older children, well-distinguished from the younger ones who were children of Pemmy. The older children were left only $1.00 each, probably because they *were* so much older and already well-established in life. (It is unclear whether the slaves to be sold and divided involved them or the other group of children; but it seems to be the latter, since a further record involving the estate indicates that the younger group were the only 'joint legatees'.) It seems evident, therefore, that the William named is the *eldest* son of Robert and not the younger son named William Hunter Cartwright who was born to Pemmy. (Who was also shown in the erroneous accounts as having died young, in any case.) At the date of the will, the eldest son William would have been in his sixties, and the daughters who are mentioned would have been in their fifties, so certainly the son William must have had a family of his own, and Martha most likely had married and produced children, as well. *Where* they were living at the time is another question, and there is a distinct possibility for William, as will be explored later. The DAR records appear to be the only readily-available source of information for the marriages of the elder daughters, indicating that Mary married James H. Wallace and that Anne married Thomas Nelson. Since Martha was supposedly deceased as an infant, there is of course no mention of a marriage for her in the DAR records. It is entirely possible that some of these older children married in Virginia and may never have left that area.

It seems apparent from the lack of mention in Robert's will of the children William Hunter Cartwright, John Hunter Cartwright, the daughter Pemmy, and the daughter Susannah, that they must have indeed died young as indicated by some of the otherwise erroneous data concerning the family. Neither does the will of Pembroke Cartwright (shown hereafter) mention the children William Hunter, John Hunter, and Pemmy, while she notes the others who were her own children in great detail. Also important to note from the will of Robert Cartwright is the reference to the son Thomas Cartwright as *'alias Hunter'*, which was a common type of reference to a child who was born illegitimately. The will gives proof, as well, of the sons

175

David, Robert, and Jesse who were noted as additions by the copier of the Bible record.

Before continuing with other abstracted records from the Davidson County, Tennessee will series, I must present here some excerpts from a source of historical memoirs which bears mentioning because the accounts refer directly at times to the Robert Cartwright family.[6] This source is a book containing the personal memoirs of a man named **John Carr**, who was personally present during the pioneer days of the Cumberland Settlement and was acquainted with many of the parties involved. Though he did not travel to the site of the settlements with the first groups led by Donelson and Robertson, he arrived soon thereafter and joined in building many of the forts and settlement sites. He was a witness to some of the attacks by natives, and had personal knowledge of many others. The book was first published in 1857, which as an important point since the author refers in his writings to persons then still living. The references in the copy to which I had access state that the memoirs first appeared as sketches in the 'Christian Advocate' and the 'Southwestern Monthly', papers published at Nashville, at some time before they were actually collected and published in book form 'for the author' by **E. Stevenson** and **F. A. Owen**, in Nashville. No date was given for those early publications, however; thus, we don't know precisely when the sketches were written, but only that it was probably no more than a few years prior to 1857 when the book itself was published, since the author was still alive at that latter date. While there is much value in the entire collection of Carr's memoirs, only those points relevant to the Robert Cartwright family will be touched upon here. An important bit is gleaned when the author refers to the fact that **James Cartwright**, son of **Robert**, was still living at the time of his writing, in the town of Gallatin (Sumner County). James Cartwright had offered to the author some of his own recollections of the dangerous journey from Fort Patrick Henry on the Holston River to the equally dangerous territory that is now Nashville. He stated that when the fleet of boats headed by **Col. John Donelson** finally met up with those which had headed down from a different starting point on the Clinch River, the boats were about forty altogether, and that nearly every one had at least two families on board. His own father's boat, he stated, carried three families; but the said families were not named. The author later relates, during the description of one attack by the natives, that the Jennings family had tied their own boat to the back of the Cartwright vessel.

The author of the work in question also relates that in the fall of 1780, 'Col. Donelson, Hugh Rogan, William Cartwright, and others' took two small boats and went 'up to Clover Bottom' (a settlement that had been made in the spring and then had been abandoned when it came under attack) in an attempt to bring down their crop of corn. One of the boats started out before the other and had gone only a little way when it was attacked, with several of those on board being killed. Among those killed was **William Cartwright**.

It is difficult to determine precisely the identity of this William Cartwright who was among the settlers and who was killed in 1780. We have seen from the will of Robert that his eldest son William was still living in 1809, so it could not have been he who was killed. The younger son named **William Hunter Cartwright** would have been only eight years old at the time of the Indian attack described, and the wording of the account certainly does not seem to be indicating that the person named William Cartwright who was killed was a child. On the other hand, the son **John Hunter Cartwright** would have been eighteen years old in 1780, clearly old enough to have been going with the men to bring down the corn. Since one of the DAR accounts claimed that he was killed by Indians in 1780, it seems possible that the author of the above memoirs simply has mixed up the given name of the pertinent Cartwright. Still, in nearly every instance where Mr. Carr describes attacks, (which were numerous and occured at many different dates over the first few years of settlement), he gives a list of names of those killed and then adds, 'as well as many others', or 'several others'. He also mentions several occasions on which children were killed. It is entirely possible, therefore, that all those persons in question here were killed by the Indians---William Hunter Cartwright, John Hunter Cartwright, and another, unknown William Cartwright. If it is not a case of mistaking the given name, then we simply do not know who the unfortumate William Cartwright was in relation to the others. Certainly as stated, however, various records indicate well enough that it could not have been Robert Cartwright's eldest son William.

Since it is pointless to speculate further on that issue, I will continue with giving the relevant references from the Davidson County area, before returning to the Virginia records.

The following abstracts are from the same source of Davidson County records as the will of Robert Cartwright, given earlier[5]:

Dated 20 February 1810 is an inventory of the 'chattels', etc. of **Robert Cartwright**, deceased. Returned Jan. term 1810. Abstract says several items listed, not detailed. Signed by **David Cartwright**, **Thomas Cartwright**, and **Jacob Cartwright**.

Dated 21 February 1810 is an Agreement involving the estate. **Thomas, Jacob, James, Robert, David,** and **Jesse Cartwright** and **Elizabeth Rutherford**, heirs of **Robert Cartwright**, deceased. Their agreement entered into 2 January 1810 between the above named heirs, the only joint legatees, to the personal estate of **Robert Cartwright**, deceased, to make an equal division of all the cotton, flax, hemp, flax seed, all the salt, wheat and all the fat hogs fit for pork among the before named persons.

Will of **David Cartwright**, deceased, of Davidson County. (proved) Feb. 15, 1814. To my beloved wife **Elizabeth** shall keep (sic) and hold together the whole of my estate both real and personal until my youngest child shall arrive to 21 years of age for raising and educating my children, also land whereon I now live lying on the south side of Dry Creek during her natural life. To my son **Albert** the balance of the tract to take possession of when he arrives at age of 21 years. Rest of my estate to be divided among the rest of my children. My will is that if the part of my father's estate now in the possession of my mother should descend to my heirs before the youngest child becomes 21 years of age, then it should be sold and divided among my heirs. I appoint **Col. William Donelson, George Wharton**, Esquire and my beloved wife **Elizabeth**, executors. This 19 January 1814. Witness: **Robert Cartwright**.

Will of **Pembroke Cartwright**, deceased, of Davidson County. (proved) 16 June 1826. To my son **Jacob Cartwright** my apple mill

with two large troughs. To my son **James Cartwright** a negro boy and other property he has received. To my son **Jesse Cartwright** a negro girl and property he has already received of me also $100.00. To the heirs of my son **David Cartwright**, to wit, **Jaconia** (probably should be Jacomine) **Cartwright, Elbert Cartwright, Pembroke Cartwright, Emily Cartwright, Eliza Cartwright**, and **Sally Cartwright**, the sum of $600.00 to be equally divided between them when they become of age or marries (sic). To my grand daughter **Pembroke Rutherford** one by mare. All the property that I may die possessed with except what is already bequeathed etc. to be divided equally between **Thomas Cartwright, Jacob Cartwright, James Cartwright, Betsy Rutherford, Robert Cartwright, Jesse Cartwright** and the heirs of **David Cartwright**. I appoint **Samuel L. Wharton** and **William Donelson**, my executors. This 13 August 1818. Witnesses: **Enoch Cunningham** and **John Cole**.
Codicil: made 16 November 1818. I give unto my son **Thomas Cartwright** the sum of $294.00 to be paid out of the proceeds of sale of my fattening hogs. To my grand daughter **Polly Cartwright**, daughter of my son **James**, a bed and furniture etc. To my grand daughter **Pembroke Rutherford** a bed and furniture etc. To my grand daughter **Betsy Kittrell** one cow and calf, set of knives and forks and other items. To my grand daughter **Nancy Butterworth** one sow and pigs. To my grand son **John Hunter Cartwright** one gray colt. To my grand daughter **Pembroke Cartwright** daughter of **Robert Cartwright**, a bay horse. Witnesses: **George Wharton** and **Samuel L. Wharton**. Apr. Term 1826.

Dated June 22, 1826 is an Inventory of the estate of **Pembroke Cartwright**, deceased. Taken by **Samuel L. Wharton**, executor, on 8 February 1826. Several items listed, notes on **James Cunningham**, on **Reuben Payne**, on **John Cunningham**, on **James Cunningham** (a second note?) and one on **George W**(illegible). Apr. Term 1826.

Dated 14 September 1826 is aa Sale of Estate of **Pembroke Cartwright**, deceased. Made by **Samuel L. Wharton**, executor. (Abstract shows only the names of persons listed.) **James Hit, David McGuire, Solomon McGuire, Douglas Puckett, Isham**

179

Butterworth, John Porter, Martin Pierce, Thomas Cartwright, Elizabeth Cartwright, James Cartwright, Mrs. Martin, William Porter, Isaac Newland, B. Thomas, Thomas Davis, William Boothe, John Wray, James Faulkner, Lewis Basye, Isaac McCaslin, Benjamin Bell, Robert Bates, William Williams, A. Cartwright, William Shaw, William Payne, L. Baker, A. Grizzard, Jas. Hunt, Isaac Walton, George Watkins, William Watkins, James Newland, John Beazley, John Cunningham, Henry Davis, John Orr, A. Cunningham, R. J. Williams, Jas. Cunningham. This 22 July 1826. July Term 1826.

Dated 15 September 1826 is a sale of estate of **Robert Cartwright**, deceased. (evidently this is the estate of Robert Cartwright the elder, the renewed sale coming as a result of Pembroke's death.) Taken on 9 March 1826. Persons listed: **James Cartwright, Jas. Cunningham, Jno. Cunnignham, John Wray, David Roulston, J. Newland, Thomas Cartwright, Elilzabeth Cartwright, Enoch Cunningham, Enoch P. Connell, John Adams, Ambrose Grizzard, John Pierce, David Ralston,** and **William Shaw. Thomas Cartwright**, executor. July Term 1826.

Dated 9 June 1828 is an Inventory of estate of **David Cartwright**, deceased. (It may be that this is when his widow Elizabeth died, or else it may be related to the estate of the elder Robert.) Made by **Reuben Payne**, admr. Note due on **Samuel S. (L.?)Wharton**, a bond on **Elizabeth Cartwright** widow of **David Cartwright**, deceased, dated 9 Dec. 1819, payable when the youngest child becomes of age. Also from **Thomas** and **Jacob Cartwright**, executors of the estate of **Robert Cartwright**, deceased, principal. Also interest paid to **William Glasgow** and his wife **Jemima** (Jacomine?) legatee of **Elizabeth Cartwright**. $151.00 paid **Ans. Brown** and **Emily Brown**, legatee $151.00, paid **Thomas** (illegible) and his wife $100.00 to Mrs. **Elizabeth Cartwright** $30.00 ___Dec. 1826, and to **Thomas** and **Jacob Cartwright** for her note $56. 62. Apr Term 1826. (It is difficult to tell which of these amounts of money went to whom.)

Dated 14 June 1828 is a Settlement of the estate of **Pembroke Cartwright**, deceased. Made with **Samuel L. Wharton**, executor. Persons listed: **A. Mathis, J. Newland, T. Cartwright, William P. Byrn, A. Cartwright, A. Brown, William Glasgow**, and **J. Beazley** and **N. Ewing. William Lytle**, Esquire and **Jno. H. Smith**, Commissioners. Apr Term 1828.

Will of **Jacob Cartwright**, deceased. (proved) 10 November 1828. To loan to my bleoved wife **Patience Cartwright** during her widowhood all the use and benefits of my farm whereon I now live except about 15 acres of the cleared land on the west side of the farm for **John Cartwright** which I want him to have possession of when he comes of age. Also to my wife seven negroes, all the rents and profits of my lands on Whites Creek and in Sumner County for the purpose of raising and educating my three youngest children and in case of her death or marriage, my executors to take possession of the same for the purpose above. To my wife forever all my household and kitchen furniture not hereafter given away and also other items. To my daughter **Harriet Mathis** a yellow negro girl **Kitty** and a sorrel mare and colt and what I have heretofore given her. To my daughter **Tabitha Cartwright** a negro girl **Harriet**, one sorrel horse, bridle and saddle, a cow and calf, two beds and furniture and one bedstead etc. To my daughter **Lizetta Hobdy** the interest of $200.00 now which sum of $200.00 as well as what she may heretofore get from my estate, my will is that the principal be put into the hands of **Enoch P. Connel** as Trustee for her and at her death to be equally divided between her heirs. To my two sons, **John** and **Marcus D. Lafayette Cartwright** the plantation whereon I now live to be equally divided between them when the youngest comes of age reserving for my wife the use of the house and as much cleared land as will support her during her lifteime of widowhood. My son **John** shall have a gray horse now and at his arrival of age to have the use of part of my farm. To my two sons, **Robert** and **Alexander Cartwright** all my lands on Whites Creek aslo 69 acres in Sumner County to be equally divided between them when the youngest comes of age. Residue of my estate to be sold and equally divided among the seven I appoint **Enoch P. Connell** and **William P. Byrn** my executors. This 22 September

1828. Witnesses: **William P. Connell** and **Martin Pierce**. Jan. Term 1828.

Also found in the records of Davidson County, Tennessee for the same time frame is the will of a **Robert Cartwright** who is not the same as the son of Robert of the current study; and records relating to the death of a **Vinson** or **Vincent Cartwright**. These Cartwrights will be dealt with in a later chapter. They were of Pasquotank descent and although found in these same areas as the Robert Cartwright family under discussion, they were apparently not closely related.

To examine further the children of Robert Cartwright of Nashville, we should first return to the Bible and tombstone records mentioned earlier, as found in the works of Jeanette Tillotson Acklen. Aside from those already given, there is a Bible record for **Jacob Cartwright** who married **Patience Hobdy**; also another record for one of his sons, **Alexander Cotton Cartwright**. Although the first is called the Bible record of Jacob Cartwright, it seems more properly to have been the Bible record of his daughter **Harriett Cartwright**, who married **Allen Mathes**; for by far the larger number of births and marriages contained in it are for the latter couple and further generations of their own family. Consequently, here I intend to reproduce only the data from the record which concerns Jacob, his wife, and their children. For anyone descended from this family, I would certainly reccomend consulting the volumes in question[1]. The Bible record below is noted in the source volume as being in the possession of **Charles Smiley**, Goodlettesville, Tennessee (in 1933).

Jacob Cartwright, born Feb. 22, 1767; died Oct. 12, 1828.
Patience Cartwright, his wife, born Nov. E, 1785; died July 25, 1837; married Nov. 23, 1803.
Their children: **Lorzettie Cartwright**, born Aug. 20, 1804.
        Harriett Cartwright, born Dec. 15, 1807; died Nov. 7, 1874.
        Tabitha Cartwright, born April 5, 1809.
        John H. Cartwright, born Jan. 1, 1812.
        Johnson Cartwright, born July 21, 1816.
        Robert Hobdy Cartwright, born July 21, 1816.
        Alexander Cotton Cartwright, born July 16, 1825.

Allen Mathes, born Oct. 19, 1779; died Mar. 29, 1848, aged 70 years.

Allen Mathes and **Harriett Cartwright** were joined in holy matrimony May 1, 1825.

The Bible record of **Alexander Cotton Cartwright** likewise contains much information about later generations, but there is a considerable amount of data concerning early births and marriages of those associated with the family, which I will reproduce here. The birthdate given for Alexander Cotton Cartwright is different in this record from the one above. Aside from recording the birth dates for Jacob and Patience Cartwright, this record gives the added data of Patience's maiden name and her birth date:

A. C. Cartwright and **Mary M. Stark**, married Jan. 7, 1844.

A. C. Cartwright born July 16, 1823.

Mary M. Stark, born Dec. 25, 1821.

Jacob Cartwright, born Feb. 22, 1767; died Oct. 12, 1828.

Patience Hobdy Cartwright, born Nov. 3, 1785; died July 25, 1837.

John Stark, born May 8, 1788.

Margaret Primm, born Oct. 1, 1787.

John and **Margaret Stark**, married Sept. 6, 1812.

John Stark and **Sarah English**, married in Virginia, Jan. 4, 1769.

Jacob Andrew Cartwright, born Nov. 27, 1844.

Talitha Cotton and **Robt. Hobdy**, married near Halifax, N. C.; came to Sumner County, Tenn. in 1791, in wagons. **Robt. Hobdy** died about 1800, and **Talitha Hobdy** married **Dempsey Powell**.

(After this the record contains a large number of births, marriages, and deaths of later generations.)

The only further data found in the volumes of Ms. Acklen which seems definitely relevant to the Robert Cartwright family is shown below. There are a number of other Cartwright tombstone inscriptions, for persons whom I have not distinctly identified as belonging to the Robert Cartwright family. Although some of them probably *do* belong in that group, they will be touched upon in a later chapter under miscellaneous data.

(In the Spring Hill Cemetery at Gallatin Pike, Nashville, Tennessee)
Jacamine J. Cartwright, wife of **Wm. Glasgow**, Oct. 27, 1803-Oct. 16, 1872. Her daughter **Elizabeth E.**, Oct., 1831.

Marriage data concerning members of the family of Robert Cartwright can be found in various sources[7,8,9] Because it is so difficult in some cases to distinguish them from the Cartwrights of other origins who moved in the same areas, I have listed below most of those which seem relevant without attempting a definitive identification in every instance. Some who have similar names but are clearly not the persons already discussed in the various records preceding may have been children of Robert's sons **James Cartwright** and/or **Thomas Cartwright**, whose families are largely unknown. It is also possible, of course, that some of those noted in the marriages below belong to the Wilson County group, even though the marriages occured in Davidson or Sumner.

Elizabeth Cartwright to **James Rutherford**, 7 January, 1791, Davidson Co., TN.

Thomas Cartwright to **Agnes Christian**, 22 January 1791, Sumner Co., TN. Bondsman Thomas Masten.

James Cartwright to **Mary Kitterlin** (?) 21 August 1798, Davidson Co., TN. (The name of the woman whom James Cartwright married has been shown in so many different ways, in varying sources, that it is difficult to determine precisely who she was. Somehow I suspect the name should be simply Mary Kittrell. One of the DAR records alluded to earlier shows a first marriage for James Cartwright, to a Frances Thompson; and then shows the second wife as 'Mrs. Kittrell'. As demonstrated, it is difficult to know how much of the data in those records is accurate. One of them indicates that James married 'Mrs. Kittness Frank Thompson', which is clearly just a mangled collage of the various bits of confusing marriage data.)

Jesse Cartwright to **Patsy P. Rawlings**, 24 December 1806, Sumner Co., TN. Signed by **James Rutherford**. (Some transcribed sources of this record show the groom as 'Alexander' Cartwright, which is a mistake.)

Nancy Cartwright to Byrd Miles, 11 February 1807, Davidson Co., TN.

Robert Cartwright to Elizabeth Vinson, 2 December 1810, Sumner Co., TN. (Since some sources show the wife of Robert and Pemmy's son Robert as Elizabeth Lawson, this may be the marriage record for that couple, with the bride's surname uncertain or mixed up.)

Sarah Cartwright to John Beasley, 12 August 1811, Davidson Co., TN.

John Cartwright to Susannah Ragan, 22 September 1813, Davidson Co., TN.

David Cartwright to Elizabeth Cooper, 13 May 1817, Davidson Co., TN. (This David may belong to the family of the 'second Robert Cartwright mentioned.)

Nancy Cartwright to Wm. Butterworth, 24 August 1818, Davidson Co., TN. (This Nancy was mentioned as a grandaughter in Pembroke's will, but with no indication of which Cartwright was her father.)

Thermy Cartwright to Edward Daniel, 12 December 1818, Davidson Co., TN.

Thomas M. Cartwright to Mary Booth, 12 September 1820, Davidson Co., TN.

Wm. Cartwright to Jeney Bell, 7 April 1821, Davidson Co., TN.

Elesette Cartwright to Joses Hobday, (sic) 12 March 1822, Davidson Co., TN. (This is clearly the 'Lizette Hobdy' and 'Lorzettie' Cartwright referred to in the will and Bible records of the Jacob Cartwright family.)

Thomas Cartwright to Polly Orton, 14 October 1823, Davidson Co., TN.

Polly Cartwright to John Stanford, 8 December 1824, Sumner Co., TN.

Mary A. Cartwright to Jno. Adams, 20 January 1825, Davidson Co., TN.

Jeremiah J. (should be Jacomine) Cartwright to Wm. Glasgow, 23 February 1826, Davidson Co., TN. (Clearly this is the 'Jaconia' or Jacomine, daughter of David, mentioned in various records given previously.)

Emily Cartwright to Aris Brown, 1 March 1827, Davidson Co., TN.

(Another of David's daughters, as mentioned in Pembroke's will.)

Pembroke Cartwright to **Thomas Watkins**, 28 January 1828, Davidson Co., TN. (Since both David and Robert had daughters named Pembroke, it is uncertain which of those the bride in this record may have been.)

Eveline E. Cartwright to **Chas. H. Noaks**, 24 March 1828, Davidson Co., TN.

Elizabeth Cartwright to **Levi Warner**, 11 May, 1829, Sumner Co., TN.

Talitha Cartwright to **Allen M. Perry**, 28 May 1830, Davidson Co., TN.

Talitha Cartwright to **Andrew Milom**, 24 June 1830, Davidson Co., TN.

Eliza Cartwright to **Robert P. Estes**, 16 June 1831, Davidson Co., TN. (Evidently this is the grandaughter Eliza, daughter of David Carwright, who was mentioned in Pembroke Cartwright's will.)

Jno. H. Cartwright to **Kitty Connell**, 17 March 1832, Davidson Co., TN. (This may have been the grandson named John Hunter Cartwright who was mentioned in the will of Pembroke Cartwright, evidently the son of Jacob as shown in the latter's Bible record.)

David Cartwright to **Sarah Pitt**, 17 September 1832, Sumner Co., TN. Bondsman Richard G. Thompson.

John Cartwright to **Laney Compton**, 16 January 1833, Davidson Co., TN.

Evelina Cartwright to **Theodrich Hall**, 10 February 1835, Davidson Co., TN.

Albert R. Cartwright to **Priscilla B. Gideon**, 5 May 1835, Williamson Co. TN. (Included because this appears to have been the son of David Cartwright, who was son of Robert and Pemmy, even though the marriage is recorded in Williamson County, where different sets of Cartwrights are also found.)

Thomas Cartwright to **Elizabeth Hooper**, 18 January 1838, Davidson Co., TN.

Bibliography of Sources for Chapter Seven

1. 'Bible Records and Marriage Bonds', and 'Tombstone Inscriptions
   and Manuscripts' by Jeanette Tillotson Acklen. Originally
   published Nashville, Tennessee 1933; reprinted by
   Genealogical Publishing Co., Inc., Baltimore, MD. 1967, 1974,
   and 1980.
2. 'DAR Roster of Members and Soldiers', Vols. II and III.
   The National Society of the Daughters of the
   American Revolution, Washington, D. C.
3. 'Princess Anne County, Virginia Land and Probate Records
   Abstracted from Deed Books One to Seven 1691-1755', by
   Anne E. Maling. Herigtage Books, Inc., Bowie, MD. 1992.
4. 'Princess Anne County, Virginia Land and Probate Records
   Abstracted from Deed Books Eight to Eighteen 1755-1783' by
   Anne E. Maling. Ibid. 1993.
5. 'Davidson County, Tennessee Wills & Inventories' (Vols. One and
   Two) compiled by Helen C. & Timothy R. Marsh. Southern
   Historical Press, Inc. P. O. Box 1267, Greeneville,
   South Carolina 29601. 1990.
6. 'Early Times in Middle Tennessee' by John Carr. The Parthenon
   Press, Nashville, TN. (No date.) First published 1857, by E.
   Stevenson and F. A. Owen, Nashville, TN. Reprinted in 1958
   by Robert H. Horsley and Associates, 24th Floor, Life and
   Casualty Tower, Nashville, TN. (Apparently there are few
   copies of this book in print, although my references may be out
   of date and it may have been reprinted more recently. My
   references were obtained from a copy held by the Johnson
   City Public Library, Johnson City, Tennessee.)
7. 'Early Middle Tennessee Marriages' compiled by Byron and
   Barbara Sistler. Byron Sistler & Associates, Nashville, TN.
8. '35,000 Tennessee Marriage Records and Bonds' by the Rev. Silas
   Lucas Emmett, Jr. and Mrs. Ella May Sheffield. Southern
   Historical Press, Inc., Greeneville, S. C.
9. 'Tennessee Genealogical Records' by Edythe Rucker Whitley.
   Genealogical Publishing Co., Inc., Baltimore, MD.

Chapter
Eight

Pasquotank and Camden Counties
North Carolina

The data concerning the numerous Cartwrights of Pasquotank County, North Carolina begins with **Thomas Cartwright**, the grandson of the progenitor **John Cartwright** as seen in Chapter Six. Aside from the brief references in Lower Norfolk County, Virginia as noted by Ms. Granberry Walter in her chart, the first mention that I have found of Thomas Cartwright in connection with Pasquotank is a land patent to him in the time period 1693-1696. He patented 640 acres of land at Spelman's Landing.[1]

Abstracts of the wills of Thomas Cartwright (Sr., at this point) and various other members of his family are given in Grimes' 'Abstract of North Carolina Wills'.[2] These abstracts are shown below, with several others of import. The first date given is the date the will was written, the second date is when it was proved.

March 4, 1706, April 15, 1707: **Thomas Cartwright**, Pasquotank Precinct. Names sons **Thomas, Robert, Job, John, William**. Daughters **Catren, Mary, Elisabeth**. Wife and executrix, **Grace Cartwright**. Executor: **John Cartwright**, son. Witnesses: **Thomas Twiddy, George Harris, William Warren**. Clerk of the Court, **Tho. Abington**.

April 23, 1714: **John Cartwright**, Pasquotank Precinct. Names brothers **Job Cartwright, Thos. Cartwright, Jos. Cartwright**. Sisters **Eliza Cartwright, Catherine Cartwright**. Friend **John Murden** (son of **Jerome Murden**.) Executors, brothers **Thomas** and **Job Cartwright**. Witnesses: **Gran Cartwright, Will Norris**. No probate. (I suspect that 'Gran' Cartwright probably should be Grace Cartwright, John's stepmother.)

December 30, 1728, June 3, 1729: **Grace Cartwright**, Pasquotank Precinct. Names daugter **Elizabeth Trueblood**; son **Joseph**. Other legatees: **Josiah Trueblood, Joshua Trueblood, John Trueblood, Elizabeth Trueblood, Miriam Trueblood, Elizabeth Murden, Jeremiah Murden, Mary Murden, John Murden, Job Cartwright, Sr., Benjamin Cartwright** (son of Joseph), **Elizabeth Cartwright** (daughter of **Joseph**), **Thomas Cartwright** (son of **Thomas**). Executor son **Joseph Cartwright**. Witnesses: **Benjamin Miller, William Lewis, Martha Lewis**. Will proven before **Richard Everard**.

February 2, 1731, February 16, 1730 (Given this way in abstract, but these dates should apparently both be 1731 by the current calendar. See later a fragmented version of this will, when deed abstracts are shown.): **William Cartwright**, Chowan or Pasquotank County. Names brothers **Robert** and **Thomas**. Other legatees: **Owen Rees, Hannah Staffard, Joseph Stockley, Mary Rees** (sister), **Elizabeth Clark**. Executors: **Jeremiah Murden** and **Stephen Delemare**. Witnesses: **Elisabeth Clark, Jonathan Hibbs, Mary Murden**. Proven before **Richard Everard**. (This is clearly William Cartwright, Jr., since he names sisters who are shown as children of William, Sr., below. But the fact that there was another William Cartwright associated with this one's brother, David, and alive after this time, is shown by the will of Owen Reese, given shortly.)

January 15, 1733, April Court 1734: **William Cartright**, Pasquotank County. Names sons **Thomas, Robert, Joseph** (plantation whereon I now dwell), **Caleb** and **David** (land called the Sandy Run), **John**. Daughters: **Hannah Cartright**, (land above the pigpens), **Tamer**

189

Cartright (tract of land called the Little For). Other legatees: **Oen Rese**, **Elizabeth Cartwright**, daughter of son **John**, deceased (forty acres of land on the South side of the Creek swamp known by the name of Maverts). Wife and executrix, **Sarah**. Witnesses: **Edward Whorten, John Richardson, James Greaves**. Clerk of the Court: **Joseph Anderson**.

April 15, 1746, July Court 1746: **Robert Cartwright**, Pasquotank County. Names sons **Hezekiah** (plantation whereon I now live), **Josiah, Ezekiel**. Daughter **Martha Cartwright**. Grandson **Claudius Cartwright**. Wife and executrix, **Martha**. Executor, son **Hezekiah Cartwright**. Witnesses: **James Pike, Edward Tadlock, Jos. Martin**. Clerk of the Court: **Thos. Taylor**.

August 25, 1755, September Court 1755: **Catrin Gaskins**, Pasquotank County. Names son and executor **Thomas**; daughter **Ann Cartwright**. Witnesses: **Samuel Davis, Joseph Pindleton**. Clerk of the Court, **Thos. Taylor**.

April 7, 1745, July Court 1745: **Owen Reese**, Pasquotank County. Names sons **John** and **Owin**. Daughters **Betty, Sarah, Mary**, and **Ann Reese**. Wife and executrix, **Mary**. Executor, **Daniell Williams**. Witnesses: **John Burnham, David** and **William Cartright**. Clerk of the Court, **Thos. Taylor**.

April 4, 1752, December Court 1758: **Robert Ednye** (Edney), Pasquotank County. Names sons **Samuel, Nuton Rensher Ednye**. Daughters **Ann Ednye** (land on the long ridge), **Ahinoam Ednye** (land on ash branch), **Elizabeth Cartwright** (land on broad neck branch). Wife and executrix, **Ann**. Witnesses: **Samuel Smith, Joseph Spence, Thos. Loads** (Rhodes). Clerk of the Court: **Thos. Taylor**.

December 3, 1748, January 19, 1748 (49): **Samuel Jackson**, Pasquotank County. Names sons **John** (upper part of plantation), **Joshua** (remainder of my land). Daughters **Elisabeth Benton, Miriam Pool, Mary Cartwright, Mary Ann Lovel**. Wife,

Elisabeth. Executors, sons **John** and **Joshua Jackson.** Witnesses: **Abraham Rankhorn, Samuel Benton, Joseph Robinson.** Will proven before **Gab. Johnston.**

July 16, 1719: **Bartholomew Hewitt,** Pasquotank County. Legatees: **Robert Lowry, Samuel Davis, Thomas Cartright, Samuel Norris.** Executor, **William Norris.** Witnesses: **William Jones, John Macky.** Original missing. Recorded in Book 1712-1722, page 243.

Plus, below, a will in which it appears the pertinent name should be Cartwright, but is spelled otherwise:

October 27, 1740, Probate not dated: **John Avery,** Hyde County. Names wife **Jane;** other legatees: **Martha Smith; Agnes Slade; Thomas, William** and **Samuel Smith** (sons of **John**); **Lydia** (wife of **Benjamin Russell**); **Elizabeth** and **Dorcas Smith; John Smith; Darcas Worldly; James Avery; Gilbert Macknary; Kezia Hadley; Elizabeth** (daughter of **Uriah Collins**); **Foster Jervis; Lydia Cathright; James Avery.** Executors, **John Smith** and **Foster Jervis.** Witnesses: **Uriah Collins, William Sylvester, William Giddens.** Clerk of the Court, **William Barrow.**

This will abstract includes a **John Cartwright** as a legatee, and he appears to be the same one who is seen later in other records as one who is unidentified as to family origins:

October 19, 1719, November 2, 1722: **Sarah Hawkins,** Pasquotank County. Names as legatees: **Thos. Merriday;** heirs of **Elizabeth Stubble,** wife of **John Stubble** of Wickham, England; **Mary Stubble; George Griffing; John Cartwright; John King; Susannah Talksey; John Everigin, Jr.; Emanuel Low; John Symons; Wm. Everigin, Sr.;** (the last two named are appointed executors). Witnesses: **Garrett Pursey, Robert Harrison, Sarah Harrison.** Proven before **Wm. Reed.**

While these wills give a great deal of information, there are other records which provide even more clarity and identification of many of the members of this group of Cartwrights. First, the earliest record I have found is is the birth and marriage of **Elizabeth Cartwright**, daughter of **Thomas Cartwright** and his second wife, **Grace**. Appearing to have come from a Bible record, the data is contained in a source of miscellaneous data for Old Albemarle County.[3]

Amos Trueblood was born Jany. 20th. 1691.
Elizabeth Cartwright was born March 3rd: 1693.
The afsd **Amos Trueblood & Elizabeth Cartwright** was married the 27th: Jany 1714.
Thomas Trueblood was born 20th: Jany. 1717(18).
Abell Trueblood was born 30th: April 1722.
Josiah Trueblood was born 18 Jany. 1724(25).
Joshua Trueblood was born 2: March 1726(27).
Meriam Trueblood was born 10: Febry. 1729(30).
Caleb Trueblood was born 14: April 1732.
all being Children to the afsd **Amos** and **Elizabeth Trueblood** and Recorded this 2d: July 1739.

Another set of very important information is found in the deeds of the county.[1] The pertinent abstracts are set forth below, with commentary following where appropriate. (One must be careful with these old records, for in some places the name Cartwright has been confused with that of John Carteret, Earl of Granville. As far as I can determine there was no relation.) I have shortened even further the abstracts, confining them to the important genealogical detail, since some of them are very long. Also, I have chosen to note signatures of the main parties only when they include more detail of the names than is otherwise given. Finally, I have included those abstracts which mention only the land of various Cartwrights when it seems helpful in some way, but not otherwise. Thus, for any one closely interested, a fuller inspection of the footnoted sources is advised.

29 November 1706: His Excellency **John Lord Granvile** Palatine....give and grant unto **William Cartwright** a tract of Land containing 200 acres lying in Pasquotank..... Witness our trusty and well beloved **William Glover Esqr.** President..... Signed: **W. Glover**,

Samuel Swann, John Ardern. Francis Foster, Edwd. Moseley.
Recorded in the Secretary's Office, 1 Dec. 1707. **T. Knight** Secy.

Thomas Cartwright Junr. and **Mary** my wife....(This deed is partially illegible and with a portion of it missing. There is no date. It is included by the compiler with the very early records, roughly 1700-1715, and thus it must have been in the earliest deed book.) ...in Consideration of the full Sum of 15 pounds....paid by **William Warren**...sold...our plantation and land containing 100 acres....on the South side of Pasquotank River in a fork between two branches, by my other Tract of Land, and running up the easternmost branch.....
Dividing this Tract from our brother **Job Cartwrite's** land.....

1 January 1707:   **Mary Cartwright** signed as a witness on an assignation of **John Jennings** and wife **Dorithy** to his daughter **Eliz. Reding,** 'all my right, title, and interest of this within mentioned Patent of Land', after our decease. Acknowledged 20 Jany. 1712/13, Reg. 25 Jany. 1712/13.

17 July 1711: **William Cartwright's** line mentioned as adjoining that of **Eliza. Garner** or **Gardner,** who is selling half of her land to **William Simson,** another whose land adjoins. **William Cartwright** also signed as a witness. (No other persons mentioned.) Reg. 18 '7ber' (?) 1711.

27 December 1712: **William Relfe Senr.** of Pasquotank doth assign over all my right title & Interest of this within mentioned plat of land unto **Wm. Cartwright**.... Witnesses: **Wm. Warren, Lidia Avery.** Reg. 5 Ffeby. 1713/14.

26 Jany. 1713/14:   **Ffran: Hendrick** with the free & voluntary consent of **Mary Hendrick** my lawful wife & for......10 pounds in hand paid by **Robert Cartwright** in the precinct of Pasquotank & Province aforesaid planter.....Sold.....bounding upon the Main Swamp of Newbegun Creek....Richd. Gray's line....100 acres. Witnesses: **D. Guthrie, Tho. Robison.** Reg. 5 Ffeby. 1713/14.

26 Jany. 1713/14: **Wm. Cartwright** of Pasquotank in the County of Albemarle & Province of North Carolina....Sum of 39 lbs. 17.6 Current money of this Province....Sold to **Jerr Munden** of the County and Province aforesaid...my plantation whereon I now live containing 200 acres situate lying & being in Pasquotank aforesaid excepting only one Neck of land beyond the bee tree branch & runing up to the Cypress Swamp....by virtue of a Patent bearing date the 29th day of 9ber 1706.... Witnesses: **Robt. Morgan, Robt. Cartwright, Jos. Glaister**. Reg. 10 June 1714. (Judging from other records, the above name should be Jeremiah Murden. Another version of this deed includes the identification of William Cartwright as 'wheelright'.)

6 Jany. 1712/13: **Jeremh. Murden** of Pasquotank in North Carolina doth assign over all my right title and Interest of this within mentioned bill of Sale unto **Job Cartwright**. Witnesses: **Wm. Relfe Senr., Wm. Relfe Junr**. Ack. Pasquotank 20 April 1714, **Jerr. Murden** and **Mary** his wife to **Job Cartwright**. Reg. 5 May 1714.

10 October 1716: **Joseph Guilford** of Albermarle (sic).....in consideration of the sum of 6 pounds Current money of North Carolina to me in hand paid....by **John Cartwright**....Sold .....a certain Tract of land ct. by estimation 50 acres more or less lying and being on the NE side of Pasquotank River beginning at the head of Joseph Gilfords line & so coming down to the first Cross Branch & bounded on the other side by the Pecoson. Witnesses: **Phil Torksey Senr., Thos. TT Torksey**. Reg. 25 June 1718.

17 June 1717: **Wm. Cartwright** witness on deed of **Emll. Low** and wife **Ann** to **John Conner**, merchant. (Long description of land genealogy, shortened here): Patented to **Major Samll. Swann** 26 Feby. 1696, 467 acres at mouth of Newbegun Creek, bounded on north by **Mr. Daniel Akehurst**....assigned on back of patent 27 Feby. 1696 to **John Archdale, Esqr.**, who gifted it to grandson **Nevil Low**, son of the abovesaid **Emll.** and **Ann Low**, and 'after his decease unto ye sd. **Ann Low**....' **Nevill Low** is since dead. **Emll.** and **Ann** now sell to **John Conner** for 150 lbs. the 467 acres, 'except ye several lots part of ye. sd. tract of land as are already sold.....' Reg. 26 July

1717. In another record of same date, also witnessed by **Wm. Cartwright, Jno. Conner** acknowledges the parts that are already sold---to **Nicholus Noy, Esqr., Jos. Jordan** Gent. & **Ffilia Christi Jordan** his now wife, being 200 acres more or less......'then called and known by ye name of Chancey's Plantation and whereon the sd. **Jos. Jordan** now liveth'. Reg. 27 July 1717. A third record concerning same, in which **Emanl. Low** apparently gives **Conner** a mortgage on the land, for 500 pounds sterling. Again Witnessed by **Wm. Cartwright**, same date of Registration. Other witnesses on all these records are **Joseph Jordan, Daniell Richardson**.

17 June 1717: **Wm. Cartwright** witnessed another transaction of **Eml. Lowe**, merchant. A long and confusing record; seems to be saying that as a result of persuading his wife **Ann** 'by special entreaty' to sell the above land to **Conner**, he has given as a 'recompense, certain Negroes' to be held specifically for the purpose of determining that she and her children shall not suffer, etc. '....have given.....unto **Edwd. Moseley** of Chowan precinct & **Daniel Richardson** all the right he now has in four following Negroes, namely **Jupiter, Hany, Bess & Hany, Nero**' (? Two 'Hanys', or is this a mistake?).....to the use & behoof of my self & my said wife during the term of our joint lives'.....then to children, etc. (Apparently Edward Moseley and Daniel Richardson are to be joint owners or else overseers?)

21 October 1718: **Joab Cartwright** of the prect. of Pasquotank & province aforsd. (North Carolina)....with the free voluntary consent of **Lydia Cartwright** my lawful wife....for the valuable consideration of 11 pounds.....paid by **George Harris Junr.** of the prect. & province afsd.....sold....100 acres by Will given unto me by my father **Thos: Cartwright** dec: & by me sold unto **Thos: Joyc**(?) & by the sd. **Joic** (sic) sold & returned unto me....known by the name of Jobs old field.... **Job J. Cartwright, Lydia Cartwright**, (marks). Witnesses: **W. Norris, Levy Purfoy**. Reg. 1 Dec. 1718. (Since Job Cartwright, Sr.'s wife was named Lydia, as seen here, it appears that she was the same Lydia 'Cathright' named in the will of John Avery of Hyde County, North Carolina. Perhaps being a grandaughter, since the will did not clarify the relationship.)

21 July 1719: **Wm. Cartwright** of Pasquotank prect: in North Carolina, in Consideration of the love & affection which I bear unto my well beloved son **Thomas Cartwright**....give....100 acres....**Henry Bugbirds** corner tree.... Signed **Wm. W. Cartwright**, his mark. Witnesses: **Gabl. Burnham, Fran: McBride**. Reg. 24 July 1719.

21 July 1719: **Wm. Cartwright & Sarah** my wife for & in consideration of (blank) paid by **Henry Bugbird** of the prect. & province aforesaid (North Carolina) being part of a greater tract belonging to me the sd. **Wm. Cartwright** containing 400 acres by Patent granted to me bearing date the 7: day of Jany 1716/17...on the South West side of Pasquotank river.....Sandy run branch.... Witnesses: **Gabll. Burnham, Wm. Cartwright Junr**. Reg. 23 July 1719.

21 July 1719: **Wm. Cartwright** of the province of North Carolina & in the county of Albermarle & prect. of Pasquotank....make over forever the within written patent & land to my well beloved son **Wm. Cartwright jun. Wm. W. Cartwright**, mark. Witnesses: **Nath. Jones, Jno. Smithson**. Reg. 24 July 1719.

19 Jany 1719/20: **George Harris** for me my heirs & Assigns do assign over all my right....of the within mentioned land to **Job Cartwright**.... Signed **George Harris Jun:**. Witnesses: **W. Norris**. Reg. 22 July 1710.

19 July 1720: **Jos. Cartwright**...for the Consideration of the exchange of a plantation, lying upon Pasquotank River, joining to **Levy Cressey**, wherewith I am fully satisfied....sold.....unto **Douglas Rood**, a piece of land lying upon the (blank) of **Jos: Reding & Wm. Relf**, given to me by my father **Thos: Cartwright** in his last will & Testament ct. 100 acres.... Signed **Jo: Cartwright, Ele X Cartwright**. Witnesses: **Levy Cressey, Isaac Scarbro**. Reg. 22 July 1720. (Presuming that 'Jos.' is Joseph Cartwright, the son of Thomas the elder, rather than Josiah Cartwright who was son of William, Sr..

Whichever he is, the obvious appearance of this deed is that his wife must have been 'Ele'. Perhaps short for 'Eleanor'?)

14 March 1718/19: **Steph: Vaughan** do assign.....all my right.....of the within mentioned Bill of Sale & platt....to **Jno. Cartwright**.... Witnesses: **Jno. Condon, Math. Vaughan**. Reg. 26 Sept. 1721.

18 July 1721: I assign over the said within mentioned unto **Jos: Harrison**. Signed: **John Cartwright**. Reg. 26 7br 1721. (No details)

17 October 1721: N. Carolina...**Amos Trueblood** of the prect. of Pasquotank & province afsd...with the consent of **Elizh. Trueblood** my Lawfull wife....for the valuable consideration of 100 pounds ster. money of Great Brittain to us paid by **Thomas Cartwright**....sold....a tract of land & Plantation ct. 330(?) lying & being upon Pasquotank...upon **George Harris's** line to the foot of old horse bridge...which land was formerly given by will to the sd. **Eliza. Trueblood** formerly **Eliza. Cartwright** by her father **Thomas Cartwright**. Witnesses: **W. Norris, Jo: Reding**. Reg. 24 October 1721.

17 October 1721: **Thomas Cartwright** for the valuable consideration of 100 pounds sterling money of Great Brittain....paid by **Amos Trueblood**....do assign over all my right...unto the within mentioned deed & land therein expressed..... Signed **Thomas T. Cartwright** his mark, **Mary Cartwright**, her mark. Witnesses: **W. Norris, Jo: Reding**. Reg. 24 October 1721.

17 Jany. 1720/21: **Wm. Cartwright's** land, formerly **Relf Gardner's**, mentioned as adjoining that sold by **William Norris & Susan** to **Joseph Stokely**. Reg. 20 July 1721.

16 April 1723: **William Cartwright**, for a valuable consideration.....give unto the Honble **Col: Willm. Reed Esqr**. all my right....unto a tract of land I have sold unto **Jeremh. Murden**....(? This is unclear to me. Appears to be just a confirmation that he has

sold the land and makes no claims on it.) Witnesses: **Josa. Markham, Danl. Richardson**. Reg. 19 April 1723.

21 April 1724: 21 April 1724: **Thomas Cartwright Junr**.......with the free voluntary consent of (left blank, but her name was Mary as seen elsewhere) my lawful wife, for the vaulable consideration of 2 pounds paid by **Jereh. Murden**.....a parcel of Land contg. 4 acres....being part of a tract of Land belonging to **Thomas Cartwright Junr.**, ...to be taken out from the largermost end of the said Cartwright land.....binding upon a tract of Land formerly belonging to **Henry Bugbird** and by him sold to **Jeremh. Murden**.....Signed **Thos. T. Cartwright**. Witnesses: **Joseph Stokely, Ann Stokely**. Reg. 29 7br. 1724. (Perhaps Thomas Cartwright's wife was the daughter Mary Cartwright named in Samuel Jackson's will, given previously.)

21 July 1725: **Jeremiah Murden** for the valuable consideration of the sum of 20 pounds....paid by **William Cartwright**....sold.....all my right......of the within written premises....by the joint consent of **Mary Murden** my lawful wife..... Witnesses: **Henry Raper, Truman McBride**.

15 October 1729: **Edward Wharton** of Pasquotank, with free voluntary consent of **Elizabeth** my wife; for 9 pounds paid by **Thomas Cartwright**, land beginning at a branch called Tarr Kill Branch, 50 acres. Signed **Edward E. Wharton**, his mark. Witnesses: **Thos. Tweedie, Esau Alberson**, (blank) **Martin**. Reg. '10 ye. 16th 1729'.

12 Jan. 1729/30: **Thomas Cartwright Senr.** of Pasquotank in the County of Albermarle; for the good will, love, & natural affection I do bear unto my son **Moses Cartwright**, 160 acres Beginning at the upper end of the sd **Thomas Cartwright's** line upon the Eastern side of the Waiding Branch & so running down to **John Harris'** line. Signed **Thos. T. Cartwright**, his mark. Witnesses: **Thos. Tweedie, Lodwick Gray** his mark. Reg. April ye 8th 1730.

14 July 1730: **John Cartwright** witnessed a record of **Ann Jones**. (Unclear in meaning, but appears to be a mortgage?) Binds herself unto **Wm. Burgess** for 800 pounds 'to be paid to him', but appears to be transferring land to him for same amount. Land was given & bequeathed to her by the last will & testament of her father **Cornelius Jones**. Signed by her mark. Other witness: **Solomon Davis**. Reg. ye 11. 1730. Another record also witnessed by **John Cartwright** shows that **Wm. Burgess** paid to **Anne** 100 pounds for land bequeathed to her by her father. On NE side of Pasquotank River....'a piece of Land out of the tract called Robertson all ye land on ye east Side of the plantation called ye water Million path Walnut tree neck & ye can dance to ye Same Containing more or Less together....' (?!! What a description. Wonder what it means?) Signed by her mark. Other witness is again **Solomon Davis**. Reg. 8 ye 11 1730.

16 Feb. 1730: (Compiler notes that the first part of this 'deed' is missing, which is unfortunate because it is clearly the will of William Cartwright, rather than a deed. Grimes apparently had access to the full will, since his abstract names other persons than those shown below. I will reproduce the fragmented version in as full a state as it was given in the source volume of deed abstracts, for edification, even though it contains only a little more colorful information than the other.): '...And two hogs unto my brothers **Robert Thomas** (sic) and ever Item I give unto my Brother **Thomas** forever one young mare they giving unto **Eliz: Clark** ye first Colt of ye said mare & I do make & give **Jeremiah Murden** & **Stephen Dellmar** my full & Sole Ex: of this my last will & testament.... Signed: **Will. W. Cartwright** his mark. Witnesses: **Eliza C Clark** hir mark, **Jona. Hibbs**, **Mary Murden**. North Carolina Chowan these are to Certify that **Stephen Delmar** personally appeared at Edenton in ye prect. afs'd & took his Solomn affirmation well & truly to perform ye afore written will of **W. Cartwright** dec: ye 16 Feb: 1730(31). Before me **W Baddham** Justice. Feb. 16 1730(31). Proved this will before me **Richd. Everrard**. Recd. June ye. 7. 1732 in y prect of Pasquotank.'

12 8br. 1730: **George Bray** of North C. and County of Albermarle, prect. of Pasquotank....and **Eliza.** my wife for 6 pounds, paid by **John**

Cartwright of same province, etc; 66 acres of land lying joining to **Thomas Raymans** line & **John Cartwright's** line. Witnesses **Will. Burges**, **Thomas Sawyer**. Reg. 2 Aug. 1733.

12 October 1741: **Joshua Perisho** (of Pasquotank) to **Robert Cartwright** for 50 pounds, 40 acres on Pasquotank River above the Great Swamp on the head said river, part of it on the middle Swamp & the rest of it **Owen Reeses** swamp....**Betty Perisho** the wife of **Joshua** surrenders all her right of Dowry. Witnesses: **Richard Pritchard, William Sawyer**. Reg. 14 Oct. 1741.

9 April 1741: (Deposition) **John Cartwright** of the County personally appeared...that about 20 years ago, he saw and read a patent for a piece...of land on North side of Pasquotank, joining to a plantation now possessed to **Thomas Merriday** of this County, which patent was in the name of **Isaac Gilford** late of this County, decd. and grandfather to **Joseph Gilford** who now possesses said piece of land and plantation bounding upon the afsd. plantation where the said **Thomas Merriday** now lives.....the patent was very much shattered and a great many holes in it he believed caused by the worms....the afsd. plantation now in poss. of the afsd. **Joseph Gilford** has been peaceably possessed by the Gilfords ever since he could remember first by the Uncle and then by the father of the afsd. **Joseph Gilford**, and further this Deponent saith that he is about 50 years of age......Signed: **James George** (? apparently the person who took John Cartwright's deposition). Exhibited in open court by **Joseph Gilford**. Reg. 3 Dec. 1741. (This John Cartwright, probably the same as shown in previous abstracts, remains completely unidentified. Most of the men named John Cartwright in the families under study are accounted for as having died before this time. There is some small uncertainty about the actual death of the John Cartwright who was the son of the elder Thomas and whose will is shown dated 1714; but that John would clearly have been the son of Thomas and his first wife Alice, meaning that he would have had to be born before 1687 and thus would have been considerably older than the John shown here. Yet, to have been the age indicated here, this John would have had to be born circa 1691, and the only John we see in the family outlines who could have been of that age is the son of William, Sr. who died before this date as

well, being mentioned as deceased in William's will of 1733. Likewise the son John of Robert Cartwright who remained in Princess Anne County, Virginia is indicated as having died prior to 1729, by his mother's will.. But there certainly Cartwrights, apparently of this family, who are not extant in the records in a way that shows any of their own families; for instanct the inventories of two William Cartwrights in Princess Anne County, Va., who are unidentified.)

9 April 1743: North Carolina, Pasquotank County. **Thomas Cartwright**, Planter, for & in consideration of the Love, Goodwill, and affection which I have and do bear towards my loving brother **Job Cartwright** of the County abovesaid planter have given one part of a registered tract of land whereon I the said **Thomas Cartwright & Lidy Cartwright** now dwells....75 acres on the S. W. side of Pasquotank River....being the uppermonst of the said Tract of land.....old House branch. Witnesses: **Thomas Trueblood, Abel Trueblood, Josiah Trueblood**. Reg. 17 Jan. 1743. (This Thomas Cartwright is the son of Job Cartwright, Sr., now deceased. Job, Jr. is the brother to whom Thomas gives the land. 'Lidy' is not Thomas's wife, as some who take this record out of context seem to presume, but his mother. Thomas is at this point still living at and in possession of the home plantation of his father Job, Sr., whereon Thomas's mother 'Lidy' still resides also.)

21 June 1744: **Jonathan Hibbs** of the County of Pasquotank in the Province of North Carolina House Joiner for and in consideration of the sum of 400 pounds Bills...paid by **Thomas Cartwright**, son to the deceased **Job Cartwright**...land   S. W. side of Pasquotank River...**Rodes** line...**Wm. Sawyer's** line...Mouth of broad Gut at the River....60 acres, being a tract of land granted by two deeds of sale, one from **Wm. Relfe** and the other from **Daniel Rodes** both bearing date 1737. Witnesses: **Danl. Rodes, Al. Jack**. Proved by the oath of **Alex Jack**. Reg. 1 Aug. 1744.

5 Jan. 1744/5: North Carolina, Pasquotank County. **Job Cartwright** for 44 pounds 7 shillings and 6 pence Virginia currency, paid by **Abel Trueblood**, sold one part of a Registered tract of land whereon **Job**

Cartwright Senr. formerly lived....75 acres...S. W. side of Pasquotank River...being the uppermost part. Signed **Job Cartwright, Martha M. Reding**, her mark. Witnesses: **Thos. Trueblood, Benja. Pritchard**, Josiah Trueblood. Ack. April Court from **Job Cartwright & Martha** his wife to **Abel Trueblood**. Reg. 7 May 1745. (It appears that Martha Reding was the same as Martha, the wife of Job, Jr.. Why she would have signed the deed as Martha Reding may have had something to do with the origins of the land, perhaps having come from her dower.)

12 Aug. 1747: North Carolina, Pasquotank County. **Stephen Scott**, for 40 pounds Virginia currency....paid by **Abel Trueblood**, sold one part of a registered tract of land whereon **Joseph Reding Senr.** formerly lived....100 acres...on the S. W. Side of Pasquotank River...beginning at the mouth of the Easternmost Branch of **Chartwrights** (sic) Creek....between **Thomas** and **Joseph Cartwright**...main creek Swamp... Witnesses: **Joseph Pritchard, Job. Winslow, Jos. Jordan, Jr.** Reg. 24 Oct. 1747.

17 March 1747/48: North Carolina, Pasquotank County. (This record reads like both a will and a deed of gift. It is difficult to tell which it is, but it appears that it was taken to be a will and thus that Martha must have died at this time.) **Martha Chartwright** (sic) Widow....for the love, good will, and affection which I have and bear towards my three loving children after named, viz **Hezekiah Chartright, John Chartright** and **Sarah Palmer** (Spouse to Robert Palmer) my daughter and to the three Grand Children of these my two Sons and Daughter afsd. have given .....viz I give to my Son **Hezekiah Chartright** the first foal that is brought of the mare called Jenny, which mare so called is given to **Sarah Palmer** my Daughter, also I give unto my sd Son **Hezekiah Chartright** a large Iron pot and pothooks, also I give unto my Grand Child **Claudius Chartright** son of the afsd **Hezekiah Chartright** a small Iron pot and a large peuter basin. I give unto my son **John Chartright** my own Bed with the whole furniture thereof and those unto belonging with two peuter Basons a peuter Dish, my own Chest a middle sized Iron pot and pothooks, one Cow and a two year old Bull, Eight old Hogs and

Sixteen pigs, fifteen barrels of Corn & nine (blank) thereof in the hands of **Josiah Chartright** and all other things whatsoever I have not mentioned is given to said **John**. Also I give unto my Daughter **Sarah Palmer** my own riding Mare called Jenny excepting the first foal she brings to my Son **Hezekiah** as afsd. I give unto the sd. **Sarah Palmer** two barrels of Corn Also I give unto my said Daughter **Sarah Palmer** a peuter Dish I give unto my Grand Child the eldest Son of **John Chartright** not yet named one cow.... Signed **Martha Chartright**. Witnesses: **Thomas Chartright, Junr., Anne, Anna Chartright** her mark. Proved April Court 1748 by the oath of **Thomas Chartright, Junr.** Reg. 2 July 1748. (This Martha is clearly the widow of Robert Cartwright, whose will abstract was given previously, and not to be confused with Martha Reding Cartwright, the wife of Job Cartwright, Jr.. But note that neither the son John Cartwright nor the daughter Sarah Cartwright Palmer was named in Robert's will, only two years earlier, unless the abstraction somehow missed them. Martha herself does not mention the son Ezekiel who is named in her husband's will. It does not seem likely that the John Cartwright of this family is the same as the one discussed previously as being unidentified in the family lines, for this one seems to have been younger than the one who testified to being 50 years old in 1741. As for the Thomas Cartwright, Jr. and Anne who signed as witnesses, this is clearly the fourth-generation Thomas, being the son of Thomas and Mary. Anne is most likely the daughter of Catrin Gaskins who was named as Ann Cartwright in the latter's will in 1755, given previously.)

28 November 1750: North Carolina, Pasquotank County. **Christopher Cartwright**.....for the exchange of a certain piece of land to me in hand delivered by **Edwd. Scott**.....sold one part of a registered Tract of Land whereon **Joseph Cartwright** formerly lived....100 acres, S. W. sid of Pasquotank River...Knobs Crook Creek...Tulley's Corner. Witnesses: **Thomas Trueblood, Josiah Trueblood**. Reg. 18 April 1751. (Though the evidence is not fully direct, it appears that Christopher Cartwright must have been the son of Joseph Cartwright, who was son of the elder Thomas, died 1707.)

26 Sept. 1750: North Carolina, Pasquotank County. **Job Cartwright** for 14 pounds, 14 shillings, & 4 pence...paid by **Edwd. Scot**...sold one

part of a registered tract of land it being a conveyance out of **Job. Cartwrights** now granted patent....100 acres...S. W. side of Pasquotank River....**Abel Trueblood's** line....**Josiah Trueblood's** line..... Witnesses: **Thos. Trueblood, John Casse**. Reg. 18 April 1751. Reg. same date is another record with same amount of money for same amount of land, sold to **Josiah Trueblood**, dated 9 Sept. 1750.

19 Jan. 1748/49: (Though there are many records which I am not including if the pertinent Cartwright has only signed as a witness, I give this abstract because it is the first mention made of an Isaac Cartwright.) **Thomas Burges Junr.** of Pasquotank County, for 50 pounds current money of Virginia paid by **Thomas Torksey** of the same county afsd. sold....N. E. side of Pasquotank River Binding on Raymon's Creek being part of a tract patented to **Stephen Burges** in his last will and testament then given from him to his son; **Thomas Burges** in his last will and testament, 100 acres...head of Targinton Gut between **Thomas Cartwright** and **Thomas Burges**....between **Thomas Burges** and **Stephen Burges** so binding on **Charles Wright's** line to the Creek... Witnesses: **John Squires, John Cartrite, Isaac Cartwright**. Reg. 18 April 1751.

18 Feb. 1750/51: **Edmund Jackson** of Pasquotank for 3 pounds, 10 shillings Virginia Currency...paid by **Hezekiah Cartwright** of the County afsd. Planter....sold 5 acres...fork of Knobs Crook...head of the land which was patented by **Henry Nichols**, bearing date 1715. Between **Thomas Pritchard** and the land formerly called Coopers.... Witnesses: **Thomas Weeks, Josiah Cartwright, Danl. Williams**. Reg. 18 April 1751.

20 December 1748: (Just as a demonstration of how the name Cartwright is occasionally confused with that of John, Lord Carteret, in these records, I show the abstract below. It should be disregarded, for as stated I have seen no indication that the Earl of Granville had any connection with the Cartwrights.): **John Coats** of Pasquotank, Planter to **John Sikes** of afsd for 2 pounds, 450 acres.....**John Coats** took up as by a patent under the hand of **Edward Mosely** and **Robert**

Halton agent for **John Lord Cartwright, Earl of Granville**, date of 20th day of Dec. 1748........etc.

Other records to be found in the source 'Old Albermarle', etc.[3]:

Thomas Chartright son of **Thomas Cartright** recorded a mar_ as follows, a Swallow-fork in the left e_r And a Crop and an under Keil in the right Ear the 29nth: of _ep: 1741.
Christopher Chartright records a Mark as follows (to witt) a Crop & an under Keel & an over square in __ Left ear, And a Crop on the right Ear, recorded the _d. day of September 1745.
Benjamin Cartright records a Mark for himself as follows (to witt), a Crop & a hole in the Left Ear An under Square in the right Ear, recorded the 1st: day ___September 1747.
Christopher Chartright, records a Brand as follows, Thus (CC) on the near Buttock the 23rd day of Aprill 1749.
These records found amidst the brands and flesh marks, clearly important for identifying the marriage of **Christopher Cartwright**, and of several others:
North Carolina, Pasquotank County. Then received of Mr. **Christopher Chartright** the full Legacy Left by Mr. **Thomas Smithson** Deceased to his Daughter **Tamer Smithson** now the wife of **John Norris** I say received by me June the 4th: 1748. (Wit.) **Banjn: Cartright**, Mark. Signed **Jo. Norris, Tamer Norris.** Rec. August 13nth: 1751.
Know all by These Presents That I **Thomas Relfe**, I have received of Mr. **Christopher Chartwright** Excr: in Right of his wife to **Thomas Smithsons** Estate I the said **Relfe** have received, in wright of his wife **Mary** Daughter to the deceast, one Case of Bottles, one Sow and Piggs, one brass Kittle, and three dishes and two Puter Plates, and Share? of the Eartorn ware, Witness my hand this 2d: day of December 1749. **Tho. Relfe. Joseph Sawyer.** Decem. 27th. 1750.
North Carolina, Pasquotank County:
Then received of **Christopher Chartwright**, And **ann** his wife Executrix of the last Will and Testament of **Thomas Smithson** of the said County deceased, one Fether bed and Furniture and two large Pillars and one Sett of Shoe-makers tools and one hunting Gun and one Six Gallon Iron pott, and one two Gallon Stone Jug and one pair

of Stilleards, one Grindstone and one fole brought by the mare Called filley, the young mare was delivered to the said **Joshua Smithson** when she was a bout Three years old then recd. all these things within mentioned I say recd. by me. **Joshua Smithson**. Test: **Jno: Norris, Dorcas Smithson** her mark.

Received of **Christopher Chartright** the full Legacy given by Mr. **Thomas Smithson** deceased to his Daughter **Dorcas Smithson** I say received by me I being Exor. August the 6th: day 1751. **John Smithson**. Witness: **Martha t Chartwright**, her mark.

North Carolina, Pasquotank County:

Then Received of ___Chartwright the full Legacy left by Mr. **Thomas Smithson** deceased to his Daughter **Merriam Smithson**, which is now the wife of **Joseph Sawyer**, all but a Negro Wench after her Mothers decease I say received by me, **Joseph Sawyer**. Decem. ye. 2d: 1749. Test: **Tho. Relfe**. Recorded the 13nth day of August 1751. By. **Tho: Taylor**, Clk. Co.

It can be seen from the above records that **Christopher 'Chartright'** married the widow of **Thomas Smithson**, and the children of said Smithson were acknowledging that he had delivered to them their legacies of the estate. Thus, **Thomas Smithson's** sons were **Joshua Smithson** and **John Smithson**, the latter probably being the eldest since he mentions himself as executor and he receives his sister's part on her behalf. **Thomas Smithson's** daughters were **Tamer**, who married **John Norris**; **Mary**, who married **Thomas Relfe**, **Dorcas Smithson**, and **Merriam** who married **Joseph Sawyer**. The identity of the **Martha Cartwright** who signed as witness is uncertain, but she could have been **Martha Reding Cartwright** who was wife of **Job Cartwright, Jr.**, as shown by previous records; or she could have been an unmarried daughter of one of the various Cartwrights.

Continuing with the other records in the same source:

Thomas Cartwright Records a mark for his son **Matthias Cartwright** (Viz) A Swallow fork and Under keel in the left ear and a Crop in the Right ear, Recorded the 6th day of October A. D. 1764.

Thomas Cartwright records a mark for his son **Thomas** as follows (Viz) A Swallow fork in the right ear and a Crop and Under keel in the left ear. Recorded the 6th. day of October A. D. 1764.

Thomas Cartwright records a mark for his son **James** as follows, towit, A Swallow fork in the left Ear & a Crop in the Right ear; Recorded the 6th day of October A. D. 1764.

Robert Cartwright Son of **Peter Cartwright** Records a Mark for himself Swallow fork in the Right Ear and an Under keel and Upper Keel in the Left Recorded this 3d. Day of September 1770.

Morgan Cartwright son of **Peter Cartwright** Records a mark for himself Swallow forks and under keel in the Right Ear. Recorded this 3d. day of September 1770. (This is the first indication that I have seen of the use of the name Peter among this group of Pasquotank Cartwrights. Whether he is still alive at this point is not indicated by this record, and thus we have little idea how old he would have been or when he might have been born, let alone to whom.)

John Cartwright son of **Thomas Cartwright** and **Sarah** his wife was born the 3th. (sic) day of July 1778.

Thomas Cartwright son __ **John Cartwright** & **Rhoda** his wife was born the 21st. of January 1779.

William Cartwright son of the aforsd. **Thomas** & **Sarah** was born the 2nd. of June 1780.

Thomas Cartwright, Sr. Records a mark for his Son **John Cartwright** as followeth a Swallow fork in the Left & under Keel in the Right Ear. Recorded this 30th. of August 1780. Test: **Enoch Relfe**, C. C.

John Cartwright Records a mark for him self as follow a Swallow fork In Each Ear & under Crop Cut? the Right. Recd. This 30th. of August 1780. Test: **Enoch Relf.**

John Cartwright Records a mark for his son **William** as followeth a Crop in the Right Ear & upper Keel & under Keel In the Left. Recd. this 30th. (blank) 1780.

John Cartwright records a mark for his son **Thomas Cartwright** as followeth a Crop & a slit and under Keel in the Right and a Crop in the Left Ear. Recorded this 12th. March 1791. Test: **Enoch Relfe**, C. C.

John Cartwright Records a mark for **Caleb Trueblood** son of **Able Trueblood** as followeth a Crop & Slit? the Right and a Slit in the Left Ear. Recorded this 12th March 1791. Test: **Enoch Relfe**.

Christopher Cartwright Records a mark for himself as follows A Smooth Crop in the left Ear & a Crop & half Crop in the right ear. Jany. 17th. 1798. Test: **Will: T. Muse**, Clk.

William Cartwright records a mark for himself as follows, a swallow fork and Over keel in the right Ear. April 10th. 1798. Test: **Will: T. Muse**, Clk.

'A list of Marriage Licenses issued by **Wm. Felluse** (same source. I have extracted Cartwrights only):

Tamer Cartwright and **James Jackson**, Jany. 1798.
William Cartwright and **Abigail godfrey**, April 10, 1798.
Sarah Cartwright and **Abijah Pendleton**, May 1798.
Nancy Cartwright and **Ephraim Bright**, Dec. 1798.
Hezekiah Cartwright and **Eliz. Pritchard**, March 26, 1799.
Joseph Cartwright and **Sarah Markham**, August 21, 1799.

Other Cartwright marriages in Pasquotank County, prior to 1800[4]:

Ahaz Cartwright and **Ann Madron**, 5 May 1772.
Jesse Cartwright and **Sarah Pendleton**, 12 January 1774.
Joseph Cartwright and **Martha Reding**, 5 September 1774. (Not to be confused with Job Cartwright, Jr. and his wife Martha Reding, shown to have been married by 1745 per deeds given previously.)
John Cartwright, Jr. and **Rhody Tweedy**, 23 November 1777.
(The one below is certainly translated wrong, somehow):
Robart Cartwright and **Matthew Zachary**, 25 August 1778.
Joseph Cartwright and **Sarah Lenness** (widow), 26 January 1781.
Thomas Cartwright and **Elizabeth Hastings**, 25 July 1786.
Chole (probably Chloe?) **Cartwright** and **Mark Sexton**, 22 September 1790.
John Cartwright alias **Davis** and **Catherine Langley**, 30 May 1794.
Jemima Cartwright and **Thomas Church**, 13 July 1799.

Wills that are available for Cartwrights in the county of Pasquotank and have not already be shown can be found in Olds' volume of 'Abstracts of North Carolina Wills', and/or listed in Mitchell's 'North Carolina Wills, A Testator Index'. Olds' work is an important and useful reference, but the abstracts are very rudimentary and it should be used only a as a guide, for I have found in almost every case that there are more pertinent details to be found in fuller sources, such as children who were left out of the abstracts, etc. Mitchell's Index is a valuable help because it gives complete references concerning the location of the wills listed, for obtaining copies. Below I give a brief synopsis of the data to be found in these sources, with commentary in some cases where the information is of help in working out the family lines.

Olds' Abstracts---from Pasquotank County. (Although the abstracts usually specify when the given name is a spouse, this is not always the case. Wives can be named without being so designated.)[5]

1760: **Christopher Cartwright---wife Ann; Joseph; Ann.**
1762: **Thomas Cartwright---Robert; Sarah; Tamer; William.**
1763: **Abram Cartwright---Ezekiel; Abram; wife Elizabeth.**
1776: **Isaac Cartwright---Caleb; Jesse; Isaac; Asa; Elizabeth; Mary; Lydia; Dinah; wife Elizabeth.**
1776: **Job Cartwright---wife Martha; Miriam.** (Clearly Job, Jr., who m. Martha Reding.)
1777: **Jesse Cartwright---son Jesse; wife Eliza.**
1778: **John Cartwright---mentions wife, not named; Caleb; Barnaby; and John, brothers.**
1790: **John Cartwright---wife Elizabeth; John.**
Also:
1772: **Charles Wright---wife Ann; Augustin; Elizabeth Cartwright** (daughter); **Levi.**
1777: **Joseph Morgan---Peter Cartright** and wife **Jean** (daughter) and their children. (This may be the Peter mentioned earlier, whose identity as relates to the other Cartwrights is unclear,

209

but who was the father of Robert and Morgan as indicated by the 'flesh mark' records.)

Aside from these, there are will abstracts in the same source for many members of the families seen to be connected with the Cartwrights, such as Trueblood, Jordan, Reding, etc.

Mitchell's Testator Index--Cartwrights of Pasquotank County only are given here[6]. All wills indicated are on record in the State Archives unless otherwise noted. The designation 'no original' does not mean that the will is not on record, but only that it was never officially recorded or proved, and was found by other means than in the will books If the will is listed in the index, a copy should be obtainable from either the county or the State Archives. I have not included here those wills dated beyond the year 1800, and there are many.

Thomas Cartwright, 1707; Secretary of State papers.   (Grimes' Abstracts.)

John Cartwright, 1714; Secretary of State papers. No proving date.

Grace Cartwright, 1729; Secretary of State papers.

William Cartwright, 1732; Secretary of State papers. (d. 1731, as shown in Grimes' abstracts. There is a **William Cartwright** listed 1730 for Chowan County, but he appears to be the same William, as shown by the deed abstracts previously given which indicated the fragmented will was proven in both Chowan and Pasquotank.)

William Cartright, 1734; Secretary of State papers. (Those from which Grimes took his abstracts. This is clearly the William who is shown as died 1733 in said abstracts.)

Abram Cartwright, 1763; Will Book H, pg. 53. (Shown in Olds' abstracts, as given previously.)

Robert Cartwright, 1746; Secretary of State papers.   (Grimes' Abstracts.)

Thomas Cartwright, 1751; no proving date. Original only, State Archives.

Christopher Cartwright, 1760; Will Book H, pg. 9. (Shown in Olds' abstracts.)

Thomas Cartwright, 1762; Will Book I, pg. 11 (Olds' abstracts.)

Thomas Cartwright, 1772; original only, State Archives.

Isaac Cartwright, 1776; Will Book I, pg. 149. No original.
Job Cartwright, 1776; Will Book I, pg. 150. (Shown in Olds' abstracts.)
Thomas Cartwright, 1777; original only, State Archives.
Jesse Cartwright, 1777; Will Book I, pg. 113.
John Cartwright, 1778; Will Book K, pg. 13.
John Cartwright, 1790, Will Book K, pg. 203.
Darius Cartwright, 1793; Will Book L, pg. 1.
Hezekiah Cartwright, 1793; Will Book L, pg. 6.
Ahaz Cartwright, 1796; Will Book L, pg. 76.
Caleb Cartwright, 1797; Will Book L, pg. 103.
Jesse Cartwright, 1798; Will Book M1, pg. 20.

A final overview of the Pasquotank area Cartwrights might be had from a look at the earliest census records. The 1790[7] census, even with heads of households only being named, can help to identify or eliminate various persons when trying to trace those Cartwrights who moved westward to other areas from Pasquotank. Listed below in alphabetical order are those Cartwrights found in Pasquotank, and in Camden County which was taken from Pasquotank in 1777. Since headings for the columns would be too long, the explanation is given here: The number in the first column after the name is Free White Males Over the Age of Sixteen; the next column is Free White Males Under the Age of Sixteen; the next is Free White Females, (all ages); the fourth column is All Other Free Person; and the last column is Slaves:

Pasquotank County

Name	FWM >16	FWM <16	FWF	Other Free	Slaves
Ahaz Cartwright	1	6	2	0	0
Benjamin Cartwright	1	0	1	0	0
Caleb Cartwright	1	4	3	0	10
Clement Cartwright	1	1	1	0	9
Darius Cartwright	1	1	2	0	2
Elizabeth Cartwright	0	0	1	0	1
Hezekiah Cartwright	1	1	0	0	0
Hezekiah Cartwright	2	0	0	0	0
Isaac Cartwright	1	2	1	0	0

James Cartwright	1	1	3	0	0
Jehu Cartwright	1	3	4	0	0
Jesse Cartwright	1	4	1	0	2
John Cartwright	1	2	4	0	1
John Cartwright	1	4	4	0	0
Martha Cartwright	0	0	1	0	3
Robert Cartwright	1	1	2	0	0
Simon Cartwright	1	1	4	0	0
Thomas Cartwright	1	4	2	0	1
Thomas Cartwright	1	0	3	0	0
Thomas Cartwright, Jr.	1	1	1	0	0

Camden County

Ann Cartwright	0	1	2	0	0
Caleb Cartwright	1	3	3	0	3
Daniel Cartwright	1	1	1	0	2
Edy Cartwright	0	1	1	0	0
Elijah Cartwright	1	0	0	0	0
Hosea Cartwright	1	0	0	0	0
Isaac Cartwright	1	1	1	0	0
Jabez Cartwright	1	1	5	0	0
Jacob Cartwright	2	1	3	0	0
James Cartwright	1	3	3	0	1
Jesse Cartwright	1	0	0	0	0
John Cartwright	1	0	4	0	0
Morgan Cartwright	1	1	1	0	5
Moses Cartwright	1	2	2	0	0
Robert Cartwright	2	1	2	0	0
Robert Cartwright	1	1	2	0	5
Samuel Cartwright	1	1	1	0	2
Tulle Cartwright	1	1	2	0	0

From a close study of the above census lists and figures, one could likely glean some idea, in certain cases, of the relation of these persons to the Cartwrights shown in the earlier records. Since many of these Cartwrights can probably be traced through later censuses, land records, and wills, there is little need for me to enter into any speculative analysis here.

At this point there should be some further discussion of Camden County. Unfortunately, there is very little that *can* be said. As stated, Camden was formed from Pasquotank in 1777, but most or all of the original early records of the county have somehow been lost. Wills on record do not begin until 1859, and the status is similar for land and court records. Testimony of various persons was that the Federal troops burned all the records during the Civil War, although Mitchell comments in his 'Testator's Index' that there is actually no evidence that the Courthouse or its contents were ever burned. All the same, the fact that no one has been able to find the records leaves us with little recourse in researching persons who resided in that specific area. The censuses are perhaps the only means we have of identifying persons who have been 'swallowed up' by Camden, as I tend to think of it. On the other hand, local historians in such places often manage to find ways to cope with a dearth of official records, at least in part. It could be helpful for anyone closely interested in the area to visit or write to the local libraries in an effort to determine what types of 'fill-in' records might be available, which I have not done.

Below are the pertinent Cartwrights, of Pasquotank and Camden Counties, who were still in evidence as of the 1800 census[8]:

Calib Cartwright	Camden Co.
Christopher Cartwright	Pasquotank Co.
Clement Cartwright	Pasquotank Co.
Daniel Cartwright	Camden Co.
Ezekiel Cartwright	Pasquotank Co.
Hezekiah Cartwright	Pasquotank Co.
Isaac Cartwright	Camden Co.
Isare (?) Cartwright	Camden Co.
James Cartwright	Camden Co.
James Cartwright	Pasquotank Co.
Jehu Cartwright	Pasquotank Co.
Jesse Cartwright	Camden Co.
Joab Cartwright	Camden Co.
Job Cartwright	Pasquotank Co.

John Cartwright	Camden Co.
John Cartwright	Pasquotank Co.
John Cartwright	Pasquotank Co.
John Cartwright	Pasquotank Co.
John Cartwright	Pasquotank Co.
Joseph Cartwright	Camden Co.
Joseph Cartwright	Pasquotank Co.
Josiah Cartwright	Pasquotank Co.
Mark Cartwright	Camden Co.
Moses Cartwright	Camden Co.
Parthinia Cartwright	Pasquotank Co.
Robert Cartwright	Camden Co.
Saba Cartwright	Camden Co.
Thomas Cartwright	Pasquotank Co.
Thomas Cartwright	Pasquotank Co.
Timothy Cartwright	Camden Co.
William Cartwright	Camden Co.
Wm. Cartwright	Pasquotank Co.
Zelly Cartwright	Camden Co.

Bibliography of Sources for Chapter Eight

1. 'Pasquotank County, North Carolina, Record of Deeds 1700-1751' compiled by Gwen Boyer Bjorkman. Heritage Books, Inc., Bowie, MD.
2. 'Abstracts of North Carolina Wills,' (1690-1760) compiled by J. Bryan Grimes, Secretary of State. Genealogical Publishing Co., Inc., Baltimore, MD. 1991.
3. 'Old Albemarle County North Carolina, Pasquotank Precinct (County), Births, Marriages, Deaths, Brands and Flesh Marks, & County Claims 1691-1833' by Weynette Parks Haun, 243 Argonne Drive, Durham, N. C. 27704. 1981.
4. Pasquotank County, North Carolina marriages, as obtained on microfilm from the North Carolina State Archives through the Interlibrary Loan System, and transcribed for the author by Willa Sorensen of Goodyear, Arizona. (Major libraries can provide information as to how to use the Interlibrary Loan system.)
5. 'An Abstract of North Carolina Wills, From About 1760 to About 1800' by Fred A. Olds. Originally published Oxford, 1925; Reprinted Southern Book Company, Baltimore, MD. 1954; Reissued Genealogical Publishing Co., Inc., Baltimore, MD., 1965-1983. Reprinted by Genealogical Publishing Co. for Clearfield Company Inc., 1990.
6. 'North Carolina Wills, A Testator Index' by Thornton W. Mitchell. Genealogical Publishing Co., Inc., Baltimore, MD. 1992, 1993.
7. 'Heads of Families at the First Census of the United States Taken in the Year 1790'. Originally published Government Printing Office, Washington, D. C. 1908. Reprinted Genealogical Publishing Co., Inc., Baltimore, MD., 1966-1992.
8. 'Index to the 1800 Census of North Carolina' compiled by Elizabeth Petty Bentley. Ibid., 1977.

Chapter
Nine

Miscellaneous Cartwright Data

There is much data to be explored concerning various
Cartwrights whom I have not been able to fit directly into the outlines
of any of the families already examined. Some of these 'unknown'
Cartwrights are certainly members of the lines discussed and are
simply without enough documentation to be connected. Others are
barely mentioned, leaving a gaping question as to their familial
identity.

By setting out here all the other important references that I
have found in various places within the pertinent regions, I hope to
give others the chance to assess the data at length and perhaps come
up with more data, or to be able to see a connection that I have
overlooked. Again, I am certainly not claiming to have found every
piece of data available on Cartwrights in the areas under study; nor
even to have included every small tidbit that I have uncovered. In
some cases where the mentions seemed so brief or inconsequential as
to be of little help, or in which the data was merely repetitive of other
sources, I have avoided complicating the work with them. I cannot
stress too much, therefore, the need for anyone who is closely
interested in any particular set of Cartwrights to make the effort on

their own to examine original sources and/or reference volumes as given in the Bibliographies. There may be other perspectives which shed more light on various bits of information, and there may be descendants of the people investigated in this volume who have more data than I have had available to me. This book should be a tremendously helpful guide, but not the final say concerning the numerous Cartwrights of the specific areas under study.

Virginia

Going back to the beginning with the Virginia records, there are Cartwrights mentioned in various sources as transportees, headrights, and immigrants to Virginia who must be shown here for a sense of thoroughness, although most of them are seemingly never heard from again insofar as later data or descendants are concerned. Aside from those already mentioned elsewhere in this volume, below I am including the remainder who are listed as being destined for Virginia in the collective source 'Passenger and Immigration Lists Index'[1] (which work is readily available for perusal in most large libraries):

Elizabeth Cartwright   to Virginia 1739
Hugh Cartwright   to Virginia 1663-1679
James Cartwright, age 30   to Virginia 1700
Sybilla Cartwright   to Virginia 1683

Aside from those early colonists already discussed such as John Cartwright, Thomas Cartwright, and Robert Cartwright, (the latter of Surry County, Virginia), there are found in the early records of Virginia[2] as headrights transported by others, the following persons:

Paul Cartwright, headright, with others, of **Samuell Mathewes, Govr.**, 23 November 1657.
Rolph Cartwright, headright, with others, of **John Williams**, 11 March 1658.
Richard Cartwright, headright, along with the **Robert Cartwright** already mentioned, of **Mr. Arthur Allin**, 24 August 1665.
Mary Cartwright, headright, with others, of **John Prosser**, 8 October 1665.

The volumes collected by the noted Beverley Fleet[3] are an important source of the early records of Virginia. (And I must say here that I just adore Mr. Fleet's work. His compilations are most entertaining to read, both in their own form and per his running commentary. Remarks in parentheses below, however, are my own) Among them are found the following abstracts concerning Cartwrights:

Paul Cartrewright (sic) shown again as a headright, this time transported by **Howell Pryse**, with a date of roughly 1655-58. (Under the records of Charles City County.)

Benjam. Cartwright---(pg. 135 of Charles City County Court Orders 1655-1658): **Antho: Allen** sworne saith That he went along w'th **Martin Quelch** to receive a hdd of tobbo from **Benjam. Cartwright** and that the sd Quelch demanded the Country Levies of the sd Cartwright and the sd Cartwright sayd he would not pay him the tobbo in the cask but the sherr should follow him and receive it where he had it oweing him and behanged if he would, and further saith not.

Beniain Cartwright (sic)---(pg. 138 of Charles City County Court Orders 1658-1661): On confession of **Beniain: Cartwright**, he is ord. to pay **Tho. Drewe** 415 lb. tobo.

Ben: Cartwright---(pg. 140, same records): Whereas **Ben: Cartwright** is arrested to this Co'rt and convict by evidences for opprobrious language uttered agst the sherr in contempt of this office and consiquently of the authority whence it derives: Itt is therefore ordered that the sd Cartwright be imediately punished w'th two lashes on his bare sholders for his sd abuse, and pay all cost occasconed in the suite agst him, als exec. (meaning, 'also the costs of the execution', etc.) Upon request and intercession of **Howell Pryse** and recantation and submission of **Ben: Cartwright** the Co'rt is pleased to remitt and release the corporall punishm't adjudged and to be inflicted on the sd Cartwright.

(Poor Benjamin was obviously a little hot-headed---a Cartwright trait to which I can personally attest. Even though all those Cartwright males whom I have known are generally possessed of impeccable manners and a rigid sense of justice, they are all somewhat reminiscent in truth of the 'Bonanza' group.)

Benj. Cartwright---(pg. 162, same records): Ordered that **Benj. Cartwright** pay **Howell Pryse** 350 lb tobo according to bill. (Evidently Benjamin was not only hotheaded, but lacking in gratitude. Then again, we don't know the full circumstances of this situation.)

Elizabeth Cartwright, Jane Cartwright, Sarah Cartwright---(pg. 545, Charles City County Court Orders 1664-1665): Order that **Wm Bushell** deliver to **Elizabeth** and **Sarah** the daughters of **Jane** his wife, who was the relict of _____**Cartwright**, each of them a cow and calf "in satisfaction of a cow and their increase given them by a deed of **Joseph Clarkes** vide orphans Booke fo: 35".

Wm. Cartwright, found on a long list of those transported by **Howell Pryse**, 1655-1658.

It might appear from these records that **Paul Cartwright, Benjamin Cartwright**, and **Wm. Cartwright** must have been related, and that the woman **Jane** was the wife of one of them, at least. But there is no direct statement to clarify any relationships among these Cartwrights. The **Henry Cartwright** below appears to be the same one who is listed as an immigrant to Maryland, as mentioned previously. It is interesting, in light of seeing the name Henry used in a family of Cartwrights to be seen presently in another part of Virginia, and which family seems to have clear connections to that of Peter of Maryland. It makes one wonder if this Henry could have been a brother of Matthew, the immigrant.

From the same source (Fleet's abstracts):

Hen. Cartwright---(Northumberland County Records 1652-1655): **Tho Hawkins** agt **Hen Cartwright**. **Cartwright** came into Court and ack. a Judgmt of 250 lb of tobo to **Hawkins**. (Here we go again.)

Hen. Cartwright---(same records): **Hen. Cartwright** agt **Tho. Hailes**. Case referred to next Court.

Hen. Cartwright---(same records): **James Claughton** agt **Thomas Phillpott** att of **Hen. Cartwright**. "Whereas **James**

219

Claughton informed the Court that he was arrested at the suite of **Thomas Philpott** Atturney of **Henry Cartwright** and the said **Phillpot** does not declare against him", The Court declares **Phillpot** nonsuited, etc.

Henry Cartwright---(same records): **Mr. Newman** agt **Henry Cartwright. Cartwright** owing **Mr. Robert Newman** 480 lb tobo is ordered to pay.

Hen. Cartwright---(same records): **Geo. Thompson** and **Hen. Cartwright** their Bill to **John Dandy**. (Entry mutilated) **Thompson** and **Cartwright** to **John Dandy** and **Thomas Maidwell**. Dated 3rd July ----. Wit: **Tho. Philpot** his mark. Rec. 20th September 1652.

Henry Cartwright---(same records): Witness on Assignment of patent, **Tho. Broughton** to **Tho. Ellis**. (notes record mutilated) fragment bears date 21 November 1653. Signed **Tho. Brough---**. Wit: **Phillip Carpenter, Henry Cartwright**. Rec. 21 Nov 1653.

hinery Cartwright---(Northumbria Collecteana 1645-1720): **hinery Cartwright** signs oath to Commonwealth. 13 Apl 1652.

Found on the quit rent rolls of Norfolk County, Virginia[4] for the year 1704 is **Peter Cartwright**, with 1050 acres. (Ms. Granberry Walter notes on her Cartwright chart that this Peter's wife was named Mary, and that the latter married 2nd John Dale, which marriage is found in various sources and given in another part of this volume; also that Peter had children Margritt, Cibell, and Afiah; will on record Norfolk County, Va.) Also shown is '**Widd'o' Cartwright**, with 800 acres. Found on the quit rent rolls of Princess Anne County are **John Cartwright**, who of course is the one already studied, with 100 acres; and **Robert Cartwright**, with 260 acres.

In a List of land patents granted during the years 1710-1718, (same source) there is found a grant of 400 acres to **Thomas Cartwright** and **Eliza. Boboe**, April 1, 1717, in King William County. What the relationship was to Eliza. Boboe is not indicated, but this Thomas Cartwright is studied further, shortly.

Early Cartwright marriages in Virginia, which are not noted elsewhere[5,6]:

Sally Cartwright with **James Hearn**, April 2nd 1763. Teste: **James Hearn, W. Nimmo, Lem. Newton**. Princess Anne Co., Virginia.

John Cartwright and **Sally Bosman**, 12 March 1787, Southampton Co,, Virginia.

Mrs. Mary Cartwright and **John Dale**, 28 August 1727, Norfolk Co., Virginia.

Seth Cartwright and **Mary Lovering**, 1 September 1792, Fairfax Co., Virginia.

Southward Cartwright and **Jacamine West**, 28 October 1797, Princess Anne Co., Virginia.

Thomas Cartwright and **Mrs. Susanah Esther**, 5 December 1772, Norfolk Co., Virginia.

William Cartwright and **Martha Biddle**, 8 December 1779, Princess Anne Co., Virginia.

William Cartwright and **Frances Weblin**, 1 November 1785, Princess Anne Co., Virginia.

The following are brief excerpts from 18th Century newspapers'[7]:

'**Cartwright, John**, gunner, upwards of 40, ran away from the *Norfolk's Revenge* galley in Chickahominy River. (Virginia Gazette as pub. by Alexander Purdie, 14 June 1776.)

'**Cartwright, Thomas**, Eng. svt., bricklayer, ca. 22, ran away from **William Shedden**, Essex Co. (Virginia Gazette, 29 June 1776.)

Found in the records of Spotsylvania County, Virginia[8] (which was taken from parts of King William County, Essex County, and King and Queen County, in the year 1721) are several references to the **Thomas Cartwright** noted previously:

23 July 1728: **James Taylor** of Drysdale Par., King and Queen Co., to **Thomas Cartwright** of the said par. and county. 140 a. in St. Geo. Par., Spts. Co.---part of pat. granted sd. **Taylor** July 21, 1722. Witnesses: **Zachary Taylor, George Taylor**. Rec. Augt. 6, 1728.

Martha Taylor, wife of **James Taylor**, acknowledged her dower in the above land to the sd. **Cartwright**.

1 June 1739: **Peter x Gustavus** and **Mary**, his wife, of Amelia Co., to **William Sandige** of Spts. Co. 25 lbs. curr. 450 a. in St. Geo. Par., Spts. Co. (witnesses) **Thomas Cartwright, George x Willcox, George Sheppard.** (Another deed of same to **Joseph Peterson**, dated 29 April 1739, same witnesses.)

7 May 1745: **Thomas Cartwright**, witness on a deed of **Nicholas Hawkins** to **Nathan Hawkins**, both of St. Geo. Par., Spts. Co.. Land was first granted to **Larkin Chew**, sold to **William Lindsay**, then to **Nicholas Hawkins.** Other witnesses: **Parmenas Bowker, Alexander Hawkins**.

6 June 1749: **Thomas Cartwright** of Spts. Co. and **Rachel**, his wife, to **Joseph Holloday** of sd. County. 43 lb. curr. 80 a. in St. Geo. Par., Spts. Co. Witnesses, **John Crittenden Webb, Wm. x Gholeston, Henry Sparks**.

7 Dec. 1742: **Thomas Cartwright** witness on the will of **John Holloday** of St. George's Parish in King William Co., who d. Nov. 4, 1742. Other witnesses, **John Waller, John Waller, Jr.** The will mentions: sons **Joseph** and **Benjamin Holloday**, son-in-law **William Pulliam**, son **William Holloday**, land where **Thomas Certain** formerly lived, son **John Holloday**, land where **James Perry, Jr.** lived, son **Daniell Holloday**, daughter **Elizabeth** now the wife of **Patterson Pulliam**, daughter **Winifred** now the wife of **Thomas Pulliam**, daughter **Sarah** now the wife of **James Rollings**, land adjoining 'tract I sold to **Thomas Burch**', daughter **Susanna Holloday**, land adjoining **Mr. Wyat's** land.

3 April 1750: **John Holloday** admr. of **Thomas Cartwright**, decd., with **Anthony Foster**, sec.

Torrence's 'Wills and Administrations'[9] lists the following Cartwrights for whom inventories of estate are on record. (Not including those who are already mentioned or studied elsewhere.) These are all of Princess Anne County:

Jno. Cartright, 1704, inventory. (Ms. Walter notes the fact that this was likely the husband of the 'Widdo' Cartwright' found on the 1704 quit rent rolls; and that the first Jno. shown hereafter may have been his son.)
Wm. Cartwright 1725, inventory.
Jno. Cartwright, 1727, inventory.
Wm. Cartwright, 1731, inventory.
Jno. Cartwright, 1733, inventory.
(One of the men named William Cartwright here may have been the father of Mary who married William Gaston, as shown in the set of abstracted Princess Anne County deeds, Chapter Seven.)

Virginia Military data[10]:

Justinian Cartwright, entered service 1776 in Amherst County, Virginia; Born 22 February 1752, moved to Caldwell County, Kentucky ca 1782. m. 1777 **Frances Gillespie** who d. late 1818; pension 1819 in Caldwell Co. Kentucky. Died there 27 December 1832. Surviving children in 1846 were: **James A. Cartwright, Polly M.**, wife of **Elisha Thurman, Bennett G. Cartwright, Nancy S. Cartwright, Levin L. Cartwright** who resided in Mississippi, **Justinian Cartwright, Winnefred Cartwright, Sally**, wife of **Leonard Brown, Terresa**, wife of **Tutt Brown**. Information from **A. J. Cartwright** of San Francisco, CA.

Peter Cartwright, entered service 1777/8 in Amherst County, Virginia; m. 1787 **Christina Garven**. (Marriage Bond 27 February 1787, signed by William Cartwright.) Moved to Kentucky 1791, and died in Caldwell Co. 1809/10. Children: **Reverend Peter Cartwright, Rosanna Vineyard, Polly Pentecost**. (Records related to pension application state that two of Peter's brothers were killed in action at the Battle of Brandywine.)

These men of the above records may possibly have been sons of the **Thomas Cartwright** of Spotsylvania, shown earlier. Both **Justinian** and **Peter**, though having moved their families to Kentucky, are seen occasionally in Tennessee records. **Peter, Jr.**, or the **Rev. Peter Cartwright**, was of course the celebrated 'Backwoods Preacher' of the Cumberland Settlement[11]. **Justinian** is noted in a couple of other different sources, as below:

17 November 1790, pg. 174 of Davidson County, Tennessee Will Book 1[12]: **Justinian Cartwright** of Davidson Co., N. C. sells a horse to **Robert Cartwright** of the same place.

Deed Book #1 of Sumner Co., Tenn. 1793-1797, pg. 13 (same source): **Just. Cartwright** to **Jas. Gambling**. (No details given.)

Justinian Cartwright, Esq., age 78, married on the 4th inst. by the **Rev. Mr. Wilcox** to **Mrs. Mary Harris** aged 75, both of Caldwell County, Ky. National Banner & Nashville Whig. (Wed., Nov. 24, 1830.)[12] Note that as per above abstracts from his military records, Justinian died just a couple of years later.

An examination of Amherst County, Virginia records is in order, considering the indication that the above Cartwrights' resided there. Among the early marriage records of the county[13], we find not only the marriage of **Peter Cartwright** and **Christina Garvin** as related above, but also the following:

John Cartwright, widower, and **Martha Patterson**, spinster, July 31, 1779. **George Galaspie**, surety. Consent of **Martha**.
Ann Cartwright, spinster, and **Samuel Bibe** (or Bybee), bachelor, November 2, 1789. **Edward Ware**, surety. **Samuel Bibe** stated that he was of lawful age. **Anny Cartwright** stated that she was of lawful age.
Lydia Cartwright, spinster, and **Thomas Fitzpatrick**, bachelor, October 21, 1793. **Joseph Roberts**, surety, who stated that **Lydia** was over 21 years of age.
Ann Cartwright, spinster, and **William Lovegrove**, widower, March 23, 1794. **Samuel Brown**, surety. Consent of **Ann**.
Sally Cartwright, spinster, and **Nicholas Moran, Jr.**, December 9,

1799. **Ambrose Moran**, surety. Consent of her father, **John Cartwright**. **Elijah Moran** made oath that **Nicholas Moran, Jr.** was above 21 years of age.

Note that the names Lydia and Ann, used in the Amherst family of Cartwrights along with Peter and John, are strongly reminiscent of Peter Cartwright's family in Maryland. Also, there is a **Notley Maddox** who is found in the records of Amherst County, Virgina. As stated in Part I, there were numerous men of that name in the Maddox family, through several generations. I can find a Notley Maddox in nearly every place where Cartwrights are present, so that the fact may not be a direct help in estblishing which line of Cartwrights were the origins of those under discussion. But taken with the other evidence of similar given names for these Cartwrights, it adds to the compulsion to identify them as Maryland Cartwrights of Peter's line. It is my inclinaton, as mentioned, to think that the **Thomas Cartwright** of King William County--Spotsylvania County may have been the son of Peter, with these Cartwrights of Amherst being in turn Thomas's children. But since there is no direct proof of either connection, I have been compelled to relegate the data to this miscellaneous section.

There are further bits of data in the records of Amherst County, Virginia, which confuse matters greatly concerning some of the other Cartwrights who are under examination. Note the name **George Galaspie** as surety on the marraige of **John Cartwright,** found among the marriage records of Amherst County. It should be recalled that **Justinian Cartwright** is shown to have married **Frances Gillespie**, by his abstracted pension records. Next, I should explain here that there seems to be some question concerning Justinian's given name in certain instances, for the source of the abstracted pension records given earlier lists a **Jesse Cartwright**, with the reference 'see **Justinian Cartwright**'. But then the reference concerning Justinian does not mention a Jesse at all. Another source containing the same pension abstract refers to the subject of the application as '**Justinian or Jesse Cartwright**'. Thus, there must have been some confusion of names in the original pension papers themselves.

In the abstracted will records of Amherst County,[14] there are a number of brief references to the estate of a **George Gillespie** (Gellaspy, Galaspy, etc.). Listed among the legatees are **Jesse**

Cartwright and wife **Fanny**. (! Is this the Blount County, Tennessee couple of the same names?) A **Jas. Cartwright** is one of the committee to file a report. Dated December 16, 1811.

While we have seen from other areas of study that there can be different Cartwrights whose given names are the same and who also have wives of the same name, it is still necessary to to consider whether this couple named Jesse and Fanny Cartwright might be the same as those found in the records of Blount County, Tennessee. There is the added clue of a James Cartwright being connected with them in both places, and it should be recalled that there was a **James Gillespie** mentioned as a neighbor of Jesse Cartwright in one of the court records of Blount County, Tennessee. Obviously there is some connection here, but an attempt to reason out the possibilities without a closer examination of the original records from which the abstracts were taken becomes rather confusing in itself. Is the Jesse Cartwright who is named in the estate of George Gillespie being confused with Justinian? Did Justinian possibly have a son named Jesse, and if so, was he the Jesse Cartwright of Blount County, Tennessee rather than the latter being a son of Matthew Cartwright of Halifax County, North Carolina?

The second possibility seems doubtful, because the Gillespie records seem to indicate that the 'Fanny' named as wife of Jesse Cartwright must have been a daughter or grandaughter of George Gillespie. Such records do not usually name the wife in such a manner unless the wife herself is the actual heir. In which case, to postulate Jesse Cartwright as a son of Justinian would mean that both father and son had wives named Frances Gillespie. This is nonsensical even if not entirely impossible. The only explanation for both men being related to this family with wives of similar or identical given names would be if Jesse's wife was a much younger member of the family than Justinian's, perhaps being a neice of Justinian's wife, etc. Even in that case, it certainly isn't likely that Jesse and Justinian were father and son, but perhaps of some less close relation.

One might briefly entertain the notion that Jesse and Justinian were the same man, but the fact that they were two different men seems beyond question, in light of the various records concerning them. Justinian was older than the Jesse of Blount County, and the woman named 'Fanny' who was apparently wife of the latter was clearly still living at the time of the 1830 census, while Justinian's wife is shown by the pension record to have died in 1818. Justinian himself was age 78 when he entered the second marriage as shown earlier. Further, Justinian is shown by that and other records to have lived in Kentucky, even if seen for a while in records of Middle Tennessee.

Notwithstanding the confusion concerning the given name in the pension papers (which could possibly be cleared up by an examination of a microfilm copy of the original record) it seems likely to me that the Jesse Cartwright of the Gillespie records was of some other relation to those Cartwrights in Virginia. If he was a cousin, for instance, it could be that he met his wife 'Fanny', heir of George Gillespie, through visiting the Virginia Cartwrights whose connections were the Gillespies. There is nothing to indicate whether the couple named **Jesse** and **Fanny Cartwright** were actually in Amherst County at the time of the administration of the estate of **George Gillespie**. Obviously it is the latter possibility that I tend to believe, since I have proffered the evidence of the trail from Halifax County, North Carolina to Blount County, Tennessee as being strong. However, it is also possible that the Thomas Cartwright of Blount County, Tennessee was a son of Matthew but that Jesse was not his brother.

Whatever the case, the appearance that nearly all the Cartwrights of divers places were related to each other becomes more and more convincing. Even those separated into the two lines of the progenitors **John Cartwright** and **Matthew Cartwright** are so intermingled with each other in Tennessee and other areas that it is very difficult to separate them. The best we can do is to examine all the available records very closely, and make further investigations where possible.

Neither are we finished with finding Cartwrights in Virginia. There is a group of Cartwrights seen in the early records of Hampshire County[15] (now West Virginia), and again the given names used seem to indicate they may have been of the family of Peter Cartwright from Maryland, and/or perhaps being the same as those already discussed per the Amherst County records. Furthermore, it can be seen again that a number of persons who are connected with the Cartwrights of both Halifax County, North Carolina and of Blount County, Tennesse are mentioned in the Hampshire County, Va.-West Va. records. But none of them seem to have been there for very long. Below are the references, with a **Peter Cartwright** shown there as early as 1765 and the other records mostly pertaining to the mid-1780's. The only one of the pertinent group who is actually seen in the census of 1782 for Hampshire Co. is a **Sam 'Cutright'**, noted as being 'gone' in 1784 even though his name is seen in other records after that date. The compiler of the abstracts notes in a foreword that many of the persons dealing in land there were never residents of the area.

Despite the mispellings in some cases, it is clear that the persons referred to in the records below are Cartwrights:

3 October 1765: **Peter Cutright** witness on lease and release, **Maunis Alkier** and wife **Lydia** to **Michael Thorn**, (all parties of Hampshire Co.) Other witnesses: **Christian Bingamon, Adam Brown**.

20 April 1778: **Samuel Cartwright** signed as a witness on a mortgage, **Mary Creamour** to **Simon Ahrsam** and wife **Mary**, (all parties of Hampshire Co.) 385 a., S. Branch R., Rec. 12 May 1778. Other witnesses are **Sam Hornback** and **Simon Hornback**.

3 March 1778: **Sam C. Curtright**, witness on the will of **Daniel Hornbeck**. Other witnesses are **Simon Hornbeck** and **Charles Myers**. Named in the will are wife **Magdelene**, executor with **William Hornback**; 3 child. **Abraham, James**, and **Solomon**; to **Abraham Coffman**; **Elizabeth Anderson**, wife of **John**, and their dau; to **Thomas Leary's** child. **Daniel, Dennis**, and one dau.; **John Anderson's** 3 child. **Mary, Thomas**, and **Margaret**.

6 March 1780: **Thomas, Lord Fairfax** of the Northern Neck of Va. to **Samuel Cutright** of Hampshire Co. 137 a. on South Branch. Rec. 14 March 1780. Witnesses: **Robert Stephen, G. Jones, Andrew Wodrow**.

24 May 1783: **Henry Cartwright** signed as a witness on a deed of **Benjamin Robinson** to **Benjamin Bean**, both of Hampshire Co. 49

a. on South Branch River. Rec. 11 November 1783. Other witnesses: **Andrew Wodrow, Sylvester Ward**.

17 September 1783: **Samuel Curtright** witness on a deed of **Abraham Hornback** to **Samuel Hornback**, both of Hampshire Co. 17 a. on South Br. R., Rec. 11 November 1783. Other witnesses: **Joseph Nevill, Charles Myers, Daniel McNeill, John Obannan, Abel Randall**.

25 August 1785: **Samuel Cartwright, Peter Cartwright**, and **Richard Cartwright** of Hampshire Co., to **Moses Hutton** of same. 86 a. on South Branch R.. Rec. 8 November 1785. Witnesses: **Andrew Wodrow, Peter Higgins, Jonathan Heath, Abel Randall, Jacob Yoakum**.

25 August 1785: **Samuel Cartwright** of Hampshire Co., to **Moses Hutton** of same. 137 a. on South Branch R., Rec. 8 November 1785. (Same witnesses)

9 May 1786: **Peter Cartwright** of Fayette Co. to **John Hornbeck**, Atty. **Power of Attorney**. Authority to make deeds of lease and release of a tract of land in Hardy Co., of 86 acres to **Moses Hutton**. Rec. 13 February 1787. Witnesses: **P. Patterson, Eli Clurland**.

Connected persons found mentioned in these records of Hampshire Co. are a **Foreman** family with many of the given names which are seen among those in Halifax County, North Carolina, related to the Tippetts. The abstracted records concerning them in this Hampshire Co. source are too numerous to reproduce here, but there is a **Benjamin Foreman**, a **William Foreman**, a **John Foreman**, etc., and several of these men's wives are named in various records. There appears to be no way to tell if these could be the same or at least a closely related group. But also, the abstracts below demonstrate the presence of a **Henry Franks**, though whether he is the same one as found in connection with the Cartwrights in Blount County is uncertain, as well:

20 October 1792: **James Waterman** and wife **Leah** to **Henry Franks**, (all parties of Hampshire Co.) 100 a. on New Creek. Rec. 30 October 1792. Witnesses: **Ed McCarthy, Samuel Ravenscroft, J. Wheeler.**

23 November 1793: **Henry Franks** witness on a deed of **John Reed** to **Henry Miller**, of Hampshire Co. 198 a. on Patterson Creek; Rec. 11 December 1793. Other witnesses are **Michael Miller, David Cotrel.**

1 December 1796: **Henry Frank** and **George Frank**, of Fayette Co., Pa. to **Osborn Sprigg** of Hampshire Co. 157 a. in Hampshire Co., Rec. 19 December 1796. Witnesses: **Samuel Beckwith, Michl. Cresap, John J. Jacob, Thomas Cresap.**

There is yet another apparent connection with Blount County, Tennessee, since there is also a **Thomas Noble** to be seen in the early records of Hampshire County. There are several other surnames which are familiar from Halifax County, North Carolina---**Hines, Barnes, Haynes**, etc. All of this is not full proof that there is a genuine relationship between the Cartwrights seen in the records of Hampshire County and those whom we followed from Halifax, North Carolina through Tennessee, but there is enough to make it unlikely that it is all just a coincidence. Most probably, as I have indicated before, the connection is that these Cartwrights of Virginia/West Virgina were descended from Peter of Maryland.

It may be some of the same Cartwrights who are found referenced in some slightly earlier records[16], when all of the territory west of the Blue Ridge Mountains was termed Augusta County, Virginia. Once again, there are many surnames of persons found in this general collection by the compiler, Chalkey, which are familiar from various places where Cartwrights have been examined. Set forth below are the pertinent references that I have found in this valuable source. I have included references in which it seems to me the name should be Cartwright, but it has been spelled otherwise:

Abstracts of Wills of Augusta County, Virginia, Will Book 1; Page 165, 19th April 1749: **James Coburn's** appraisement. (Many names listed, including a Hornback, which seems to connect this Cartwright with the Hampshire County records). Due from **Henry Cartwright**. (No details.)

Deed Book No. 1, Augusta County: 22d February 1753. **Hendrick Cortreght**, witness on a deed of **Peter Reed** and 'Cathern' (his wife?) of So. Fork of So. Br. of Potomac, to **Peter Hoos**, of same. 680 acres, Gr. So. Br. of Potomac. Other witnesses: **Peter Thorn, Tobias Decker**.

Augusta County Will Book 1, page 491: 22nd March 1753, **Benjamin Scot's** bond as administrator c. t. a. of **James Scot**, with sureties **Michael Harness, Henry Curtract**.

Augusta County Order Book No. 3, page 419: March 22, 1753. A list of militia officers, including **Henry Cartwright**, 'qualified Ensign of Foot'.

Augusta County Court Records, Order Book No. IX., page 91. August 24, 1764: With little detail about the context, and apparently just as a list of names of those present in court, the record lists among others **Sarah Cartwright**, servant of **John McNeill**.

Same Order Book, page 307, dated March 23, 1765: (Perhaps not very appealing as a reference, but important all the same) **Sarah Cartright** and **James Burns**, servant of **John McClenachan**, cured of venerial (sic) disease. (Note by compiler says 'many of same'.)

Found on a list of Delinquents: 1767, **Col. Preston's** list: (among many others) **Peter Cutright**, runaway. And on 'A List of Levys returned bad by **John Smith** for 1773-1774', a person who *may* have been a Cartwright, though the name seems mangled: **Jno. Counrodright**.

Will Book No. 4, page 411: 13th August 1771, **John Berry's** estate appraisement. Among several others, **Peter Cutwright**, solvent.

Military Records. Compiler notes that these declarations were gathered by **Dr. Joseph T. McAllister** of Hot Springs, Virginia, from many different counties. (But presumably all from areas which were once included in the frontier territory of Augusta.): **Alexander Scott's** Declaration, August 21, 1832. Free man of color, born in Culpepper 1752; in 1781 he entered the Artillery Company of **Capt. Ambrose Bohannon**, Regiment of **Col. Samuel Hawes**, as a substitute for **Jestima Cartwright**; first marched to the Barracks at Cumberland Court House to guard prisoners; remembers **Major Landrum**, Captains **Eskridge** and **Brown**, and **Lieut. Drew**. **William Thurman** testifies that he saw Scott in the Army. **William Lavender**, a Revolutionary soldier, also testifies to Scott's services.

It seems to me that the 'Jestima' Cartwright mentioned above is probably <u>Justinian,</u> in which case this is another example of confusion concerning his given name. This one puts it even closer to Jesse, making one wonder if Justinian may have sometimes gone by Jesse as a nickname, etc.

Perhaps at this point I should summarize by recalling data from the Maryland investigation which might give possibilites for the origins of these Virginia Cartwrights. Recall that the will of Peter Cartwright named sons Robert, Thomas, Samuel, and Gustavus, with the indication that there were sons not named. Recall also that there was a marriage record for a Jesse Cartwright, in those early Maryland sources; and that there seemed to have been a John Cartwright who was not satisfactorily accounted for among the other sons of Matthew the Immigrant, and their children. The possibilities are that the Jesse Cartwright in question was a son of Peter; and that his own descendants moved westward through Virginia, being the origin of the given name Jesse as used in several branches of the family; that the son Thomas of Peter was the same as the one shown in the records of King William and Spotsylvania Counties, Virginia; and that Justinian Cartwright was of one of these families. On the other hand, there is an equal possibility that the Thomas Cartwright of King William/Spotsylvania, Virgina was the original son Thomas of Matthew the Immigrant, who was not seen in any of the records of Maryland after the mention in his father's will. Since the latter was one of the younger sons of Matthew, the date of death for the Thomas

232

of Spotsylvania in 1749 seems a reasonable correlation. And though I have postulated in Part I of this work that the said Thomas, son of Matthew Cartwright the immigrant to Maryland, was the first husband of Sarah Burroughs Carter, it is still possible that the deceased husband of said Sarah was some other Cartwright who was completely unseen in any of the records due to his early date of death. It is this kind of open-minded reasoning that is the best we can do when there is an absence of records to delineate the lines, but in some of the cases of speculation there is a chance of solving the puzzles with more definitive attempts to locate other records.

North Carolina

I have not found a great deal of data concerning Cartwrights in other parts of North Carolina, before the turn of the Nineteenth Century. For starters, however, there is what I tend to think of as some 'spillover' of the Pasquotank Cartwrights into Perquimans County, which neighbors Pasquotank to the southwest. It appears to me that the data there may answer the question of the origins of the name Peter among the Pasquotank group. And there is a **John Cartwright** in evidence in Perquimans County quite early, so that he most likely was the son of Thomas the elder who seems to have died in 1714. This leaves the parentage of the Peter Cartwright shown in later Perquimans records unknown, unless the fact that the will of John dated 1714 was unproved is an indication that he did not actually die at that time. (Usually that is not the case, since there are many reasons why a will would not have been proved and recorded, in those days. If it was found by the Secretary of State in some official group of records as indicated, then it was probably due to the man's death having occured as suggested by the date.) Below is the brief but important data found among the Perquimans records[17]:

Deed Book A, No. 134: 14-10mo. 1697 (October 14). **Wm. Edwards**, with consent of wife **Elizabeth**, doth assign 200 acres 'upon the Wide of Little River, up Deep Creek' to a Branch called

'Shelton's Gut' adj. **Arnold White, & John Cartrite**. Witnesses: **Henry White, Robert White**.

Deed Book A, No. 230: April 25, 1704. **Thomas Cartwright, Sr.,** to **Samuel Right**--95 acres on South side of Deep Creek, adj. **Wm. Godfrey, & Wm. Hunt**, 'belonging to me **Wm. Terrell** in New England'. Witnesses: **Thomas Twedie, Wm. Twedie**. (There is no indication of what the reference to Wm. Terrell means, but evidently he must have been the person who owned the piece of land before Thomas Cartwright, Sr.; or else had empowered Thomas to sell the land for him.)

Deed Book A, No. 256: Jan. 10, 1705. **Arnold White, & Parthene** his wife, to **John Cartrett** (Cartwright, inserted by compiler) of Albemarle Co, for 6 pounds pd by **Aughter** (Arthur, again by compiler) **Carlton**, of same, sold 200 acres on West side of Little River, up Deep Creek, on a Branch called 'Shelton's Gut'. Witnesses: **Tho. Snoden, John Stepney**.

Deed Book G, No. 25: Nov. 12, 1760. **Peter Cartright** of Perquimans, Planter, for 400 pounds pd by **Jarvis Jones**, Merchant, of Pasquotank County, 'doth sell 30 acres in Perquimans' on the head of Deep Creek, patented by **Albert Albertson Sen.**, Jan. 1, 1694, & Jan. 7, 1721, assigned to **Albert Albertson, Jr.** (son of sd Albert), & by will of **Albert Albertson, Jr.**, given to said **Cartright**. Witnesses: **Jacob Madon, Daniel Koen, Edward Halstead**.

Deed Book G, No. 26: April Court 1762. **Peter Cartright**, for 3 pounds pd by **Col. Jarvis Jones**, sold 200 acres in Perquimans 'where said **Peter** now lives', near the mouth of Tomblins Branch, being part of 300 acres, granted to **John Tomblin**, July 1694. Witnesses: **Jacob Madren** (Madre, inserted by compiler; but I have seen this name many times in Pasquotank as Madren and Madrun.), **Daniel Roen, Edward Halstead**. (The name 'Roen' here probably should be 'Koen', as above. Note later in this chapter that a Vincent Cartwright of Davidson County, Tennessee married Thoney Koen. This could be some indication that Vincent Cartwright was a descendant of this Peter.)

It is certainly probable that this Peter was son of one of the sons of Thomas the elder, in Pasquotank, and he may have been the same Peter shown earlier as father of Robert and Morgan, in the 'flesh mark' records of Pasquotank. We do have a clue to the possible identity of Peter's mother, who may have been a daughter of Albert Albertson, Jr., given that land was willed to Peter by him. The other land, indicated as having belonged to John Tomblin, was bought by Albert Albertson, Sr. as shown in another deed, not reprinted here.

A look back to Grimes' volume reveals the abstracted will of Albert Albertson, Sr., the will of Mary Albertson who is clearly his wife, and the will of one of their sons, Nathaniel, along with some other Albertsons who were probably kin. There is a listing in Mitchell's 'Testator Index' for the will of another Albert Albertson of Pasquotank, 1759, who is undoubtedly Albert Albertson, Jr.; but the latter will is not abstracted in Grimes' volume, even though it is listed as being among the Secretary of State Papers. Neither is it found in Olds' abstracts, and I have not attempted at this date to obtain a copy from the Archives, though certainly that would be in order to find out whether the will names a grandson Peter Cartwright or gives any other indication of such a relationship. Below are given the abstracted wills of Albert Albertson, Sr., his wife Mary, and their son Nathaniel, for the purpose of elucidation on the matter[18]. It may be seen that if the postualtion about Albert, Jr. being the grandfather of Peter Cartwright is correct, this may be where the name Peter originated for his branch of the Pasquotank Cartwrights.

February 10, 1701, April 14, 1702: **Albert Albertson, Sr.,** Perquimans Precinct. Names sons **Peter, Nathaniel, Albert,** and **Easaw** (sic). Wife mentioned but not named. Executors, sons **Peter** and **Nathaniel Albertson**. Witnesses: **John Falconer, Nathaniel Nickolson, Joseph Suton.** Clerk of the Court, **John Stepney.**

January 10, 1720/21, (proved. will not dated.): **Mary Albertson,** Perquimans County. Names son **Albert**. Grandchildren, **Mary, John,** and **Elizabeth Albertson.** Executor, son **Albert Albertson.**

Witnesses: **Thomas Stafford, Albert Albertson, Jr..** Clerk of the Court, **Richard Leary**.

December 4, 1751, January Court 1752. **Nathaniel Albertson**, Perquimans County. Names sons **Joshua** (land on Long Branch and Creek Swamp), **William** ('my manner plantation'), **Aaron**. Grandsons, **Benjamin** and **Chalkley Albertson**. Daughters, **Hannah Albertson, Elizabeth Newby, Lydda Trueblood**. Negroes bequeathed to sons. Three sons appointed executors. Witnesses: **Joshua Perisho, James Henbe, Mary Morris**. Clerk of the Court, **Edmund Hatch**.

Also, the will of **John Tomlin** of Perquimans Precinct, dated July 7, 1715, shows **Albert Albertson, Sr.** and **Albert Albertson, Jr.** signing as witnesses, along with **Thomas Stafford**. **Tomlin** names only a son **William** and a brother **William**. No probate.

Further information concerning this group of persons can be obtained from the source of Perquimans County data as shown above.[17] There is an enormous amount of genealogical data on numerous families included by the author Mrs. Winslow (unfortunately with that part of the work not indexed, making it tedious to try and extract information from it). The collections were apparently collated from many different records, including the deeds of the county, volumes of Quaker records, Berkley Parish Register, and other sources. It seems that the collections occasionally contain some presumptions with which I do not agree, but on the whole the data is a very valuable. To be found in it is the following information:

Marriage of **Martha Cartwright**, daughter of **Robert Cartwright** of Pasquotank County, to **Zachariah Jones**. No date is given, but a **Zachariah Jones** who is apparently the same man is shown as deceased intestate April 20, 1762, with **Thomas Jones** 'praying for Adminstration'. The marriage of course must have occured many years prior to this date; but after 1746, for the will of Hannah's father at that date names her as Hannah Cartwright, indicating she was unmarried at the time..

236

Concerning the Albertson family, I have extracted the following data from Mrs. Winslow's volume, much of it apparently obtained from Berkley Parish Register; but again, the author notes numerous sources, including Quaker records, county records, and data submitted by others which she had no chance to verify:

Albert Albertson (Sr.) m. **Mary Gosby**, Cec. 20, 1668. Children: **Albert**, b. July 15, 1669; **Susanna**, b. Feb. 19, 1670; **Esau**, b. Sug. 19, 1672; **Hannah**, b. Dec. 11, 1675; **Peter**, b. 'Last of June' 1677.
Hannah Albertson m. **Joseph Nicholson**, son of **Christopher & Hannah**. (No date.)
Albert Albertson (Sr.) died 'att his on house' Feb. 28, 1701.
Albert Albertson, Jr. m. **Elizabeth Mullen**, (d. of **Abraham**) 'who m. 2d, **Wm. Bateman**, before Oct. 18, 1768.' [This is a part of the data which I find to be probably in error. The author cites a deed, Book H, pg. 41. It is abstracted in the same work, and names a William Bateman and Betty his wife of Perquimans, noting 'Albert Albertson in his will did bequeath unto Bettie Mullen (dau. of Abraham) a tract of land, (purcharsed by said Albertson of Richard Grey) & said Bettie did since marry sd. Bateman.....'etc. Sold to 'my son John Bateman'. Dated Oct. 18, 1768. The reason for doubting that this could refer to the wife of Albert Albertson, Jr. is obvious, though of course it is based on my own presumption that the Albert Albertson for whom a will is listed in Mitchell's index, 1759, is the same as Albert Albertson, Jr. If so, then his wife was not a widow until that date, and would have been at the very least some seventy-nine or eighty years old by the time her husband had died, since she had children born in 1694 and 1696 as shown previously. That she would have married again seems improbable, if not impossible. In any case, it seems much more likely that the Bettie Mullen to whom Albert Albertson bequeathed land was a younger relative, and hardly his wife at the time. Most wills do not bequeath land to a wife by giving her maiden name. This leaves the question of where the data concerning Albert Albertson's marriage to an Elizabeth Mullen came from, and whether it was merely presumed from the mentioned deed rather than being taken from the Berkley Parish Register where most of the other data seems to have originated. It is possible, of course, that Albert's

wife was Elizabeth Mullen and there was also a younger relative by that name.]

Albert Albertson, son of **Albert & Elizabeth**, b. ye Nov. 23, 1694.

John Albertson, son of **Albert & Elizabeth**, b. Nov. 27, 1696.

Peter Albertson, (son of **Albert & Mary Gosby**) m. **Ann Jones** (dau. of **Mary Beesly**, widow) Aug. 27, 1701. Children: **Samuel**, b. Oct. 25, 1702; **Peter**, b. Oct. 7, 1704; **Joseph**, b. Feby 5, 1705/06; **Ann**, b. Aug. 4, 1708 (d. young.); **Mary**, b. Mch 12, 1710; **Patience**, b. Dec. 5, 1711; **Hannah**, b. June 15, 1715; **Anne** (2nd by that name) b. Aug. 4, 1718; **Martha**, b. Aug. 15, 1721.

Esau Albertson, (son of **Albert & Mary Gosby**) m. **Sarah Sexton** (dau. of Darby & Doroty) ye 27 Jany. 1700/01, by **Rev. Richard French**.

Nathaniel Albertson m. **Abigail Nicholson** (dau. of **Samuel**) 'at a meeting at ye house of **Samuel Nicholson**', July 12, 1704. Children: **Sarah**, b. Nov. 2, 1706. (He had other children, shown is his will, given previously, while Sarah is **not** shown there.)

There is much more data concerning the Albertson family given in Mrs. Winslow's volume, but I reproduced the above information only in an effort to track down the relation between Peter Cartwright and the Albertsons. It seems rather fruitless, except for the demonstration of mutual connections with the Jones family, but there is not that much information given on the children of Albert Albertson, Jr., and that is where I suspect the connection to Peter Cartwright would be found. If he was the son of Robert, mentioned in the earlier abstracts of Old Albemarle, then the speculation is that Robert must have married a daughter of Albert Albertson, Jr. It seems very likely, at least, that the two sons mentioned in the birth records were not Albert's only children, and thus he could have had a daughter who married a Cartwright..

Another few bits of data that I have found in North Carolina is evidence of a **John Cartwright** in Anson County[19]:

Deed Book 6, pg. 221: 26 September 1761. **John Cartwright** to **John McDaniel**, both of Anson; 12 pounds for 100 acres north of Peedee; **Francis's** corner. Witnesses: **Wm. Terry, Mary Terry**.

Deed Book 7, pg. 470. 20 August 1774. **John Cartwright** witnessed a deed of **William Coleman** and **James Pickett** of Anson to **George Jefferson** of Lunenburg County, Virginia. 60 pounds for 200 acres on northeast side of the Peedee, etc. Other witness was **John Chiles**.

Deed Book K, pg. 113: 17 Jany. 1772. **John Cartright** to **Wm. Coleman** and **James Pickett**, all of Anson, for 82 pounds, tract on north side of Peedee on northeast side of Mountain Creek. Witnesses: **Joseph Hinds, Jno. Almond, J. Duncan.** proven in open court by **Joseph Hinds.** (Presuming that this name 'Hinds' is the same as 'Hines', as indeed it is seen so in other records of the same county, then this seems to indicate some kind of connection with the Cartwrights of Edgecombe-Halifax, since there was obviously a connection with a Hines family there. There is also a William Barnes found among the records of this county. And a Noble family, etc. But we have seen time and again that these connected names being present do not help us identify the Cartwrights in question.)

Court Minutes for 13 January 1772; A recording of a deed, **John Carwright** and wife to **John Almond**, proved by **Joseph Hinds**.

Court Minutes for 17 April 1774: A recording of a deed, **John Cartwright** and wife to **Wm. Coleman** and **James Pickett**. Proved by **Joseph Hindes**.

In the marriages of Rowan County, North Carolina, there is the following[20]:

Joseph Cartwright and **Eve Miller**, 24 March 1770. **Michael Miller**, bondsman. **Thos. Frohock**, witness.

William Tippett and **Rebecca Mills**, 3 March 1796. **Philemon Mayfield**, bondsman. **J. Troy**, witness.

John Mills and _____.   23 August 1797.   **Wm. Tippett,** bondsman. **Jno. Rogers**, witness.

And possibly the same Joseph Cartwright as seen above in Rowan County, is indicated just briefly in Old Tryon county records, by witnessing a deed:[21]

Deed Book A#1, pg. 51: 11 Dec. 1778. **John Fleeman** to **William Langhorn**, 50 pounds proclamation money, 200 acres, Second Broad River, first Creek that runs in on the E side, below **Thomas Robertson** Creek. (300 acres granted to **Thomas Fleeman** and conveyed by deed to sd. John.) Witnesses: **John Morgan, Joseph Cartwright, William McGaughy**.

The question in my mind concerning the Joseph Cartwright of the above records is whether he might be the one who was the father of the group in Smith County, Tennessee, as seen in Chapter Five, Part I. However, some researchers have indicated that this Joseph Cartwright and wife Eve went to Kentucky. Perhaps one does not necessarily negate the other.

Tennessee

Aside from the knowledge that the noted Robert Cartwright and family were in or around the area of the Watauga settlement by 1779 or perhaps even before that time, the earliest reference to a Cartwright in Tennessee seems to be the presence of an **Alexander Cartwright**. This name is included on a long list of those petitioners from the 'lost' State of Franklin, who sought to be freed from the control, and thus the taxation, of the authorities in North Carolina in 1787[22]. I have not seen any reference to this Cartwright either before or after the appearance of the name on the petition, and neither have I seen the name Alexander used in any of the Cartwright families we have examined. (Except for generations later in the family of Jacob Cartwright, son of Robert of Nashville; which given name seems to have come from a maternal side of the family.) There are, however, several names found on the petition which are familiar from our other areas of study, such as a **John Lee**, several **Gibsons**, a **John Sawyer**, numerous **Taylors**, etc.

There is next the important matter of the Sullivan County, Tennessee Cartwrights, and I have alluded to the possibility that they may have been the descendants of **William**, the eldest son of **Robert Cartwright**, which William was shown *not* to have died in infancy. Unfortunately, I cannot do more here than to present a few bare facts and engage in some speculation. I present the subject in order to air an idea and to make an appeal for anyone who may have more helpful information to make it public, in the interests of exploring the question. I must state from the beginning that I have not had the opportunity to do in-depth research among Sullivan County records concerning these Cartwrights, though a brief foray into the matter has not turned up more than some sparse data on the earlier generations of the family. Even from that standpoint, however, there seems to be some strong evidence for believing that the Sullivan County Cartwrights might have been descended from **William Cartwright**, the eldest son of **Robert Cartwright** of the Nashville area, and the matter warrants a deeper investigation.

The information that is undoubted concerning the Sullivan County Cartwrights is that a **William Cartwright, Sr.** came to the county at an early date and built a log home complex called 'Walnut Shade', which has been placed on the National Register of Historic Sites, but with its date of construction apparently unknown. **William Cartwright, Sr.** was still living in the county as of the 1830 census, with his wife and one son also still in residence. Evidently he died sometime before 1840, as he is not found on that census. His son **William Cartwright, Jr.** is known to have built another log cabin in the county circa 1822, which also still stands and is privately owned and occupied. **William, Jr.** and his wife **Elizabeth** had a number of children, twelve according to family data, most of whom are easily found on the subsequent censuses of the area. The names John, Lemuel and Martha were used in this family, reminiscent of the Princess Anne County, Virginia records.

For one of the most important bits of data, I am forced to rely at this point on some written family accounts which were published by descendants; and this is not to say that the data isn't well-founded, but simply that I cannot attempt to validate the matter here, not having seen the references directly. The family accounts were published by **Amy Cartwright Robinson**, of Florida, and few copies of the book exist now, one being held by Mountain Press, Inc. of Signal Mountain, Tennessee. The data shows that **William Cartwright, Sr.** was born circa 1745, and the descendants appear to have no knowledge of where he came from or of his own parentage, as of the writings that I have seen (printed a number of years ago.) Clearly, however, even this small amount of data makes it very tempting to guess that **William Cartwright, Sr.** of Sullivan County may have been **Robert Cartwright's** eldest son **William**, who did not die in infancy as previously believed. The Bible record of the **Robert Cartwright** family, as shown, gives the eldest son William's date of birth as 1746; and with the known fact that **Robert Cartwright** was in the area of the Holston territory circa 1779, all of this information taken together certainly makes it seem possible that his eldest son could have followed him that far and then chose to remain in the slightly more settled area of Sullivan County, with his own family. An important point to note in connection with this speculation is that, although Robert's will names the son William to prove the latter was alive at the time (1809), there is little evidence of this William having ever resided in the Davidson County area where Robert lived. There is, however, data to demonstrate that a **William Cartwright** who was most probably the one of Sullivan County was indeed living in that general area at least as early as the year 1800, and probably before. The will records of Washington County, Tennessee (adjoining Sullivan) show a **William Cartwright** who signed as a witness on the will of **Samuel Wood**[22]. dated April 26, 1800. (Will Book 1, pg. 52.) The will names wife **Sarah**, sons **William**, **James**, **Samuel**, **Thomas**, **Abraham**, **John**, and **George**; and daughter **Mary Handrick** (Hendricks?). Executors, wife **Sarah** and sons **John** and **Abraham**. Other witness, besides **William Cartwright**, are **Martin Seamer** and **Calvin Finch**.

Later records show that a **William Cartwright** of Sullivan County had a wife named **Rebecca** who left a will in Washington County, Tennessee in 1878, but since this is beyond the time scope to which I have restricted myself, I will not go into those details here.

The published accounts of Ms. **Amy Cartwright Robinson** give much data on the family as to those later generations.

Leaving the area of East Tennessee, it is time to examine that 'second' **Robert Cartwright** of the Nashville, Tennessee area. First, there is a record of his military service[23]:

Robert Cartwright: **Susannah** (wife); NC & VA Line; soldier was b. and raised in Camden County, NC & his parents lived there during the war & soldier married there to **Susanah Spence** in Oct. 1784 & she was also born & raised there; soldier d. in Apr. 1816 or 1818 in Davidson County, TN; widow applied 25 Oct. 1839 Williamson County, TN aged 74; widow d. 15 Oct. 1850 williamson County, TN leaving children: **David** (2nd child) aged 64 in 1853 & a resident of Williamson County, TN; **John Cartwright**. (no other children named) In 1853 a William Cartwright was a res of Davidson County, TN, but no relationship to soldier was stated.

The will of this Robert Cartwright, in Davidson County, TN[24]:

Will of **Robert Cartwright**, deceased, of Davidson County. (proved May 22, 1816) To my son **David** one bed, bedstead and furniture formerly called **Polly's**. To my son **John** one bed, bedstead and furniture second choice of those which was called **Polly's**. To my grandson **Grandberry** one bed and furniture. To my grandson **Edney Armstrong McCoy** all the property I lent to my son-in-law **Daniel McCoy** and **Nancy** his wife I will that the property be sold and proceeds be out in interest (sic?) for the use of said child until it comes of age. To my friend **Fanny Haily** one two year old heifer. To my son-in-law **Daniel McCoy** one small bed which is at his house. To my well beloved wife **Susanna Cartwright** all the balance of my property after paying my debts and at her death to descend to my sons **David** and **John** and grandsons **Grandberry Cartwright** and **Edney Armstrong McKoy**. I appoint my son **David Cartwright** my executor. This 16 April 1816. Witnesses: **Robert Johnston, Henry West,** and **Samuel McCutchen**. Apr. Term 1816.

These marriages in Davidson County seem to relate to this family[25]:

Jno. Cartwright to **Fanny Hailey**, 14 October 1824, Davidson Co., TN.
Nancy Cartwright to **Daniel McCoy**, 10 September 1813, Davidson Co., TN.

It may be that one of the several marriages involving the name **David Cartwright**, as given previously in Chapter Seven, may have been the son David in the above family. It is shown by the military pension abstract that he lived in Williamson County, TN by 1853, and possibly earlier. But clearly the family was first in Davidson County. In researching several available sources of records such as deeds and wills concerning Williamson County, I found nothing more than the indication of the presence there of both **David** and **John Cartwright**. I have not gone into the matter in depth, so that there most certainly are sources relating to Williamson County that I have not seen.

The use of the name 'Edney' in this family is interesting in light of the will of **Robert Ednye** of Pasquotank County, given in Chapter Eight. Recall that he named a daughter, **Elizabeth Cartwright**. One must presume at least tentatively that this may have been the mother of the **Robert Cartwright** in the above records. To which Cartwright she was married is another question, seemingly impossible to investigate at this point, with the records of Camden County, North Carolina being lost.

As mentioned, there was yet another Cartwright, seemingly related to the above family, found in the Davidson County records[24]:

Nov. 13, 1815: Inventory of sale of estate of **Vincent Cartwright**, deceased, who died at New Orleans, by **Levin Edney**, executor. Aug. 15, 1815, persons listed: **Tiny Cartwright, Dicy Cartwright, Matilda Cartwright, Levin Edney, Thiny Cartwright, James Rhodes, Charles R. Saunders, William Roach, Bryan Boon, Demsey Jones, Shelton Hartgrave, James Conner, John Jones, Arthur Axum** (Exum), **Thomas Loftin, Frederick Joy, Demsey Sawyers, John Stephenson, Thomas Williams, Alson Linton,**

Abner Rhodes, James Gillam, Matthew Lee, Costin Sawyer, Daniel Cartwright, Barnet Vardon, Lodrick Williams, James Haley, Abraham Ballance, John E. Nevan, James Perrel, Enoch Cartwright, Absalom Taylor, Seth Davis, Abraham Demoss, and James Smith. Oct. Term 1815.

Nov. 12, 1817: Settlement of estate of **Vincent Cartwright**, deceased. Ordered at July Term 1817 for **Josiah Horton**, **Eldridge Newsom**, and **Zachariah Allen** to settle with **Leven Edney**, admr. of said estate, find $544.00 in the hands of said **Edney** belonging to the estate of the orphans of said **Vincent Cartwright**, deceased. This 13 Oct. 1817. **Eldridge Newsom** and **Zach. Allen**. Oct. Term 1817.

The marriages below seem to relate to the above family[25]. (Some, of course, may not; and there may be marriages here which have been included elsewhere simply because of relation to the county involved.):

Vincent Cartwright to **Thone Koen**, 7 September 1802, Davidson Co., TN.
Daniel Cartwright to **Polly Hailey**, 15 July 1807, Williamson Co., TN.
Daniel Cartwright to **Sally Murphy**, 27 October 1819, Williamson Co., TN.
Enoch Cartwright to **Hannah Ragins**, 4 February 1818, Williamson Co., TN.
Dicy Cartwright to **Nathaniel L. Overall**, 12 March 1849, Wilson Co., TN.
Matilda Cartwright to **Joseph Caker**, 6 January 1849, Sumner Co., TN.
Thermy (Thiny?) **Cartwright** to **Edward Daniel**, 12 December 1818, Davidson Co., TN.
Nicy Cartwright to **Winfield Knight**, 30 October 1836, Davidson Co., TN.

Since I have touched upon the issue of African American genealogy in other parts of this work, I include here the remainder of the Cartwright marriages in Tennessee that I have found with the couples designated as Blacks[25]:

Darthula Cartwright to **Allen Hearn**, 13 May 1866, Wilson Co., TN.
Mary Cartwright to **Isac Duncan**, 7 April 1866, Smith Co., TN.
Isaac Cartwright to **Jenny Pitman** 12 April 1866, Sumner Co., TN.
A. Cartwright to **Angeline Walker**, 5 February 1869, Fayette Co., TN.

In addition to all else that has been shown concerning Davidson County, Tennessee, there are these records[24] found among the will books, with the relation of the Cartwright in question to any of the others being unknown:

May 27, 1797: Bill of Sale. I, **John Cartwright** of Pasquotank County, NC sold unto **Jno. White** of Davidson County, TN a negro woman named **Viner**. This 4 September 1796. Witnesses: **Benjamin White, John Gray**.

May 27, 1797: Bill of Sale. I, **John Cartwright** of Pasquotank County, NC sold unto **John White** of Davidson County, TN a negro child named **Dik**. This 1 October 1796. Witnesses: **James Davis, Zachariah Jackson**.

The court records of Davidson County[27] show the presence of a **John Cartwright** who is likely the same one of the above records, for he is clearly not the son of the noted Robert, being older even if that child did not die young as seems to have been the case. The John in question is shown as a constable in 1789, and serves on juries during that time period, etc. There are likewise many such records concerning **Justinian Cartwright**, as well as Robert and all of his sons who were known to have lived to adulthood. (Except for the elder William, as noted earlier.)

These same court records indicate the presence of a **Jesse Cartwright** who could not have been the son of the noted Robert's family, unless the year of birth as given for that Jesse by the copier of the Bible record was wrong. Dated 10 April 1788, the reference in the

246

court records is to an order that 'Robert Cartwright, Daniel Frazer, Jesse Cartwright, Thomas Cartwright...' and others mark a road from John Walker's to Gasper's Lick. If Robert's son Jesse was born in 1778 as shown by the record given earlier, then this could not have been him. (Since Justinian is shown to be in the Davidson County area at this time as well, could this be another reference to him, under the name Jesse?)

There is, further, a Caleb Cartwright who is found mentioned briefly in the records of Davidson County[26,27], and not otherwise seen in any sources that I have noted. It seems possible that he may have been the parent of some of those not otherwise accounted for, such as the William Cartwright who was killed by Indians in 1780, perhaps of Vincent Cartwright, and the men Jesse and John Cartwright who seem to have been too old to be Robert's sons by those names. This seems particularly likely if he was the *elder* Caleb Cartwright who was the son of William, son of Thomas, in the Princess Anne-Pasquotank area. Below are the record abstracts concerning this Caleb Cartwright:

16 January, 1799: Ordered that Joshua Balance have letters of administration on estate of Caleb Cartwright, dec'd. Bond and security given.

In addition, one of the sources of the above records[26] notes also that a Robert Cartwright died before 10 April 1799 when the administrator Joshua Balance returned an inventory of the estate. I have not seen this record in the other source, and it seems that it is probably a mistaken abstract, for there *is* a second reference to the estate of Caleb Cartwright, with same administrator returning an inventory, same date of 10 April 1799.

In relation to Sumner County, Tennessee, I have found little aside from data already shown, although many of those Cartwrights of both the Wilson County and Davidson County areas seem to have moved about or had dealings in Sumner as well. One record of note is a will on which a William Cartwright signed as a witness[28]. I believe that this William was probably of the Wilson County group (son of Hezekiah), though there is nothing to attest that for certain:

247

17 December 1791, 15 April 1790: (Will Book 1, pg. 28.) **Joseph Barnes**. Names daughter **Molly Clay**, wife **Lelah** to have plantation until son **William Barnes** is 21. Sons **John Barnes, Kintchen**. Daughters **Polly Barnes, Juslan** (?), **Lelah, Milly**, under age. Executors **Lelah Barnes** and **John Barnes**. Witnesses: **John Deloach, William Cartwright, John Roberts**.

I have researched the area of West Tennessee less closely than the rest, mainly because there are few very early sources of data relating to the area. But there are some Cartwrights to be noted in the area in the early part of the nineteenth century, doubtless descendants of the other Cartwrights already studied. In Sistler's will index[29] there is a listing for a **Robert Cartright** who died in Weakley County in 1829, with the reference given being Will Book 1, pg. 44. But an attempt to obtain a copy of said will resulted in a letter from the County Court Clerk's office stating that no such record could be found in said will book or any other of Weakley County. It is possible that a copy of the will might be on microfilm at the Tennessee State Archives, which I have not pursued.

The only Cartwright marriage that I have found in West Tennessee, earlier than the 1830's, is that of **Robert Cartwright** to **Sarah Hamblin**, 7 April 1828, Hardeman Co., TN[25].

I should note that early marriage records for some of the counties of Tennessee, such as Hardin, are not extant. And I must say again that there are many records in various counties of Tennessee concerning Cartwrights of later time periods (some only *slightly* later than those studied) that have not been touched upon here. Particularly there are Cartwrights found in counties that I have not mentioned at all, mainly because they are not found in those areas until later than the time period to which I have confined the data in this volume. Most likely, all of said Cartwrights are descendants of those investigated in this work. Some of the Tennessee counties in which records concerning Cartwrights can be found after the general time period of 1830 are Marion, McMinn, Monroe, Warren, Hardeman, etc.

Finally, a word about the 1820 census. Though it is frustrating because so many of the Tennessee counties are missing from this census, the data that does exist can be useful for placing and identifying certain specific Cartwrights.

A brief analysis of the Cartwrights found on the 1820 census for Tennessee[30]:

John Cartright	Williamson Co.
Daniel Cartrite	Williamson Co.
David Cartwright	Davidson Co.
Elizabeth Cartwright	Davidson Co.
Elizabeth Cartwright	Smith Co.
Elizabeth Cartwright	Wilson Co.
Isaac Cartwright	Franklin Co.
Jacob Cartwright	Davidson Co.
James Cartwright	Smith Co.
James Cartwright	Sumner Co.
Joseph Cartwright	Smith Co.
Joshua Cartwright	Warren Co.
Robert Cartwright	Wilson Co.
Samuel Cartwright	Wilson Co.
Thomas Cartwright	Davidson Co.
Thomas Cartwright	Davidson Co.
Thomas Cartwright	Smith Co.
Thomas Cartwright	Wilson Co.
William Cartwright	Wilson Co.

Though this is merely an index, from a close comparison of this with other data discussed in this volume, one can work out well enough the identities of most of those shown.

In summary, I should reiterate the fact that there are undoubtedly some important sources of information that I have missed, that would be more useful if viewed from the most original form, or that have yet to be found by anyone interested in the surname, for that matter.

I would also like to stress that it takes some effort to gain a good understanding of all of these Cartwrights, even when the data is set out as clearly as possible. It has not been easy to do that here, with so many bits of data concerning various persons who cannot be placed and yet who seem to belong to a certain group, etc. It can no doubt be confusing when taken at a brief reading or when simply referring to a specific person through the index. If nothing else, the study of genealogy takes time and perseverance. To be truly successful at tracking down family lines requires a willingness to pore over records concerning many persons in whom one may not be interested at first, and to compare various references almost ceaselessly. One can often benefit from going over the same records many, many times. Even while putting together this volume, after years of research, I have found myself realizing new and important tidbits which I had not noticed or considered before. Likewise, I hope that readers who wish to glean useful data from this work will take the time to go over the references in depth, perhaps time and again if necessary, to help solve some of the Cartwright puzzles.

Bibliography of Sources for Chapter Nine

1. 'Passenger and Immigration Lists Index' by P. William Filby with Mary K. Meyer. Gale Research Co., Book Tower, Detroit, MI. 1981.
2. 'Cavaliers and Pioneers, Volume One' by Nell Marion Nugent. Genealogical Publishing Co., Inc., Baltimore, MD. 1963-1991.
3. 'Virginia Colonial Abstracts' by Beverley Fleet. Ibid., 1988.
4. 'English Duplicates of Lost Virginia Records' compiled by Louis des Cogents, Jr.. Ibid., 1981, 1990.
5. 'Virginia Marriage Records From the Virginia Magazine of History and Biography, the William and Mary College Quarterly, and Tyler's Quarterly' Indexed by Elizabeth Petty Bentley. Ibid., 1982, 1984.
6. 'Virginia Marriages, Early to 1800' by Lithonia Research, Inc., P.O. Box 740, Orem UT 84059-0740. 1991.
7. 'Genealogical Abstracts from 18th Century Virginia Newspapers' by Robert K. Headley, Jr. Genealogical Publishing Co., Inc., Baltimore, MD. 1987.
8. 'Virginia County Records, Volume I, Spotsylvania County', by William Armstrong Crozier. Originally published New York, 1905. Reprinted Ibid, 1990.
9. 'Virginia Wills and Administrations, 1632-1800' compiled by Clayton Torrence. Originally published by The National Society of the Colonial Dames of America, Richmond, Virginia, 1930. Reprinted Ibid. 1990.
10. 'Virginia--West Virginia Genealogical Data From Revolutionary War Pension and Bounty Land Warrant Records, Volume I' compiled by Patrick G. Wardell, Lt. Col., U. S. Army, Retired Heritage Books, Inc., Bowie, MD.
11. 'Red River Settlers--Records of the Settlers of Northern Montgomery, Robertson, and Sumner Counties, Tennessee' by Edythe Rucker Whitley. Genealogical Publishing Co., Inc., Baltimore, MD. 1980. Reprinted by same for Clearfield Company, Inc., 1993.
12. 'Marriages from Early Tennessee Newspapers 1794-1851' by the Rev. Silas Emmett Lucas, Jr.. Southern Historical Press, P. O. Box 1267, Greeneville, S. C. 29602. 1978.

13. 'Marriage Bonds and Other Marriage Records of Amherst County, Virginia 1763-1800' compiled by William Montgomery Sweeny. Originally published Lynchburg, Virginia 1937. Reprinted Genealogical Publishing Co., Inc., Baltimore, MD. 1973, 1980; and by same for Clearfield Co., Inc., 1991.
14. 'The Wills of Amherst County, Virginia 1761-1865' by The Rev. Bailey Fulton Davis. Southern Historical Press, Inc., Greeneville, S. C. 1985.
15. 'Early Records Hampshire County, Virginia -Now West Virginia-' compiled by Clara McCormick Sage and Laura Sage Jones. Originally published Delavan, Wisconsin, 1939. Reprinted Genealogical Publishing Co., Inc., Baltimore, MD. 1969-1990.
16. 'Chronicles of the Scotch-Irish Settlement in Virginia', 3 Vols. by Lyman Chalkey. Originally published 1912. Reprinted Ibid. 1965-1989.
17. 'History of Perquimans County, North Carolina' by Mrs. Watson Winslow. Originally published Raleigh, North Carolina, 1931. Reprinted Regional Publishing Company, Baltimore, MD, 1974. Reprinted Genealogical Publishing Co., Inc., Baltimore, MD. 1990.
18. 'An Abstract of North Carolina Wills compiled from Original and Recorded Wills in the Office of the Secretary of State' by J. Bryan Grimes. Originally published Raleigh, North Carolina 1910. Reprinted Ibid., 1967, 1975, 1980.
19. 'Anson County, North Carolina Abstracts of Early Records' compiled by May Wilson McBee. Originally published Greenwood, Mississippi 1950; reprinted Ibid., 1978, 1980.
20. 'Marriages of Rowan County, North Carolina 1753-1868' compiled by Brent H. Holcomb. Ibid. 1986.
21. 'Deed Abstracts of Tryon, Lincoln, & Rutherford Counties North Carolina 1769-1786; Tryon County Wills & Estates' Abstracted by Brent Holcomb, C.R.S. Southern Historical Press, Greeneville, S. C. 1977.
22. 'Tennessee Cousins' by Worth S. Ray. Originally published Austin, TX., 1950. Reprinted Genealogical Publishing Co., Inc., Baltimore, MD. 1960-1989.
23. 'Genealogical Abstracts of Revolutionary War Pension Files,

Volume I, A-E' Abstracted by Virgil D. White. The National
Historical Publishing Company, Waynesboro, TN. 1990.
24. 'Davidson County Tennessee Wills & Inventories, Volumes One
and Two' compiled by Helen C. and Timothy R. Marsh.
Southern Historical Press, Greeneville, S. C. 1990.
25. 'Early Tennessee Marriages' series by Byron and Barbara
Sistler. (Three sets of two volumes each dealing with the three
parts of Tennessee.) Byron Sistler & Associates, Nashville,
TN.
26. 'Tennessee Tidbits, Volume I' by Marjorie Hood Fischer.
Southern Historical Press, Greeneville, S. C. 1986.
27. 'Davidson County, Tennessee County Court Minutes' by Carol
Wells. Heritage Books, Inc., Bowie, MD. 1991.
28. 'Sumner County, Tennessee Will Abstracts 1788-1882' by Shirley
Wilson, CG. (No publisher or location stated. Copy
referenced in Cobb County Public Library, Marietta, Ga.)
29. 'Tennessee Wills & Administrations' by Byron Sistler. Byron
Sistler & Associates, Nashville, TN. 1990.

Slave Index

Cartwright Index

General Index

261

269

273

275

276

278

279

280

286

288

290